Monica Kennedy

Workplace learning and organisational knowledge in the public sector

An exploration of workplace experience

VDM Verlag Dr. Müller

Impressum/Imprint (nur für Deutschland/ only for Germany)
Bibliografische Information der Deutschen Nationalbibliothek: Die Deutsche Nationalbibliothek
verzeichnet diese Publikation in der Deutschen Nationalbibliografie; detaillierte bibliografische
Daten sind im Internet über http://dnb.d-nb.de abrufbar.
Alle in diesem Buch genannten Marken und Produktnamen unterliegen warenzeichen-, marken-
oder patentrechtlichem Schutz bzw. sind Warenzeichen oder eingetragene Warenzeichen der
jeweiligen Inhaber. Die Wiedergabe von Marken, Produktnamen, Gebrauchsnamen,
Handelsnamen, Warenbezeichnungen u.s.w. in diesem Werk berechtigt auch ohne besondere
Kennzeichnung nicht zu der Annahme, dass solche Namen im Sinne der Warenzeichen- und
Markenschutzgesetzgebung als frei zu betrachten wären und daher von jedermann benutzt
werden dürften.

Coverbild: www.purestockx.com

Verlag: VDM Verlag Dr. Müller Aktiengesellschaft & Co. KG
Dudweiler Landstr. 99, 66123 Saarbrücken, Deutschland
Telefon +49 681 9100-698, Telefax +49 681 9100-988, Email: info@vdm-verlag.de
Zugl.: Canberra, University of Canberra, Diss., 2006

Herstellung in Deutschland:
Schaltungsdienst Lange o.H.G., Berlin
Books on Demand GmbH, Norderstedt
Reha GmbH, Saarbrücken
Amazon Distribution GmbH, Leipzig
ISBN: 978-3-639-23051-2

Imprint (only for USA, GB)
Bibliographic information published by the Deutsche Nationalbibliothek: The Deutsche
Nationalbibliothek lists this publication in the Deutsche Nationalbibliografie; detailed
bibliographic data are available in the Internet at http://dnb.d-nb.de .
Any brand names and product names mentioned in this book are subject to trademark, brand or
patent protection and are trademarks or registered trademarks of their respective holders. The use
of brand names, product names, common names, trade names, product descriptions etc. even
without a particular marking in this works is in no way to be construed to mean that such names
may be regarded as unrestricted in respect of trademark and brand protection legislation and
could thus be used by anyone.

Cover image: www.purestockx.com

Publisher:
VDM Verlag Dr. Müller Aktiengesellschaft & Co. KG
Dudweiler Landstr. 99, 66123 Saarbrücken, Germany
Phone +49 681 9100-698, Fax +49 681 9100-988, Email: info@vdm-publishing.com

Printed in the U.S.A.
Printed in the U.K. by (see last page)
ISBN: 978-3-639-23051-2

DEVELOPING A HOLISTIC PERSPECTIVE ON LEARNING AND KNOWLEDGE IN A PUBLIC SECTOR ORGANISATION – AN EXPLORATION OF WORKPLACE EXPERIENCE

THIS THESIS IS SUBMITTED IN FULFILMENT OF THE REQUIREMENTS OF THE DEGREE OF

DOCTOR OF PHILOSOPHY

UNIVERSITY OF CANBERRA

SEPTEMBER, 2006

MONICA KENNEDY

BA (Comm) (UC), MEdLeadership (UC)

ABSTRACT

Organisational learning and knowledge management theories are illustrated in this study as converging around discussion of three major themes: the role of the individual in the knowledge of the organisation; the increasing problematisation of the nature of knowledge; and debate over the role of mental models and organisational schema in the learning of the individual and organisation. In this study it is argued that these themes are aligned with central themes in complexity theories, and complexity is posited as an appropriate lens through which organisational experience might be viewed.

The confluent themes and complexity underpin a methodological approach that is inspired by grounded theory, but which recognises the value that complexity provides as a sensitising device to the research. Narrative methods are used to collect data and participants' sense-making informs the researcher's analysis of the results.

The emergence of a complex adaptive systems heuristic from the analysis of the collective narratives provides a ground for exploration of organisational members' experience using the grammar of complexity. This exploration leads to discussion of the ways in which complexity accommodates the consideration of learning and knowledge within a single frame.

While the experience of organisational members in many ways reflects the properties and mechanisms of complex adaptive systems, in this study the theory does not adequately describe the nature of their learning and knowledge development in the organisation. In this exploration, tension between the formal organisation and the emergent organisation leads to a disconnect between the local learning of members in interaction and the knowledge of the organisation. The nesting feature of complex adaptive systems, where levels of aggregation build hierarchy, is not apparent in this study and this finding is discussed as having important implications for learning and knowledge sharing in the organisation. In addition, the participants of this study do not describe their learning as simply mechanical, involving the building and rebuilding of mental models, as complex adaptive systems would suggest. Learning is described as far more elaborate than the theory immediately implies.

The findings of the study provide insight into the relationship between learning and knowledge in organisations through the lens of complexity as well as providing some input into developing theories of complexity. These insights are discussed with reference to the literatures across organisational learning, knowledge management and workplace learning fields and a number of implications for practice are suggested as a result.

The study supports the integration of organisational learning and knowledge within a single theoretical frame and points to more integrated organisational practice. That learning and knowledge management in organisations should remain discrete in practice is at odds with the theory and with the findings of this study.

Except where clearly acknowledged in footnotes, quotations and the bibliography, I certify that I am the sole author of the thesis submitted today entitled –

DEVELOPING A HOLISTIC PERSPECTIVE ON LEARNING AND KNOWLEDGE IN A PUBLIC SECTOR ORGANISATION – AN EXPLORATION OF WORKPLACE EXPERIENCE

I further certify that to the best of my knowledge the thesis contains no material previously published or written by another person except where due reference is made in the text of the thesis.

The material in the thesis has not been the basis of an award of any other degree or diploma except where due reference is made in the text of the thesis.

The thesis complies with University requirements for a thesis as set out in http://www.canberra.edu.au/secretariat/goldbook/forms/thesisrqmt.pdf

....
Signature of Candidate

....
Signature of chair of the supervisory panel

Date:

ACKNOWLEDGEMENTS

I have looked forward to writing this acknowledgement almost since I began. Thinking about this statement has been a wonderful motivation, and a really important chance for me to reflect on the privilege I have in this opportunity.

Firstly, I am hugely indebted, emotionally, intellectually (and fiscally) to Robert who has continually supported me in my curious attachment to study and research. I don't have the words to express the depth of my gratitude.

I was genuinely blessed to have met early in this research experience two wonderful research students, Jane Stirling and Sally Carters. It was well into the second year before I could talk about my thesis in a way that didn't make them roll their eyes, yet they helped me to work through the myriad methodological issues that emerged in the study, and continually made fun of me! I will never forget their help and friendship.

Trish Milne took over my candidacy as primary supervisor when I was six months into my research and her support has been flawless. Trish has been wise in her guidance, acting like a resource, linking me to her network, encouraging me to stretch and was a champion of every attempt I made to challenge myself. This PhD experience has been the richest learning experience of my life, and I acknowledge Trish's enormous contribution to it.

I introduced myself to Margaret Kiley on Trish's suggestion when I was struggling to link the theoretical frame of the thesis with a methodological approach. I felt immediately at home with Margaret and she became not just a great advisor on methodology and a central member of my supervisory panel, but a ceaseless source of encouragement. I thank Margaret for her unflagging attention to me, not just in terms of the research content and process, but as a research student.

John Collard was my sage in my Masters study and continued to challenge my thinking in my Doctoral research. John suggested I undertake research in the PhD and I am in his debt for starting me on this incredible journey.

I thank the participants of the study for their generosity and the organisation within which they work for allowing me access. I would like to also acknowledge the contribution of my Australian Postgraduate Award and Research Training Scholarship; the University of Canberra which supported my study in every way; the research structures which offered me opportunities to be involved as a student representative; the research community which included me as a full member; and Ting Wang with whom I shared an office in my first year and who I hold as my model PhD candidate.

I want also to thank Jessica Gibbons, Madison Kennedy and Bobby Kennedy for 'keeping it real'. These are the young people who yawned through rehearsals for my initial seminar, University competitions, conference presentations, and in the case of Jessica, my final seminar. I have never been more thrilled than when Jessica told me after my final seminar that she finally understood what it was I had been talking about for the previous three years. I took this as an indication that finally *I* understood what it was I was talking about.

This research prompted a number of conference presentations and publications. These were important in the progress of the thesis as they provided opportunities for feedback on the literature, approach and developing arguments. They are listed below:

Kennedy, M. (2004). 'Are We There Yet? Developing Methodology in a Knowledge Management Research Project.' actKM Online Journal of Knowledge Management 1(1).

Kennedy, M. (2004). Knowledge Management and Workplace Learning - Changing Perspectives, Issues and Understandings. 3rd International Lifelong Learning Conference., Rockhampton, Australia, Central Queensland University Press: 179-185.

Kennedy, M. (2004). 'Learning and Knowing in Organisations - an Exploration of Experience in the Public Sector.' actKM Online Journal of Knowledge Management 1(1).

Kennedy, M. (2005). 'Exploring Experiences of Learning and Knowing at Work: Findings from a Public Sector Case Study.' actKM Online Journal of Knowledge Management 2(1).

Kennedy, M. (2005). 'Learning and Knowing in Organisations: An Exploration of Experience in the Public Sector'. Complexity, Science and Society Conference. Liverpool, UK, Centre for Complexity Research.

Kennedy, M. (2005). 'Learning and Knowing: An Exploration of Workplace Experience Using Complexity Theory'. Complexity, Science and Society Conference. Liverpool, UK, Centre for Complexity Research.

Kennedy, M. (2005). 'Learning and Knowing: Findings in an Exploration of Workplace Experience (a Work in Progress)'. Complexity, Science and Society Conference. Liverpool, UK, Centre for Complexity Research.

TABLE OF CONTENTS

TABLE OF FIGURES

1   INTRODUCTION

Surprisingly, learning and knowledge functions are commonly dealt with quite separately in organisations through separate human/technical systems. Treated as discrete and situated within different organisational systems and structures they are supported by separate theoretical frameworks, policies and practices.

This study follows the literatures in rejecting simplistic and mechanistic views of learning and knowledge in organisations. It explores, instead, their entwinement with each other, the learning individual and collective, and the context of their emergence.

This dissertation offers a perspective on workplace experience in which learning and knowledge are placed within a single frame which acknowledges their entanglement in practice. It does so in an attempt to provide insight into the ways in which people learn at work and how this learning interacts with organisational knowledge. Learning in this study is recognised as an activity which can only be understood in terms of context and interaction, knowledge emerging from such engagement – situated, active and social.

This research has as its impetus a desire to uncover perspectives which are representative of whole experience, to contribute to understandings that are less granular than observations familiar in organisational research. These perspectives may inform learning and knowledge facilitation approaches which recognise their interdependence and lead to more satisfying workplace experiences and better organisational knowledge outcomes than those supported by their segregation.

In this initial chapter the 'red thread' (Rugg and Petre 2004: 120) or plot of the dissertation is presented, highlighting links between the research problem, the contributing literatures, the theoretical frame, and the impact of these on research approach. It draws attention to the significance of both the problem and this study in considerations of learning and knowledge in organisations and their relationship to organisational effectiveness. The chapter concludes with the goals of the research and this thesis and an overview of the monograph's structure, introducing the chapters and their aims.

1.1   BACKGROUND TO THE STUDY

'Pressure is mounting on all types of organizations to learn faster and to manage their knowledge better' (Loermans 2002: 285). It seems impossible to begin discussion of contemporary organisation without reference to the world as increasingly complex and turbulent, and change as discontinuous. So much literature for so long has begun with opening paragraphs and chapters on the increasing prevalence and rate of change in the global environment that the reference has almost become redundant. It is these conditions, however, that lead to the importance of this research project, pointing as they do to the increasingly critical role of learning and knowledge management in organisations.

Globalisation and advances in information and communication technologies are frequently cited by influential writers such as Prusak (2001) as the impetus for a focus on knowledge in organisations. In addition, 'technological discontinuities, regulatory upheavals, industry deverticalization... abrupt shifts in consumer tastes and hordes of non-traditional competitors' (Hamel and Valikangas 2003: 52) are also indicated as impacting on organisations' success. Changing expectations and understandings of work and learning (Burns 2002), awareness of organisational knowledge as complex, valuable and elusive (Malhotra 2002) and clearer understandings of the new sciences in their application to organisations (for example, Stacey 2001; Stacey 2003b) are cited as altering understandings of the ways in which organisations might improve their effectiveness.

This dissertation draws on three main bodies of literature:

1.   Organisational learning

2.   Knowledge management, and

3.   Complexity theories.

Review of the extant literature in the fields informs the argument that new perspectives on organisational experience are available through the integration of what have traditionally been quite discrete discourses. This study claims that the convergence of themes in organisational learning and knowledge management are coherent with the

13

central tenets in developing complexities theories and a view *across* these fields prompt both the research question and the research approach.

1.1.1   ORGANISATIONAL LEARNING

Organisational learning imperatives reflect the recognition of learning as 'the new form of labour' (Zuboff 1991: 6) and drive an organisational focus on the continual development of individual and organisational knowledge. This focus responds to the conception of change as increasing in prevalence and rate. Organisational learning discourse has long debated the relationship between the individual and the organisation in assumptions about the learning of the firm and the anthropomorphism apparent in assumptions that an organisation can learn. Increasingly, educational theory is contributing to more sophisticated discussion of learning in organisational learning and debates about the nature of knowledge and its emergence in individuals and collectives are challenging the enduring optimism of organisational learning literatures.

With its interest in the relationship between the individual and the learning of the organisation, reference to workplace learning is apparent in much of the organisational learning literature. There is a clear resonance between the domains, particularly in the growing reference to complexity and educational theory. In many organisations, including the organisation at the centre of the research reported here, learning 'sits with' the human resources department and focuses on the uptake and distribution of organisationally endorsed information, primarily through formal training approaches.

Workplace learning strategies based on a competency model of training remain focused on transfer of canonical knowledge and on the development of consistent individual skills and standardised competencies. Such approaches are antithetic to notions of organisational learning which focus on flexibility and change, and challenges to the epistemological base of these approaches are creating opportunities for new perspectives in the field.

1.1.2   KNOWLEDGE MANAGEMENT

In traditional settings knowledge management 'sits with' the information systems section of organisations (Vera and Crossan 2003: 123) and focuses on capture and dissemination of explicit knowledge. Having emerged from a concern for ongoing organisational learning, knowledge management has been preoccupied with the codification of information for its transfer throughout the organisation in pursuit of increased performance.

Knowledge management in the 90s reflected notions of knowledge and learning as unproblematic; simplistic, positivist notions (Spender 1996: 65). As a result practice was largely unsupported by rigorous investigation of the epistemology underpinning their development (Blackman and Henderson 2005: 166). Instead, practice remained informed by constructions of knowledge which underlined its value in extraction and dissemination, and of learning as the transfer of such codified knowledge from expert to novice, aimed at standardisation and consistency. Centred on the development of information and communication technologies and the consultancies inherent in their implementation, these approaches were largely unlinked to the weighty theoretical discourse available in the literatures. Developing theory in the fields of learning and knowledge management, however, challenges these traditional perspectives and highlights convergence of themes across discourses.

An important advance in knowledge management theory is the closer attention paid to the epistemology on which specific knowledge management approaches are built. A clearer separation between dimensions on the data-wisdom continuum and differentiation between knowledge bases (Earl 2001) has the opportunity to contribute to more appropriate knowledge strategies, ones which recognise the complexity of knowledge and its entanglement with the experience of human learning.

1.1.3   COMPLEXITY

Developing focus on the epistemological underpinnings of organisational learning and knowledge management theory and practice progresses alongside developments in complexity theories and their application to organisational contexts. Complexity theories focus on the dynamics of interaction, self-organisation, connection, holism and emergence. A complexivist view shifts focus from assumptions of clear and linear relationships between action and effect, reductionism and direction to the emergent outcomes of nonlinear interaction.

Increasingly, organisation theory incorporates complexity in attempts to represent observations and understandings of organisational experience in holistic ways. Complexity provides an opportunity for interdisciplinarity and there is a growing body of literature that seeks to integrate discourse across the areas of interest in this study through the complexity metaphor set (for example McElroy 2000; Kennedy 2004; 2005).

Hawking predicts that this century will be the century of complexity (2000). Just as Newtonian science informed industrial notions of organisation and management operationalised by Taylor and practiced throughout the past century, organisational theorists are now looking to the new sciences for insight into organisations and their processes (Capra 1983: 31-33). In organisational learning and knowledge management complexity offers a gateway for the integrated investigation of the learning that occurs in organisations and the interaction of that learning with the knowledge of the organisation.

1.1.4   CONVERGENCE

Across the literatures of organisational learning and knowledge management increasing attention is paid to the role of the learning individual in the development of organisational knowledge, the emergence of knowledge through interaction, and the problematic role of schema in knowledge generation and development.

The convergence in the literatures triggers myriad questions about the experience of learning and knowledge in organisations. It prompts discussion about the elusiveness of knowledge, its construction within and between individuals, its emergence through individual and collective engagement with the workplace, the role of sense- or meaning-making, the process (rather than the content) of learning, and the role of the social in knowledge development and its contribution to the organisation. This convergence of themes is enriched by metaphors arising from complexity theories and insights gained through cross disciplinary perspectives on organisation.

1.2   PROBLEM

These contemporary understandings of learning and knowledge in organisations call into question the familiar separation of learning and knowledge management and challenge their fragmented practice. The literatures support the recognition of learning and knowledge as entwined in the experience of interaction in the work context (Stacey 2001; Fenwick 2003; Stacey 2003a; 2003b). Workplace practice however, persists in its focus on formalised training programs and information and communication based knowledge management interventions which are discrete from each other and distanced from informing theory.

Workplace learning strategy in Australia is underpinned by a Nationally endorsed competency based training model which is criticised for its focus on the transfer of individualised skills, knowledge and attitudes from expert to novice (ANTA 2003, 20). Knowledge management practice, too, continues to maintain a focus on the dissemination of explicit knowledge through codification and transfer through electronic channels (Malhotra 2002).

That learning and knowledge remain discrete in *practice* is in contradiction to their convergence in *theory*. Their separation points to a problem that lies in the contrast between increasingly sophisticated treatment of the notions of learning and knowledge which recognise their inherent interconnectivity in theory and the reductionist perspectives that underpin divided practice. Converging theories in learning and knowledge management point to their integration, while the disparate organisation of, and practice in, each of the fields maintains their separation. This disconnect highlights an important problem for organisations in pursuit of more effective learning and knowledge outcomes. The problem prompts investigation of organisational experience with a view to illuminating the relationships between learning and knowledge management and developing understandings which contribute to improved practice in organisations.

1.3 PURPOSE OF THE STUDY

While the integrated consideration of learning and knowledge management through complexity in organisations is prominent in the literatures, there is no empirical research available which explicitly explores their interaction.

The purpose of this study is to investigate the relationship between learning and knowledge in organisations in the experience of organisational members. The question,

'What is the relationship between workplace learning experience and organisational knowledge?' is designed to lead to fuller understandings of learning and knowledge in organisations than their separate investigation can provide, and contribute to holistic perspectives on their relationship. This study progresses from the convergence of themes in the literature to provide a background for the development of improved practice in both learning and knowledge facilitation in organisations.

1.4 AIM OF THE RESEARCH

The aim of this research is to develop a holistic perspective on learning and knowledge in organisations through exploration of workplace experience.

1.5 APPROACH

The alignment of complexity theories with converging themes at the intersection of organisational learning and knowledge management theories is strongly argued in this dissertation. In addition, the prominence of complexity metaphors across the literatures prompts sensitivity to the features of complex systems in the development of a methodology closely aligned with the thesis' theoretical frame.

The research approach in this study reflects important themes in the literature, and is designed to avoid reductionist assumptions about knowledge and research. Complexivist ideas are apparent in this study's incorporation of methods that: permit participants' responses to self-organise; allow for the emergence of novel perspectives; provide richly interconnected data; recognise the iterative and interactive nature of knowledge; and value the personal lived experience of participants in interaction with their work contexts.

The selection of a public sector organisation as a case for investigation is prompted by the typical disconnection of learning and knowledge management sections in large, bureaucratic structures and the tension that exists between policy or 'organisational' knowledge and training approaches and applied or 'local' knowledge and learning. The dissertation's focus on the convergence of themes is intended to provide justification for perspectives on learning and knowledge in organisations that recognise their interrelatedness.

1.6   SIGNIFICANCE OF THE STUDY

The relationship between learning and knowledge in organisations through the lens of complexity is suggested in the literatures, but presents a gap in empirical research. This study makes four significant contributions to the literature in addressing this gap:

1. This research makes a significant empirical contribution to the weighty theoretical discourse that uses complexity to discuss organisation. Using the language of complex adaptive systems, the research focuses on experiences of individual and collective learning, of the nature of broader organisational learning, and of managing emergent knowledge. The findings of this study support assumptions about the value of the complexity metaphor set in understanding workplace experience, although they problematise the direct application of complex adaptive systems frameworks to human organisation.

2. The study is significant in its provision of empirical support for the development of practice which recognises the problematic nature of knowledge and the nonlinear interactions that characterise organisational behaviour. The findings illustrate the entwinement of learning and knowledge in organisations and point to implications for the integration of knowledge and learning systems.

3. This research utilises an innovative research approach which draws on complexity theories in its development.

4. It illustrates the convergence of several central themes in contemporary organisational learning and knowledge management literatures and links these in the research. In its investigation across discourses, this study offers a novel perspective on each field as well as on their integration.

1.7   DISSERTATION OVERVIEW

This dissertation follows a standard format in eleven chapters, progressing through literature, methodology, and data collection and analysis before presenting findings with some discussion of their relevance to the literature and implications for practice.

Following on from this first introductory chapter, Chapter 2 presents the informing literatures and features organisational learning and knowledge management, particularly in relation to their development and intersection. Discussion of workplace learning as it relates to the fields is provided, and complexity theories are introduced.

Chapter 3 develops an argument to support the claim that the fields are converging in a number of areas, and that this convergence is coherent with central themes in complexity. A review of calls for research and an analysis which highlights the absence of research focused on examining the convergence more closely is then presented in support of need for the current research.

The literature review is followed by Chapter 4, Theory, which details the development of a research design sympathetic to the theory that underpins the study. It is followed by a method chapter (Chapter 5) which describes the iterative process of collecting and analysing data.

Following the method, an introduction to the findings (Chapter 6) is presented in which some discussion of the ways participants make sense of terms precedes the categorisation of findings. Chapters 7, 8, and 9 detail the research findings, each chapter presenting dimensions of learning experience with reference to complex adaptive systems theory. The relationship between this learning and the knowledge of the organisation emerges in a single framework and is illustrated as problematic and inherently linked to the ways in which organisational members self-organise to maximise their success in the immediate environment.

In Chapter 10 the findings are discussed with reference to the converging literatures and organised under the three major themes that emerge in the meeting of the fields of discourse. These chapters draw together the findings under the three themes and compare and contrast them with published theoretical assumptions about the nature of workplace experience. In this chapter the experience of learning related through narrative precedes discussion about the ways in which the experience reflects learning and knowledge co-emerging through the interaction of organisational members. Chapter 10 also provides a brief overview of implications of the findings for learning and knowledge facilitation in the organisation and a critique of the theoretical model used to make sense of the findings.

The monograph concludes with some broad remarks about the research and its contribution to understandings of organisational experience. It identifies issues that arise in this research as inviting further investigation, and reviews the research in terms of its goals.

This dissertation provides a perspective on organisational experience that acknowledges the interconnectedness of organisational members with each other, their work and context. It illustrates the intricate entwinement of learning and knowledge and challenges the inherent contradictions of organisation and learning and of knowledge and management (Alvesson and Karreman 2001: 995).

2   LITERATURE REVIEW

This chapter lays out the literatures that inform the study, highlighting the confluence of themes across organisational learning and knowledge management and their implications for workplace learning. These themes are investigated and then related to emerging theories of complexity.

The integration of organisational learning with knowledge management focuses on future development of the fields within a single discourse. Vera and Crossan's (2003: 127) diagrammatic representation of the boundaries between organisational learning and organisational knowledge is adapted and extended below (figure 1) to highlight the convergence of organisational learning and knowledge management literatures in relation to workplace learning and complexity theories. This model illustrates the relationship between informing literatures for this study and serves as a base for the development of an argument about convergence of theory in the following chapter.

Organisational Learning   ## Knowledge Management

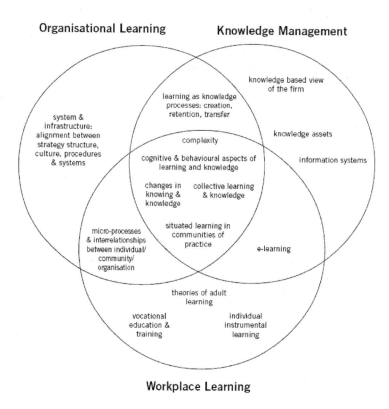

Workplace Learning

Figure 1 Convergent themes in the literatures building from Vera and Crossan 2003

This chapter begins with an overview of organisational learning which introduces changing notions of learning and organisation in the literatures. Knowledge management theory is then discussed in relation to changing conceptions of knowledge and links to organisational learning theories are highlighted. Strategies for facilitating learning practice are then critiqued in light of the contributions to theory of organisational learning and knowledge management discourses.

In this chapter complexity is introduced as an integrating device which promises new perspectives in the fields. Complexity is described as an emerging theory, based in metaphor and developing in a range of disciplines and the characteristics of the complexity metaphor set are described.

2.1 LEARNING AND KNOWLEDGE IN ORGANISATIONS

The body of literature that deals with learning in organisations and knowledge management is immense. This survey of the literature aims to summarise some major themes in the discourses and discuss some influential paradigms and debates over the history of the subject areas. The focus for the review is on the definitions, developments and metaphors prominent in the discourses of organisational learning and knowledge management and on the points of intersection between the two. It does not aim to be exhaustive, rather to develop a history and context within which this research is conceived and lead to discussion of the ways in which complexity theories support their integration.

2.1.1 ORGANISATIONAL LEARNING

The following review of organisational learning literature discusses: definitions of learning in organisation learning; definitions of organisational learning; the impetus for development of theory in organisational learning; and a brief history of the organisational learning theory that informs this research. The review also visits prominent debates and metaphors in the literatures before summarising contemporary perspectives in the field.

2.1.1.1 *Defining learning in organisational learning*

The meaning of the word 'learning', visited so frequently in management texts, is broad and often ambiguous. Even the discourse on organisational learning leaves learning itself ill-defined, unlinked to educational theory and 'simplistically mechanical' (Spender 1996: 64). In many accounts, learning is seen as the unproblematic diffusion of objective, uncontested knowledge to expert to learner (Huzzard 2004: 351), learning nothing more that direct transfer of knowledge quanta from a definitive source to a receptive individual.

Some early critical attention was paid to simplistic assumptions about cognition as the basis for organisational learning. Discussion about the role of behavioural change provided a fundamental contrast to strongly cognitivist notions of organisational learning and led to some debate which pivoted about cognitive and behavioural perspectives. Fiol and Lyles (1991: 811), for example, assert that '...one must separate behavioral and cognitive development from each other' if a theory of organisational learning theory is to be developed. Their definition is rooted in the behavioural – 'Organizational learning means the process of improving actions through better knowledge and understanding' (1985: 803).

A focus on cognition is said to inappropriately limit the premise of organisational learning (Appelbaum and Goransson 1997: 118). Cognitivist assumptions which build from individual learning theory and are based on studies of individual speech and motor skills, for example, are unable to provide insight into organisational learning theory where experience is '...mainly unique and nonrepetitive...' (Fiol and Lyles 1985: 804). Argyris (in interview with Crossan 2003: 41) maintains, however, that organisational learning work is still, '...importantly influenced by cognitive theory'.

Definitions of learning available from theorists allied with the 'community-of-practice' thread in organisational learning theory highlight its situatedness and lead discussion away from cognitivist preoccupation (Lave and Wenger 1991; Brown and Duguid 2000; Lave and Wenger 2000). Such definitions reference the practical nature of learning and its embeddedness in everyday human action, where 'Learning is a practical, rather than a cognitive, process and cannot be separated from the creation of (professional) identity' (Elkjaer 2004: 422).

Definitions of learning in more literatures also reflect authors' recognition of and grappling with its complex nature. Attempts to define learning are more frequently drawing on educational representations, Dewey (1859-1952), Vygotsky (1986 -1934) and Piaget (1896-1980) referenced with increasing frequency (for example Piaget in Mirvis 1996; Vygotsky in Spender 1996; Dewey in Elkjaer 2004; Vygotsky in Ghosh 2004).

Links to educational theory inform understandings that enrich discussions about the role of experience, participation, instrumentality, situatedness, construction, critical thinking and cultural process in learning. Definitions anchored in such discourse, and utilised in organisational learning theory, include references to its nature as an unavoidable part of human activity.

Definitions extend, too, beyond the individual learner to conceptions of learning as a collective activity. Backstrom (2004: 471), for example, describing learning as '...rather enduring changes in a collective as a result of interaction between the collective and its context'.

A challenging definition of learning in Stacey's work provides a further shift away from simple and mechanistic notions of transmission in organisational learning,

> *'Learning is the activity of interdependent people and can only be understood in terms of self-organising communicative interaction and power relating in which identities are potentially transformed. Individuals cannot learn in isolation and organisations can never learn' (Stacey 2003a: 331).*

The increasing sophistication with which learning is discussed in the literature promises new opportunities for improved learning practice and provides important contributions to organisational learning theory.

2.1.1.2 *Defining organisational learning*

Organisational learning is described as a 'fashionable' field of theory and practice (Appelbaum and Goransson 1997: 115) that has at its roots the 'conventional wisdom' (Argyris and Schon 1996: xvii) that organisations must continually anticipate and respond to perpetually changing environments in order to survive. There is a great deal of confusion over organisational learning (Burnes, Cooper et al. 2003: 458) and the concept '...is vast in scope, diffuse and suffers from an absence of conceptual clarity and theoretical coherence' (Lakomski 1998: 98). It continues to be, it seems, a 'black box' of a concept (Easterby-Smith, Antonacopoulou et al. 2004: 378).

This deficit of conceptual clarity, however, does not derive from lack of available definitions, indeed they abound. Their diversity, however, is vast. Fiol and Lyles' (1985: 803) slender definition, 'Organisational learning means the process of improving actions through better knowledge and understanding' provides an umbrella across these varying definitions.

Definitions are shifting from themes rooted in individual acquisition to a greater focus on sense-making, participation and interactivity. Ikehara's (1999: 66) focus on the individual is apparent in his definition,

> *'A learning organisation exists when the individuals in the organisation continually learn not only to realise efficiency in the work role but also to develop as an individual and be creative in the organisation as it pursues its unknown future'.*

Notions of acquisition are also apparent in the focus on new knowledge and insights obvious in Hedberg's (1980) work and in the substantial work of Argyris and Schon (Argyris and Schon 1978; Argyris 1995; Argyris and Schon 1996; Argyris 1999). In these works themes developed to define organisational learning relate to '…recognizing, surfacing, criticizing, and restructuring organizational theories of action' and applying 'double-loop' learning when considering organisational problems (Argyris and Schon 1996: xix).

This definition of organisational learning provided by Argyris and Schon focuses on the cognitive, and Garvin's definition (1993: 80), 'organizational learning occurs with an organization skilled at creating, acquiring, and transferring knowledge…' shows his similar commitment to acquisitional notions. The collection of definitions he provides for organisational learning (Garvin 1993), however, also highlights strong themes around behaviour change, and sharing of knowledge and experience.

Later definitions also problematise the role of the learning individual and the intentionality of organisational learning strategy in improving organisational effectiveness (Lam 2001; Loermans 2002). Senge (1992: 3) describes a learning organisation as one '…where people continually expand their capacity to create the results they truly desire, where new and expansive patterns of thinking are nurtured…'. Hitt (1995: 17) focuses on change, with his definition of a learning organisation as 'an organisation that is striving for excellence through continual organisational renewal'. Crossan, Lane et al. (1999: 352) highlights tension between exploration and assimilation, '…organizational learning is a dynamic process. Not only does learning occur over time and across levels, but it also creates a tension between assimilating new learning (feed forward) and exploiting or using what has already been learned (feedback)'.

Contemporary definitions even more deeply reflect the problematisation of the notion of organisational learning and of the field. Elkjaer's (2004) work brings intuition and emotion to the fore in her 'third way' of organisational learning. In her definition, organisational learning is

> *'...a combination of skills and knowledge acquisition (product) and participation in communities of practice (process) [and]...intuition and emotion are important triggers for the development of experience and knowledge in organizations' (2004: 429-430).*

In 2003 Wang and Ahmed presented a conceptual framework for organisational learning based on five focuses: Individual learning; process or system; culture or metaphor knowledge management; and continuous improvement (2003: 15). In this framework they provide a summary of definitions that illustrate these prominent themes and practices in organisational learning. The table below utilises Wang and Ahmed's structure for illustrating the concepts in organisational learning that are central to this current study.

Table 1 Different foci in definitions of organisational learning

Individual learning	'Organizational learning occurs when individuals within an organization experience a problematic situation and inquire into it on the organizational behalf' (Argyris and Schon 1996: 16)
	'...individual learning leads to individual knowledge; organizational learning leads to collective knowledge' (McElroy 2000: 198)

Collective learning	'Organisational learning is…the collectivity of individual learning within the organization. Collective learning occurs in addition to the learning process at the individual level and may even occur independently of each individual' (Wang and Ahmed 2003: 9)
Cognition and behaviour	'Change resulting from learning need not be visibly behavioural. Learning may result in new and significant insights and awareness that dictate no behavioural change.' (Huber 1991: 89) 'Continuous ongoing change in organizational cognitive structures' (Nicolini and Meznar 1995: 727)
Culture	'In order to change, an organizational learning process needs to take place that pushes the organization beyond its currently held understandings of itself and its ways of dealing both with its internal and external reality' (Lakomski 2001: 69)
Knowledge Management	'An organization learns if any of its units acquires knowledge that it recognizes as potentially useful to the organization' (Huber 1991: 89)
Complexity	'Like KM and OL, complexity concerns itself with the nature and role of learning and knowledge in human organizations' (McElroy 2000: 202)

The table illustrates a wide range of important issues that emerge in the literatures in organisational learning and underpin a number of key debates. The definitions point to varying interpretations of both learning and knowledge, with the range of theoretical standpoints highlighting the density and breadth of the field. Through these varying definitions the thesis' central themes are suggested. Individual and collective learning, the problematic nature of knowledge, and the role of cognition and mental models in learning are indicated in the definitions as critical to understandings of organisational learning. These themes recur across the fields of discourse that support this study and provide a ground for their integrated investigation.

2.1.1.3   *Impetus for the development of organisational learning*

Organisational learning theorists quote environmental turbulence, new forms of organisation, multidimensional, prevalent and increasingly fast paced change, the changing nature of knowledge, increasing complexity and uncertainty and the competitive advantage of innovating organisations, knowledge as a primary resource and internationalisation as primary drivers for organisational effectiveness. Aspin (1997), Field (1997), Loermans (2002) and Burns, Cooper et al. (2003) are among a broad field of authors to provide a range of perspectives along these lines.

Organisational learning is seen as the key to aligning organisations with the changing environments within which they operate. Fiol and Lyles (1985: 804) describe the 'ultimate criterion' of organisational performance as an organisation's ability to align itself with the environment in order to compete and innovate in a complex world.

The centrality of learning as a key to organisational performance is common in each of the driving forces for change. The main message about success in this fast changing, complex, global and knowledge-intensive context is captured in Stata's oft-quoted statement '…the rate at which individuals and organizations learn may become the only sustainable competitive advantage…' (Garvin 1993: 78; Hitt, Hoskisson et al. 1994: 42; Burnes, Cooper et al. 2003: 453). 'The organizational advantage' (Nahapiet and Ghoshal 1998), then, lies in the organisation's ability to exploit the learning that takes place within it.

This broad assumption that organisational learning is a key to competitiveness and performance underpins the development of organisational learning theory and practice and is apparent in the work of Appelbaum and Goransson (1997), Lam (2001) and Loermans (2002). While theorists acknowledge the *assumption* of positive outcomes from organisational learning, without discussion of the tension that exists between those who set the agenda for learning and those whose benefits are associated with the learning and clear definition and measurement techniques, empirical support is problematic.

Much effort is expended, however, to substantiate the assumption. In a study of research in organisational learning from 1981 to 2004 Bapuji, Crossan et al. (2005: 535) find that the term 'performance' dominates papers as the most common dependent variable. Baker and Sinkula's (1999) work is an example of research which attempts to demonstrate a causal link between organisational learning and organisational success. Indeed, their research does find that a learning orientation is significantly related to business performance. Slater and Narver (1995) similarly find that learning facilitates behaviour change that leads to improved performance and Farrell's (2000) own findings support the empirical evidence provided in both studies.

Much of the optimism that surrounds organisational learning as a precursor to organisational accomplishment hinges on the supposition that all learning is positive learning. Occasional reference to the possibility of organisational learning that is negative in its effect is apparent in the discussion over time of Fiol and Lyles (1985) Huber (1991) and Wang and Ahmed (2003). It reveals a consideration of learning and human complexity that deviates from the deterministic literature that dominates organisational learning discourse. As Huber (1991: 89) attests, 'Entitites can incorrectly learn, and they can correctly learn that which is incorrect'.

It is this problematisation of the very basis of organisational learning impetus that leads this study to explore experiences of learning in the organisation and links it to the knowledge the organisation holds. This exploration takes place within a reflection on the development of discourse over time and its contemporary discussion.

Figure 2 A timeline of organisational learning

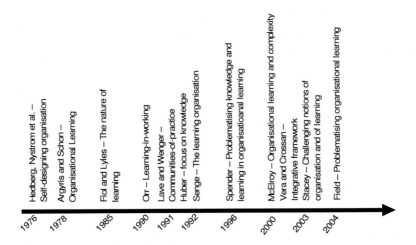

Argyris and Schon's 'Organizational Learning' (1978) drew early attention to the field, focusing on learning as the detection and correction of error. The *enabling* and *producing* of organisational learning (Crossan 2003: 41) was central to this early discussion. Implications for practice developed in Revans' (1978) action learning process and more prescriptive accounts were popularised through practitioner guides on 'the learning organisation' (Senge 1992; Drew and Smith 1995; Hitt 1995; Senge 1999). Lakomski (1998: 98) asserts that the prescriptive, positivistic approach of practitioners and consultants which led to guides for 'structuring' learning organisations did so at the same time as scholars questioned whether such organisations actually exist. Hedberg, Nystrom, et al.'s (1976) early forays into 'self-designing organization' provided a backdrop for increasing interest in organisational flexibility alongside perceived increases in the prevalence and rate of change.

By the time organisational learning became prominent in management discourse in the early 80s, it had at its core a debate about the nature of learning. The debate focused on types and levels of learning and the application of human abilities like learning to inanimate structures such as organisations (Fiol and Lyles 1985: 804; Easterby-Smith, Crossan et al. 2000: 785). Other important themes that linked with these ones related to contextual factors in the learning of organisations, the theory reflecting traditional management preoccupation with corporations' cultures, strategies and structures.

In the early 1990s empirical work by researchers such as Lave and Wenger (1991) and Orr (1990) (whose work is used extensively by Brown and Duguid 2000) drew attention to the concept of 'learning-in-working'. For these researchers, the 'legitimate peripheral participation' that occurs in 'communities-of-practice' refocused organisational learning theory on participation as learning. Within such work organisational learning is presented problematically, stressing contradictions and conflicts in learning, development of identity and transformation of practice.

The 90s also saw a shift in the discourse through which the divide between the learning organisation and organisational learning became obvious. The focus at this time was on a systemic approach to learning from four bases – knowledge acquisition, information distribution, information interpretation and organisational memory (Huber 1991: 88) and related to the emergence in the literature of knowledge management as a facilitator of organisational knowledge.

In many ways, the burgeoning knowledge management discourse took over the mantle from organisational learning scholars and practitioners attempting to develop a strategic and practical framework for the 'information distribution' base of organisational learning. This focus was reflected in a spike in knowledge management publication (Scarbrough, Swan et al. 1999: 14) and provided a path for divergence of knowledge management from organisational learning theory.

Connections between organisational knowledge, learning and memory, are made in Spender's (1996) important work which investigates the underlying epistemology upon which the concepts are built. This work attempts to move beyond the positivistic focus of organisational learning theory of the time. For Spender, continued debate around the cognitivist/behaviourist and system-structural/interpretive dualities limit the ongoing development of organisational theory. In his 1996 paper, Spender looks to philosophy and psychology in an attempt to integrate knowledge, learning and memory as interdependent parts of a single system.

In recent years, the literature has followed Spender in concerning itself to a far greater extent with integrationist themes, drawing heavily on psychological and educational theory and philosophy. Published book and article titles increasingly include key words such as symbiosis (Koopmans 2005), contextuality (Haggis 2005), complexity (McElroy 2000), collectivity (Cross and Israelit 2000; Backstrom 2004), and social construction (Visser 2005). Authors appear less interested in prescriptive, 'how to' approaches to the development of learning organisations and more interested in 'understanding the nature and processes of learning' within context and in reference to broader educational and socio-cultural understandings (Stacey 2003a: 326).

2.1.1.5 Prominent debates and metaphors

This history of organisational learning has featured a number of central debates. The prescriptive nature of learning organisation literature, and its assumptions about improving organisational effectiveness drew some serious debate in the mid- to late-nineties. The contested claim that organisations learn only through individuals who learn continues to trigger discussion. The very assumption that organisations can learn is, of course, pivotal to any argument in organisational learning. The varying perspectives in the field provide fuel for hotly argued debate in the literature and for the continual development of theory.

2.1.1.5.1 Organisational learning/ the learning organisation

A major debate in organisational learning discourse relates to the divide between 'organisation learning' and 'the learning organisation' (Easterby-Smith, Crossan et al. 2000: 784). The dual paradigm describes a divide between the former which is descriptive, non-prescriptive and distanced from practice, and the latter as a practitioner-focused, prescriptive approach to the field which uses 'learning organization' as a catchphrase (Argyris and Schon 1996: xix) (the divide is also discussed in the work of Lakomski 1998; Burnes, Cooper et al. 2003; Sun and Scott 2003; Wang and Ahmed 2003). While 'organisational learning' writing is positioned as primarily theoretically driven and academically informed, 'the learning organisation' is more commonly derided as pop-management, reductionist, even described as an '… inherently unartistic prescriptive notion' (Huzzard 2004: 350).

Senge's (1992) practitioner guide 'The Fifth Discipline' popularised 'the learning organization' literature of the mid-nineties that led to the subsequent debate. Given its practitioner focus, the learning organisation discourse waned in the presence of knowledge management approaches in the late 90s and continued to wane against organisational learning literature through the late 90s to early 00s.

Scholarly writing over the past decade questions the existence of 'the learning organisation', identifying the construct as an 'idealised goal' (Field 2000: 159), however, development of key foci of organisational learning continues. Field's work of the time questions the comment of some authors on the learning organisation, suggesting that while they describe learning organisations as 'tangible', it is in the journey toward the end goal of a learning organisation (that is, organisational learning) where value resides. These notions of 'being' and 'becoming' are used to great effect by Burns, Cooper et al. (2003) and provide a clear differentiator between the discourses.

Articles continue to be published exhorting the value of 'the learning organization' (Loermans 2002; Sun and Scott 2003) and, indeed, a popular journal which carries the phrase as its title publishes authors such as Stacey, Field, Blackman, Firestone and McElroy. Discourse, however, now tends to focus more prominently on organisational learning, and '…practitioners who seek to implement the more prescriptive models of the learning organization often draw on the more academic literature in order to help them understand the challenges they face' (Easterby-Smith, Crossan et al. 2000: 786).

2.1.1.5.2 Individual/organisational learning

One of the important challenges for practitioners is the practical imperative of linking the learning of organisational members to organisational learning, understanding the relationship between the individual and organisational in order to facilitate organisational development. As the definitions and history of organisational learning reveal, the relationship is also a critically important theme in the literatures, however the link is one which remains elusive (Critten 2003: 17). Much of the discourse (Argyris and Schon 1996; Lakomski 1998; Schein 1999; Wang and Ahmed 2003) focuses on the role of the individual learner in an organisation's adaptive and generative learning, while other work attempts to enrich and integrate the 'levels' at which learning is discussed (individual, collective and organisational) by focusing on the processes of learning (Crossan, Lane et al. 1999).

Knowledge is observed to be firstly individual by Nonaka (1994: 17) who explicitly describes the role of knowledge creation (learning and innovation) as that of the individual, with the role of the organisation to provide '…a context for such individuals to create knowledge'. Organisational learning, in this frame, is the process by which the resultant knowledge derived through individual learning is crystallised through 'organizational amplification' to become organisational knowledge.

There is huge variety in the discourse, however, regarding the importance of the individual learner to the organisation's ability to learn. At one end of the spectrum Srivastava's (1983) early research constructs organisational learning as wholly dependent on learning individuals within the organisation rather than any social construction, knowledge sharing, collective learning or organisational institutionalisation of knowledge.

This individual learner is also primary and prior to the organisation's learning in Argyris and Schon's (1996: 16) seminal work,

> *'Organisational learning occurs when individuals within an organization experience a problematic situation and inquire into it on the organisation's behalf. They… restructure their activities so as to bring outcomes and expectations into line, thereby changing organizational theory-in-use'.*

The sharing, reconstruction and institutionalisation of organisational knowledge results in its persistence independent of the individuals through which it was created in the work of Walsh and Ungson (1991). Similarly, Farrell (2000: 9) revisits organisational learning as collective individual learning, 'It is the task of the learning organisation to integrate individual learning into organisational learning'. Fiol and Lyles summarise that organisational learning '...results in associations, cognitive systems, and memories that are developed and shared by members of the organization.' (1985: 804).

For other authors, however (Hedberg 1980; Scarbrough, Swan et al. 1999; Sun and Scott 2003; Wang and Ahmed 2003), a more complex relationship exists in the role of the individual learner in the learning of the organisation. For Wang and Ahmed (2003: 9) '...organizational learning is not simply a collectivity of individual learning processes, but engages interaction between individuals in the organization...'. Hedberg's discussion (1980: 9) asserts that organisational learning is more than the sum of the learning of its members, and focuses on the ability of any organisation to develop 'world views and ideologies' which are impervious to change in the organisation's membership and which are demonstrated through pervasive organisational behaviours, memories and values. In Hedberg's argument, individual learning stems from the organisation's learning.

Other work, still, carefully differentiates between individual and organisational learning, and highlights 'collective learning and shared insights, mental models and organizational memory' (Burnes, Cooper et al. 2003: 455) and the interactions of members of the organisation and the social construction of knowledge that occurs as a result. Lam (2001: 214) sees 'the conversion of the acquired information or knowledge into organizational memory' as the final stage in the process of collective learning. Further, in his view organisational learning is only possible when '...there is a collective mind which is doing the learning'.

The 'collective nature of each socialized individual thinking, learning and remembering process' (1996: 69), is central to Spender's argument that a focus on individual knowledge and thought limits the development theory of organisational learning. For Spender, it is the interaction of individual and organisational knowledge, learning and memory, and the body of collective knowledge that is most vital to organisational learning. Spender strongly contends that he '...must hold to a different view [to that of Walsh and Ungson] if we believe that the organization is capable of activities unlike those of individuals'. He goes on to describe crowd behaviour as a construct of collective thinking and acting and summarises that

> '...*organizational properties had no correlate at the individual level and were not summations of individual capabilities, they were systemic properties that emerged unforeseen at the social level.*' *(Spender 1996: 69).*

Following Spender's argument, the emergence of culture reflects the non-sum effect of individuals in collective. His concept of 'culture as confident activity' (1996: 68) prompts an understanding of a learning culture as one which supports, promotes and values learning so that learners within the organisation are consistently confident to create, develop and innovate within and through the organisation.

Connectionism provides another perspective for consideration in the relationship between individual, organisational and cultural. It is, Lakomski states, the cognitivist perspective that ensures that organisational learning theory '...maintains the analytical base unit... as the learning of the individual within an organizational context' (2001: 68). In the connectionist cognitive perspective, what it is to know is redefined in terms of a boundarylessness between private knowledge and public culture. In this view the individual and personal, and the external and other, rather being separate worlds, are recognised as one world.

Connectionism informs a discussion of the collective mind by providing insight into the form of connections within a group, a focus which

> '...*is at once on individuals and the collective, since only individuals can contribute to a collective mind, but a collective mind is distinct from an individual mind because it inheres in the pattern of interrelated activities among many people*' *(Weick 2001: 262).*

The introduction of complexity to the debate (McElroy 2000: 201) further develops the connectionist perspective apparent in the work of Lakomski and Weik. McElroy refers to the relationship between individual and organisational as a cyclic one, where individuals' mental models are formed through organisation which in turn is modified through the learning of individuals.

It is in this frame that Argyris and Schon's question about the construction of 'organisation' is revisited, seen as critical to reducing the paradox inherent in the relationship between individual and organisational learning. In order to address the paradox, they believe, one must look at the organisation – 'what is an organization that it may learn?' (1978: 3).

2.1.1.5.3 *What is an organisation that it may learn?*

Notions of 'organisation' have shifted in response to changing understandings of the complex relationship between individual, collective, and context. Argyris and Schon's (1978) problematisation of 'organisation' drew together questions about the role of the individual in the organisation as well as the role of the organisation in controlling and directing individual behaviour.

The question is taken up as a challenge by Stacey (2003a: 330), extending discussion by questioning the very notion both of organisation and of learning and highlighting the tension described by Weick and Westley (1996) as existing between learning, which requires disruption and disordering, and organisation, which demands stability and order. His treatment of the problem highlights organisation as an emergent property of the iterative interaction of human beings. Stacey's argument pivots on one's inability to point to the organisation or to define it in terms other than the people and the artefacts they use with each other in their interaction. For Stacey, '…organisation is the thematically patterned activities of interdependent people, which constitute their closely interconnected individual and collective identities'.

Elkjaer (2004) contends that two understandings of organisation are apparent in conceptions of organisational learning. In her argument, organisation is represented either as a system or as a community of practice. Elkjaer's work goes to develop a metaphor for organisational learning built on a third understanding of organisation where the individual is neither a 'free agent', nor 'subjugated to the community', rather choosing whether or not to commit to participation in organisational life.

2.1.1.6 *Metaphor*

Organisational learning theory is saturated in metaphor. These metaphors are important to developing nuance in the theory and reflecting the variation in focus of understandings of organisational learning. In the following paragraphs these metaphors are italicised to represent their use as heuristic tools in the various discourses. Indicative authors and works are presented as examples of those which utilise the particular metaphors.

Metaphor is an important tool in creating new knowledge (Nonaka 1991: 5). Metaphor for Nonaka is a 'distinctive method of perception…Through metaphors, people put together what they know in new ways and begin to express what they know but cannot yet say.' The range of metaphorical bases on which the discourse on organisational learning lies includes those that are '…philosophical, mechanistic, educational, adaptive and organic' (Lam 2001: 212). Elkjaer's (2004) discussion of metaphor suggests development of nuance over time from *acquisition* through *participatiom* and posits a *third way* which synthesises the two.

While these metaphors are useful, aligning the myriad metaphors available in the literature with Elkjaer's *acquisition/participation* dualism is difficult. Much of the literature reflects the interweaving of the two. Argyris and Schon's (1996) work, for example, while strongly acquisitionist in nature, also concerns itself with the interaction between individual, context and group. In their view, participation in the workplace leads to cognitive shifts influenced by participation in the work and with other organisational members. Lave and Wenger's (1991) interest in participation, on the other hand, which pivots on notions of community, social practice, meaning and identity also includes notions of acquisition. This entwinement of acquisitionist and participative metaphors are evident where '…participation and reification act as distinct forms of remembering and forgetting' (Stacey 2003b: 208).

In the *third way* proposed by Elkjaer to encapsulate the synthesis of *acquisition* and *participation*, a base is suggested upon which the most contemporary understandings including complexity concepts might be developed.

2.1.1.6.1   Acquisition
Most prominent in the literature within the *acquisition* metaphor set is Argyris and Schon's (1978) *single- and double-loop* learning metaphor which focuses discussion on *routine* versus *radical* learning which leads to incremental or transformational change. While this metaphor has been useful for distinguishing between simple stimulus-response learning and reflective learning, Easterby-Smith, Crossan et al. (2000: 786) argue that the

distinction between the two has become blurred and that *innovation* now reflects investigation and understanding of *double-loop* learning. *Higher-* and *lower-level* learning (Fiol and Lyles 1985: 807-808) is a similar metaphor set for the learning at strategic, structural level (that of double-loop learning) and focused learning that is short-term, shallow and limited to association-making. Applebaum (1997: 116) describes the two main perspectives on the learning organisation as *generative* or *transformational* learning and *incremental* or *adaptive* learning.

In early discourse Hedberg (1980) and Fiol and Lyles (1985) differentiate between 'Learning - the development of insights, knowledge, and associations between past action, the effectiveness of those actions, and future actions' and 'Adaptation - The ability to make incremental adjustments as a result of environmental changes, goal structure changes, or other changes' (Fiol and Lyles 1985: 811). Others, such as Lakomski (2001: 68), argue that 'The terms learning, adaptation, change, innovation, and unlearning are all used in the attempt to account for organizational learning and contribute little to clarifying this concept'.

The acquisition metaphor incorporates *mechanistic* and *structural* understandings of learning as knowledge *accrual, transfer* or *transaction*. Learning described as *stored* (Easterby-Smith, Crossan et al. 2000), as *stock* or *system* (Bontis, Crossan et al. 2002) connotes rigidity and commodification. The use of this metaphor group reflects an intellectual *capital* and knowledge *management* focus on the role of learning in organisations.

Inherent in acquisition metaphors is assumption of the 'fundamentally additive' conception of learning (Fenwick and Tennant 2004: 60) and the individual learner as of primary consideration in understanding the organisation's learning. This assumption situates the learner as separate from, and independent of, the organisation and context. Interpretations of learning in this group focus on cognition, and include metaphors around learning as *congenital, vicarious,* involving *grafting, searching, information interpretation,* and *memory* (Huber 1991).

Aligned with the cognitivist focus coherent with the acquisition metaphor set is a group of metaphors around *mental models* or *schema, patterns* of neuronal *connection* which must be *dislodged* if generative learning is to occur. These schema provide *frameworks* within which disconfirming evidence is *overridden* and learning through novelty is hindered (Lakomski 2001).

Learning organisations are described as having *cultures* of *empowerment*, learning emerging from organisational members' empowerment to act. Nonaka (1994), relates empowerment to employees' ability to *interpret, absorb* and *apply* knowledge. Schein's (1999) interest in *culture* in organisational learning is rooted in acquisitionist assumptions including cognitive *redefinition, reframing* and *converting* resulting from *brainwashing* and *coercion* and the metaphor *empowerment* is questioned within such discussion. Field (1997; 2004) highlights the dilemma inherent in notions of organisational learning in which employees are *equipped* by managers to behave in new ways. *Empowerment* in these discussions is seen as a *mechanism* for *investing* responsibility in organisational members, '…a process in which power flows down from the enterprise's vision to leaders and on to those below' (Field 1997: 149) where organisations are *flat and lean* and creating *transparent channels* for information exchange.

2.1.1.6.2 Participation
This problematic theme, *empowerment*, however, is an important one within the literature, for example in the work of Field (2000), and much of its discussion sits firmly within the *participation* metaphor set, linked to organisational *flexibility*, where attempts are made to *open things up* by reducing *barriers*. Field's (1997) earlier work in organisational learning presents metaphors around participation that focus on *partnerships* between managers and staff, where *common goals* assist members to *collaborate* in *shared awareness* and *common* understanding.

Communities of practice highlight participation, the work of Lave and Wenger, (Lave and Wenger 1991; Lave and Wenger 2000; Wenger, McDermott et al. 2002; Snyder, Wenger et al. 2004; Wenger 2004) in particular illustrating knowledge emerging from the *social fabric* of members *exchanging* and *contributing* to the community. These communities are *cultivated*, members *energised* through *engagement* with each other and their work. When the engagement is appropriate and relevant these groups *congeal* around a common issue to increase their learning and productivity. In this way, the learning is *situated* in the doing.

The use of metaphors of *canonical* and *noncanonical* practice are prominent in the work of Brown and Duguid (2000: 145-149) which highlights the gap between actual and espoused practices in organisations and this gap's primary importance in the performance of the organisation. In this perspective, workers are seen to develop sophisticated *noncanonical* approaches to *bridge the gap* between *directive* documentation and reality, workers saving organisations from their own *short-sightedness* that may lead to *chaos*. Analogy in this frame draws on work as *journey*, *canonical* guides as *maps* and points to the importance of *reconnecting map* and *mapped* through recognition of actual *noncanonical* practice.

Echoing some of the issues raised by Argyris and Schon (1996) this domain points to learning relating to *loss of face*. In Argyris and Schon's account, organisational members do not surface gaps between theory of action and theory in use because of embarrassment, and as a result the organisation cannot learn from the difference. In Brown and Duguid's (2000: 147) analysis the *baffled* worker looks to the *trouble-shooting* consultant and together the two *construct* new knowledge through their problem solving.

2.1.1.6.3 The third way
Elkjaer stresses '…body, emotion and intuition' (2004: 429) in her *third way*. She also highlights the synthesis of thinking and doing, organisational learning refocused on the transactionality through continuous and mutual formation of both individual and organisation in a *social world*.

The *third way* metaphor opens up the discourse to integrationist perspectives which accommodate the marriage of cognitive and interactionist perspectives, but does not limit itself to these. Philosophical metaphors, metaphors of interdependence and complexity reside in this set alongside those of ecology and politics.

Spender (1996: 66) uses the analogy of Ohm's law to describe the interdependency of knowledge, learning and memory within a single system. For Spender, like voltage, current and resistance, knowledge, learning and memory may only be understood in terms of each other. Metaphors of *dynamics* and *interdependency* are critical to organisational learning in the *third way*.

The alignment of learning and *adaptation* as described earlier is increasingly prominent in the literature, the words increasingly interchangeable, particularly with reference to complexity theory, and evident in the work of McElroy (2000), Englehardt and Simmons (2002), Snowden (2003a), Kurtz and Snowden (2003) and van Eijnatten (2004). Through complex adaptive systems theory *adaptation* is expanded to '...include learning and related processes' and refers to 'change in strategy based on system experience' (Holland 1995: 9). *Adaptation* in the *third way* assumes different connotations to those assumed within the *acquisition* metaphor set. In Holland's (1995) work *adaptation*, rather than pointing to incremental change as a response to *single-loop* or *lower-level* learning and contrasted with *generative* learning, directs attention to novelty which *emerges* through the interaction of *agents*. Adaptation occurs through interaction of agents' *mental models* or *internal models* within context.

Snowden's use of *complexity* as a metaphor set (Snowden 2002; Kurtz and Snowden 2003; Snowden 2003b) incorporates both *acquisition* and *participation* metaphors; *acquisition* illustrated in his positioning of learning as developing *internal models*, knowledge both a *thing* and a *flow*. Snowden's work discusses learning *cultures* that deal with *ambiguity* through *patterning*, *adaptation* reliant on diversity and *relating*. In complexity, knowledge *unfolds* through autonomous agents' participation in their world, acting in accordance with individual and collectively held rules. In this view, cognitivist notions of *patterning* and *adaptation* sit comfortably alongside those of *relating*.

The entire *complexity* metaphor set is similarly utilised in Stacey's (2001; 2003b; 2003a) work, *paradox*, *amplification* of difference into widespread *pattern making* leading to *shifts* in meaning. Snowden (2000: 2) suggests that the shift to complexity thinking in organisational learning is analogous to *the enlightenment*, the *ephemeral* process of relating leading to knowledge that is unable to be owned or managed. *Emergence* is a critical metaphor in this set.

Linked to *complexity* are *ecological* and *evolutionary* metaphors frequently used to describe organisational learning processes and the environment in which knowledge and learning emerge. The *evolutionary* metaphor set provides a language for the discussion of organisational learning as a natural and emergent process in organisations. Sharing within *evolving* communities results in *ecologies of knowledges*. On the other hand, the *third way* also captures *non-unitary* perspectives where *political* interests reveal *struggles* to achieve *equity*. Exemplified in the work of Field (2004) are metaphors around *social defence, self-protection and enhancement, tension* and *incompatibility,* metaphors which have become prominent in literatures which challenge the pervading optimism of organisational learning theory. These literatures and others (for example, Schein 1999, Easterby-Smith, Crossan et al, 2000, Fenwick 2003 and Huzzard 2004) disrupt notions of the superiority of the expert and highlight issues around coercion, oppression and control.

The metaphors used in organisational learning provide a range of heuristic devices through which the notion might be explored. While each set of metaphors prompts consideration from differing perspectives, recent metaphors highlight increasingly sophisticated treatments of the nature of organisational learning, its emergence in patterns of human interaction and the tension which characterises adaptive response. The complexity metaphor set enlivens discussion of organisational learning by providing a vernacular which encompasses these contemporary perspectives and extends conceptualisation of learning, organisation, and of organisational learning.

2.1.1.7 Contemporary perspectives on organisational learning

The concept of organisational learning lacks clear definition (Lakomski 1998: 98) and is 'excessively broad' (Wang and Ahmed 2003: 8). For many years, however, it has been premised on the understanding that 'organizations "learn" by capturing the experiential lessons of history in routines, and they tend to retain those routines that are functional' (Colarelli 1998: 1047). Changing notions of learning and organisation are now challenging this premise as organisational learning theory focuses more closely on their nature and emergence.

The *third way* illustrates a contemporary perspective on organisational learning which is characterised by its challenge and reassessment of notions of learning and organisation. Drawing more heavily on educational, socio-cultural theory and complexivist ideas, contemporary perspectives provide a ground for convergence of diverse discourses and development of integrationist understandings.

While Lakomski (2001: 68) claims that organisational learning theory '…continues to be dominated by the cognitive perspective of the behavioral tradition', much work is moving beyond such constructions. Wang and Ahmed (2003) in a critical review of organisational learning, describe the concept and practice of organisational learning as adopting a new focus – one of triple-loop learning and unlearning, knowledge creation through radical change, creative thinking, competence-based strategy, organisational sustainability through creative quality and valuing innovation. Contemporary work takes a second look at organisational learning refocusing on learning in work (Lave and Wenger 2000), community involvement (Wenger, McDermott et al. 2002; Snyder, Wenger et al. 2004; Wenger 2004), continual adaptation of shared interest groups in ontological and political interest (Field 2004), embodiment, reflection, everyday life (Elkjaer 2004) emotional connectedness (Fineman 2003), social identity (Child and Rodrigues 2003) and inter-subjectivity (Dovey and White 2005).

Stacey (2003a: 325), in his work on learning as an activity of interdependent people, states that '…claims that organisations learn amounts to both reification and anthropomorphism'. His focus on learning as iterative interactive action makes important contributions to the developing understanding of organisations and learning. Stacey's work (2001; 2003a; 2003b) which draws on complexity adds new perspectives to the extant constructions of organisational learning theory, as does that of Snowden (2002; Kurtz and Snowden 2003; Snowden 2003b), McElroy (2000; Firestone and McElroy 2002; 2003; 2004), Fenwick (2001; 2003; 2004; Fenwick and Tennant 2004), Anderson (1999), Eijnatten (2004) and Field (2004). Importantly, this new wave of literature that looks to combine complexity theory with organisational learning may be the point at which organisational learning and knowledge management remerge and research may progress toward more holistic understandings of workplace experience.

In this review of knowledge management, definitions of knowledge in the literatures precede definitions of knowledge management. The impetus for development of knowledge management theory and practice, a select history of their development, and prominent debates and metaphors are then discussed. These then lead to remarks on contemporary theory.

2.1.2.1 *Defining knowledge in knowledge management*

Early definitions of knowledge management are surprisingly limited in development of meaning around the term knowledge itself. Nonaka as early as 1991 recognises that despite the interest in knowledge management, managers '…misunderstand what knowledge is' (1991: 96). His view is echoed in recent work, Tsoukas and Vladimirou (2001: 973), for example, proposing that a contributing factor to the naivety of definitions is that organisational knowledge is 'much talked about but little understood'.

Knowledge is often represented as dualistic, existing either as tacit to the individual or explicit and external to the individual. Nonaka (1991: 26) focuses on the interplay between the two forms, a treatment which, though reductionist, begins to address some of the more complex issues inherent in knowledge creation and dissemination. His work begins to convey the importance of commitment, serendipity, metaphor and collective identity to knowledge development.

The vast majority of early definitions, though, represent very limited sophistication in their representation of knowledge. Some early authors, in fact, quite explicitly equate knowledge with information. In 1988 for example, Drucker, identified the growing focus on knowledge in organisations, stating in the paper's introduction that '…the typical business will be knowledge-based… it will be what I call an information-based organization' (1988: 45).

For some authors, deliberation on the nature of knowledge dilutes and distracts from discussion of knowledge management, their argument that 'Conceptual analysis is of little use to practitioners faced with questions about what specifically they should do as managers of knowledge' (Davenport and De Long 1998: 43) and Swan and Scarbrough (2001: 918) question '…the dangers, perhaps, of overly abstracted argument'. For others, however, consideration of the nature of knowledge is central and primary. Spender (1996: 64), for example, is critical of perspectives which presume that knowledge is '…made up of discrete and transferable granules of understanding about reality which can be added to an extant heap of knowledge'. This presumption is exemplified by phrases such as '…a quantum of knowledge' (Appleyard and Kalsow 1999: 288) and Spender is disparaging of the naivety they reveal. His work persistently challenges epistemological naivety in the pursuit of more useful approaches to developing knowledge in organisations (Spender 1996; 2003; 2006a; 2006b).

Contemporary literature is increasingly preoccupied with addressing the naivety revealed in the definition of knowledge, and the aligning of knowledge management approaches with epistemological standpoints. In his treatment of organisational knowledge, for example, Spender (1996: 63), posits a 'pluralist epistemology' and describes two radically different kinds of knowledge existing side by side and in interaction; data and meaning. Spender asserts data and meaning are generated, stored and applied differently, intelligence shaping and being shaped by their interactivity.

The representation of knowledge in Wenger's (2004: 1) work on knowledge management is inherently linked to participation and hinges on community of practice as its 'social fabric', '…what our human communities have accumulated over time to understand the world and act effectively in it'. Cavaleri's point of view is in accord with those authors interested in challenging underlying assumptions about knowledge in the knowledge management literatures and in practice. In his opinion, approaches to knowledge management driven by managers rushing to '…automate unrecognized and unseen primitive knowledge processes' (2004: 160) lead to unanticipated outcomes and injuries to performance.

The work of Blackman and Henderson (2005) addresses epistemological issues in knowledge management and provides a rich analysis of foundations for knowledge management approaches. Using Earl's (2001) classification of schools of knowledge management, they assert that,

'...it is the application of KMS [knowledge management systems] 'solutions' without commensurate regard for the philosophical issues, that is the chief reason for the continuing disappointment with knowledge management in many quarters' (Blackman and Henderson 2005: 166).

In this analysis they describe a knowledge anatomy in which knowledge management recognises and transfers knowledge in four dimensions – knowledge, community, organisational process and problem solving routine.

Conceptions of knowledge that underpin knowledge management are explored in Tsoukas and Vladimirou's analysis, and they conclude that knowledge is '...the individual capability to draw distinction, within a domain of action, based on an appreciation of context or theory, or both' (2001: 973). The shift to a more sophisticated treatment of knowledge triggers an appreciation of more problematic aspects of its management. In Tsoukas and Vladimirou's discussion, for example, the heuristic aspect of knowledge is recognised as unmanageable.

Knowledge management definitions which explicitly problematise knowledge and its nature illustrate important variations which influence nuances in knowledge management thinking and practice. Firestone and McElroy (2004: 178), for example, with their strong focus on systems thinking, and complex adaptive systems in particular, define knowledge as '...an encoded, tested, evaluated, and still surviving structure of information that helps the adaptive system (agent) that developed it to adapt'. Stacey (2003b), on the other hand, rejects systems thinking in complex responsive processing (Stacey 2003b: 312-314) and discusses knowledge as an activity of interdependent people, '...continuously replicated and potentially transformed in the communicative interaction between people' (Stacey 2001: 222).

Recent definitions highlight, too, the interplay between learning and knowledge, learning is linked to knowledge as '...participation in the cultural practice in which any knowledge exists is an epistemological principle of learning' (Lave and Wenger 2000: 171) and

'Learning and knowledge are intertwined in an iterative, mutually reinforcing process. While learning (the process) produces new knowledge (the content), knowledge impacts future learning' (Vera and Crossan 2003: 131).

These various definitions of knowledge in its relationship to organisation inform definitions of knowledge management, contemporary perspectives questioning the very notion of knowledge management.

2.1.2.2   *Defining knowledge management*

Growing sophistication in the representation of knowledge within knowledge management is illustrated in the shifts from the tacit/explicit dualism central to Nonaka's early work (1991) to recognition of its interactive, provisional, controversial and contestable nature (Swan and Scarbrough 2001).

Definitions of knowledge management, then, are as diverse as the epistemologies that underpin their theory and practice. Gates (1999 in Call 2005: 20), a founder of Microsoft, sees knowledge management as '…nothing more than managing information flow'. Firestone and McElroy (2004: 181) view it as '…the set of processes that seeks to change the organization's present pattern of knowledge processing to enhance both it and its knowledge outcomes'. Tsoukas and Vladimirou (2001: 990) contend it is

'…the dynamic process of turning an unreflective practice into a reflective one by elucidating the rules guiding the activities of the practice, by helping give a particular shape to collective understandings, and by facilitating the emergence of heuristic knowledge'.

Scarbrough, Swan et al. (1999: 1) attempt to portray a broad understanding as they recognise knowledge to be 'complex, multilayered, multifaceted'. Their definition of knowledge management is '…any process or practice of creating, acquiring, capturing, sharing and using knowledge, wherever it resides, to enhance learning and performance in organizations'.

Stacey, on the other hand, (2001: 220) insists that

'Knowledge cannot be grasped, owned by anyone or traded in any market and its creation is a process of communicating and power relating … it is not only impossible to manage knowledge, even asking the question makes no sense',

an opinion supported by the work of Alvesson and Karreman (2001: 995).

2.1.2.3   Impetus for development of knowledge management

Impetus for the emergence of a knowledge focus in organisations and its subsequent development through knowledge management theory and practice grew out of the identification of knowledge as a strategic asset of capital value in individuals, corporations and nations (a range of perspectives are offered in the work of Spender 1996; Davenport and Prusak 1998; Choo and Bontis 2002). Lyotard (2004) describes as '…widely accepted' the recognition that knowledge has been a principal force of production for recent decades.

The 'narrowly managerialistic focus' (Swan and Scarbrough 2001: 913) of knowledge management practice is driven by 'globalisation, ubiquitous computing and the knowledge-centric view of the firm' (Prusak 2001: 1003). Organisations of all types, from knowledge-intensive organisations, such as pharmaceutical and information technology firms, through to those whose core business is more stable, such as schools and government departments, are said to have to utilise organisational knowledge more quickly and more effectively than in the past to improve organisational performance and maintain advantage in increasingly turbulent and competitive environments.

Wiig (1997: 9) describes economic transition over time from the pursuit of operational excellence, through product leadership to the current focus on customer intimacy. Wiig relates the current focus to an emphasis on '…adding competitive value to products and services by application of direct or embedded human expertise – knowledge'. Linked to this quest is a changing understanding of work and organisations from product orientation to service orientation. The shift demands new ways of managing organisations, people and, it is suggested, knowledge.

Figure 3 A timeline of knowledge management

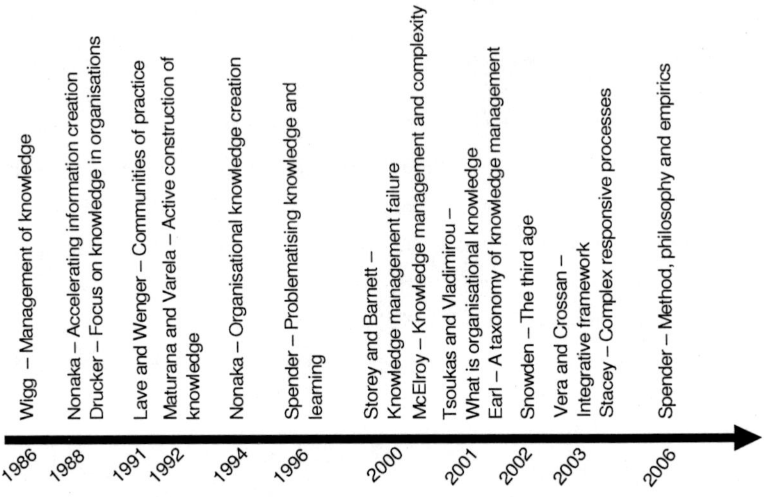

Histories of the development of knowledge management begin with a discussion of civilisations' management of tacit knowledge through focused learning (Wiig 1997: 9) and management of explicit knowledge through the development of libraries (Ives, Torrey et al. 1998; Scarbrough, Swan et al. 1999). These two understandings of knowledge management reflect the dual paradigm (Gloet and Berrell 2003) described by Swan and Scarbrough (2001: 917) as a Cartesian separation between 'knowing subject' and 'knowable object'. This duality is apparent in definitions of knowledge and knowledge management that persisted throughout the 1990s and it continues to dominate discussion into the 2000s.

Prusak claims a pioneering role in the field of knowledge management '…when the cry first went out' (2001: 2) and cites a 1993 Boston conference as the mark of its inception. Prior to this conference, however, discourse on knowledge management had been steadily growing. In 1986 a paper was presented at a European management conference entitled 'Management of Knowledge: Perspectives of a New Opportunity' (Wiig 1997) and the contributions of Nonaka (1988; 1991) and Stewart and Kirsch (1991) reflect a clear focus on knowledge development and retention as providing organisational competitive advantage and value. Nonaka's early work (1991) describes the Japanese management experience of the creation, dissemination and embodiment of knowledge in technology and product in organisations. Nonaka uses case studies to identify the characteristics of Japanese companies that have as their focus the creation and management of knowledge.

In contrast to some theory of the time (including the work of Nonaka 1991), early knowledge management practice focused on knowledge as an explicit product of organisations, and busied itself with its extraction from organisational members and distribution throughout the organisation via information technologies. This practitioner focus prevailed in defining knowledge management in its early iterations, managers looking to facilitate business process and outcomes through improvements derived from the '...perceived efficiencies of process engineering' (Snowden 2002: 100) by codifying knowledge and developing tools for its effective capture and transfer. In this 'technocratic' paradigm (Earl 2001: 218) the primary concern for organisations is the improvement of business performance through the identification and accurate, efficient transfer of knowledge held within the organisation's boundary.

Knowledge understood in this way underpins the information-processing approach to knowledge management reflected in the first age of knowledge management (Snowden 2002) (an alternative discussion of generations in knowledge management is available in Firestone and McElroy 2002). In this view, knowledge equates to data or information - a commodity to be harvested and stockpiled. It is 'without' rather than within organisational members. Knowledge in this paradigm is the responsibility of the information technology areas of the organisation rather than those concerned with human resources. This 'technocratic' knowledge relies on a process whereby '...it is extracted from the person who developed it, made independent of that person, and reused for various purposes' (Hansen, Nohria et al. 1999: 108).

Individually developed and held knowledge, although difficult to articulate, must be made explicit in order to be leveraged by the organisation in Nonaka's (1991) work. Inherent in this and other early perspectives in knowledge management is a clearly cognitivist understanding of personal knowledge and a preoccupation with the individual as the site of knowledge production. Concepts of learning in this paradigm are underdeveloped and the value of socialisation in knowledge development is downplayed.

With its focus on the extraction of knowledge from the individual, this paradigm situates information systems as the stable structure of the organisation's knowledge (Malhotra 2002: 3). In the period 1993 – 1998 the most frequently occurring key word or phrase in knowledge management was 'information technology' followed by 'intellectual capital' and 'information system'. Seventy percent of articles in 1998 about knowledge management appear in the information systems and information technology literatures. 'Training', the first keyword associated with a human dimension of knowledge management occurs at less than half the rate of 'information technology' (Scarbrough, Swan et al. 1999: 17).

The information technology focus lay the ground for a lucrative market in knowledge management information systems. It was during this period that knowledge management became identified broadly as an IT issue. The narrow information systems perspective, however, neglected the role of the learner in the organisation, their knowledge needs and the value of their tacit knowledge. It is unsurprising, then, that knowledge management initiatives in this paradigm were overwhelmingly disappointing, failure rates cited as high as 84% (Storey and Barnett 2000: 145), practice predicated on a narrow interpretation of knowledge and promulgated by vendors focussed on tools rather than people (Rossett and Mohr 2004 provide a broad discussion of problems inherent in system use).

By the mid-1990s practitioners and scholars were becoming focused on a second generation in knowledge management more focused on the value of 'tacit' knowledge in organisations - knowledge embedded and embodied (Lakomski 2001: 69). Nonaka's (1994) contribution in this period highlighted the interplay between tacit and articulated knowledge rather than the transfer between the two. In these later developments knowledge is recognised as more elusive, more problematic and more personal. With an obvious trend toward workplace mobility, knowledge management attention turned to the retention and transfer of embrained intellectual capital, and strategies shifted from those dominated by information systems to more human systems of knowledge sharing (Wenger, McDermott et al. 2002; Snyder, Wenger et al. 2004; Wenger 2004). The literatures became increasingly focused on the value of embodied individual knowledge within organisations and strategies for its retention. In this generation the underlying conceptualisation of knowledge management remained '…in spite of arguments to the contrary…largely focused on cognition' (Crossan 1999: 524).

Communities of practice also gained prominence in the discussion about facilitation of knowledge transfer in organisations at this time (Lave and Wenger 1991) and tools were focused on networking individuals for knowledge sharing and provision of knowledge repositories where knowledge elicited from individuals could be stored.

The next age of knowledge management has evolved out of the recognition of the complexity and elusiveness of knowledge, its situatedness, plurality, and entwinement with human understanding and interaction. While knowledge is represented as ontologically and processually distinct from learning, the value of knowledge for organisations and their members is increasingly linked with its construction within rapidly changing, often ambiguous and very specific contexts as well as in social settings. Knowledge is discussed in the literatures as the held between individuals and collectives as well as organisational processes and systems in stock as well as flow. Recognition of the personal yet collective nature of knowledge is leading to consideration of personal and sociological needs of individuals and collectives in knowledge genesis and learning. Additionally, the influence of political, structural and cultural organisation environments on the phenomenon of knowledge and its availability and use to the organisation are similarly brought to the fore in 'third age' (Snowden 2002: 100) or 'the new knowledge management' (Firestone and McElroy 2002: 2).

2.1.2.5 Prominent debates and metaphors

Knowledge management is a widely diverse field. Core themes range from taxonomy, to records management, network analysis, sense-making and narrative. Like definitions, what has persisted across these themes is debate over the nature of knowledge itself. Debate is no less common or passionate today than it was 2000 years ago (Wiig 1997: 6). Indeed, current academic discussion expends great energy in attempting to clarify the truth/sense-making divide (McElroy 2003; Snowden 2003a), and highlights core paradigmatic differences in approaches to managing knowledge. If knowledge is about 'truth' then an information focus to knowledge management becomes critical. If knowledge is about 'sense-making' then tacit knowledge and learning predominate. The duality of knowledge management paradigms have this basic dichotomy at their base, whether they pivot on codification/personalization (Gloet and Berrell 2003), positivist/social constructionist perspectives (McAdam and McCreedy 1999: 97), information handling/strategic management (Martensson 2000: 209-210), or supply-side/demand-side approaches (Scarbrough, Swan et al. 1999: 35).

This basic dichotomy underpins knowledge management discourse, although an analysis of the metaphors used in the field reveals huge diversity in understanding and practice. Dominant in the literature is the economics/biology (Ponelis and Fairer-Wessels 1998: 7) dyad which largely reflects the epistemological divide described. A number of other enlightening metaphors arise, however, to highlight nuance within the discourse and prompt consideration of broader perspectives on knowledge in organisations.

2.1.2.5.1 *Economics metaphor*
In much discourse the metaphor of economics, with it themes around the fiscal and industrial, dominates. Prusak (2001) in his review of knowledge management emergence refers to knowledge *commodified*, its *valuation*, *investing* in individuals and systems, in *human capital*, *intellectual capital* and *productivity* underpinning a resource based view of the firm. Knowledge *assets* and their *audit* are discussed as though they were literal and tangible (for example, Ponelis and Fairer-Wessels 1998: 3).

This collection of metaphors is most frequently used where tacit-to-explicit and explicit-to-explicit (Nonaka 1991) transfer is central, that is, discourse focused on codification and dissemination. The inorganic metaphor of *knowledge economy* resonates with discussion around knowledge *objects* and sits with the engineering set of metaphors.

There is a strong set of metaphors around the *assembly-line*; once knowledge is objectified as a commodity that exists as units within organisations it can be *seen* and theory and practice focuses on *making knowledge visible*. From this understanding grows an long list of metaphors that relate to its *production* and *warehousing*, within *knowledge factories* (Malhotra 2002). Similarly, knowledge assets can be *mined*, *tapped in to*, *dug* and *drilled*, *wellsprings* exploited for organisational benefit. Knowledge as *object* also supports discourse around knowledge *architecture*, *building* of knowledge *infrastructure* and defines and limits knowledge management to a disembodied *construct* (Malhotra 2002).

This metaphor set maintains a focus on *management* of *static* knowledge in knowledge management, with *planning*, *organisation*, *coordination* and *control* central. The focus of discourse in this vein is '…controls, rewards and incentives' (Malhotra 2002: 13) supporting traditional perspectives on management.

2.1.2.5.2 Biological metaphor

On the other hand, the biology metaphor is also strong and used with increasing frequency in the literature as discourse integrates conceptions of knowledge as *alive*, *interactive*, *iterative*, *situated* and *emergent*. The broad metaphor of biology incorporates three main interpretive metaphors –*growth*, *ecology*, and *evolution*.

Knowledge management is linked to biology in Nonaka's (1991: 2) important work where he states that 'A company is not a machine but a living organism'. Through the organic metaphor set authors describe knowledge as *growing*, and *harvested* as organisational *food*. Knowledge is *agile and flexible* (Marquardt 2002), *active*, *affective*, and *dynamic*.

Work on social networks in organisations adds to the biological metaphor, highlighting the importance of *nurturing*, *intricate webs* of communication where organisational members *buzz around* those with information (Cross, Parker et al. 2001; Cross and Prusak 2002: 106).

Knowledge ecology exists within organisations through the integration of diverse information, and is discovered through observation and description rather than modelling and prescription (Davenport and Prusak 1998: 80-87). Through this metaphor, the focus is directed to people and information behaviour, to *supply chains* within changing *environments*. The influence of environment on the ecology results in *evolution* arising from *self-adaptive* (McElroy 2000) systems.

These *self-adaptive*, *complex* systems, however, include an entire set of metaphors that provide new insights into knowledge in organisations. Complexity is discussed below and this metaphor set is addressed in detail in later discussion of the convergence of organisational learning and knowledge management theory.

2.1.2.6 Contemporary perspectives on knowledge management

In his article 'Integrating complexity theory, knowledge management and organizational learning' McElroy makes an important contribution to the discourse on knowledge management. In this article, he describes complexity theory as 'systems thinking applied to the behaviour of natural systems' (2000: 201) a perspective which has received strong criticism in different quarters, and one which reflects a critical juncture in complexity thinking in organisational settings (Stacey 2003b). McElroy draws heavily on the work of John Holland (1995), a pioneer in the science of complexity, to relate the theory of complex adaptive systems to the emergence of knowledge in organisations.

Complex adaptive systems theory emerges from the observation that complex groups of agents engage in self-regulating activities to maintain 'coherence…in perpetual flux' (Holland 1995: 1). McElroy relates Holland's theory of rule sets to knowledge in organisations, focusing further on the relationship between 'declarative' (know-what) or 'procedural' (know-how) knowledge (2000: 202).

In this work McElroy recognises organisations as '…complex adaptive systems – that is, groups of independent, autonomous agents, all of whom share certain goals and operate in accordance with individually and collectively held rules' (2000: 201). Further, he claims that the ways in which knowledge naturally develops and disperses in organisations lies with the theory of complex adaptive systems.

One of McElroy's primary critics is Snowden (2003a) whose use of complexity highlights the organic, social, nonlinear and emergent features of complex systems. This perspective contrasts with McElroy's focus on the interlinking systems of wholes and boundaries that give rise to higher levels of organisation, features foregrounded in his systems-thinking perspective on the process of complex adaptive systems. McElroy and Snowden's differing emphases reveal a basic epistemological divergence, one which points to a gap between thinking or meaning-making and non-thinking or fact based foci in the development, dissemination and use of knowledge in organisations.

The emergent nature of knowledge through participative self-organisation in Stacey's (2001; 2003a; 2003b) representation of complexity in relation to knowledge management shares some similarity with Snowden's focus. Stacey's work differs substantially from Snowden's, however, in his rejection of the focus on the individual as primary and separate from the collective, the cognitivist perspective inherent in personal heuristics, and of prescriptive approaches to managing knowledge.

Complexity metaphors are central to Stacey's (2003b) work, but he does not subscribe to the theories proffered by Kauffman (1993; 1995) and Holland (1995) on complex adaptive systems, nor to the chaos and complexity work of popular organisational theorists such as Wheatley (1999). Stacey stresses the nature of knowledge as contextual and complex and points to the non-deterministic properties of agents in complex interactions as evolving and learning through their interaction in language. The participative nature of social evolution from Stacey's perspective is the basis for knowledge development and occurs in unpredictable and novel ways that may not be managed or controlled.

Emerging themes in the literature in knowledge management are pushed to new extremes in Stacey's work. His dynamic perspective offers an entirely new slant on knowledge in organisations that is at odds with notions of organisations as structured processes for control and coordination. While themes of individual and collective knowledge, knowledge as complex, contextual, active and emergent, and debates around cognitivist perspectives on knowledge in organisations have emerged in recent years, Stacey's work challenges the very premise upon which notions of organisation preside.

Much recent theory from a range of knowledge management perspectives shares some affinity with Stacey's quite radical opinion in knowledge management. For example,

Baets (2005) edited a volume of work for the information systems audience which included articles on complexity and knowledge, cultural complexity, dialogue in knowledge exchange, contextuality, emergent learning, and an interesting chapter titled 'Knowledge management and management learning: what computers can still do' in 2005 as part of Springer's Integrated Series in Information Systems (Baets and Van der Linden 2005). Clearly, the shift away from a techno-centric perspective on knowledge management has occurred in the literatures. The themes emerging in the once quite discrete 'organic' stream of knowledge management are influencing those of the technological to produce more complete understandings of knowledge and of learning in organisations.

2.1.3   FACILITATING LEARNING PRACTICE

If knowledge management increasingly has at its focus 'dynamic adaptation of tacit knowledge to new and unfamiliar situations' (Malhotra 2002: 13) and organisational learning is increasingly preoccupied with themes of personal engagement in work, the implications for facilitating learning practice are inherently linked to those of organisational learning and knowledge management.

This link has been made in the literatures, and attempts to strengthen theoretical rigour in their integration is progressing. Quite recent work is available which contributes to a growing body of literature that specifically highlights and develops theory around the relationship between organisational and workplace learning (for example, Davis and Sumara 2001; Garavan, Morley et al. 2002; Critten 2003; Field 2004; Kennedy 2005). In workplace learning literatures the contribution of knowledge management and organisational learning perspectives to workplace strategy is apparent in the work of Kennedy (2004), Critten (2003) and Burns, Cooper et al. (2003).

Limitations of current paradigms in workplace learning are highlighted and challenged by the contribution of contemporary organisational learning and knowledge management perspectives. In problematising simplistic cognitivist perspectives of workplace learning they add weight to critiques of workplace practice available within adult and workplace education literatures (Karakowsky and McBey 1999; Garavan, Morley et al. 2002; Winch and Ingram 2002; Chappell, Hawke et al. 2003; Oval 2003).

The focus for this critique is on formal constructions of workplace learning with Bryans (2000: 230) highlighting the main issue, that,

> *Training, which by its nature pre-specifies outcomes, inevitably forecloses on the kinds of knowledge that are taken to be relevant to the knowledge economy (this is a particular irony if the knowledge economy is premised on rapid and exponential change)'.*

Assumptions about the learner as rational, individual, and logical, separate from context or relationship are inherent in the cognitivist and behaviourist perspectives that commonly underpin workplace learning interventions supported by the competency model of training in Australia (Oval 2003). Contrary to developing notions of learning and knowlege in organisations, competency based training has been embraced in Australia as the primary model for workplace learning. Competency based training emerges from

> *'...an empirical analytic paradigm, which takes the view that reality is objective and that individuals and the world are separate, knowledge involves objectively proven facts and what cannot be legitimately quantified is not worth knowing' (Burns 2002: 56).*

Reductionist perspectives on learning are informed by behaviourist theory and scientific management and privilege skill over thought, 'the manual over mental, skills over knowledge and body over mind' (Chappell, Hawke et al. 2003: 15). By prescribing consistent reproduction of mass-produced skill, this paradigm provides organisations with a '...disciplined and predominantly deskilled workforce' (O'Donnell 1999: 257).

The 'contextless' perspective of learning apparent in formal learning approaches which separate work and worker blinds workplace learning to the emergence of learning from the interaction of learners with their environment. This perspective is criticized for its prioritisation of the individual learner, workplace competence seen as held by individuals rather than collectives and stripped of context and the social nature of their learning. Individualism, driven by '...increasing levels of education, mobility and competition' (O'Donnell 1999: 251), and parallel to Cartesian perspectives of atomisation, is obviously privileged in this construction of competence.

Competence in this paradigm suggests that learning is primarily a mental process occurring in a vacuum (Fenwick 2004) and, in the words of Bryans and Smith (2000: 232), 'suspect'. For them, the landscape of competencies '…lends itself to 'dwelling in' rather than 'mastery''. Competency based training situates learning in a teleological frame and discusses it in terms of the technological-economic interest (Field 2004), learning contructed as valuable to work, for work and at work.

In the competency tradition learning is about the determinants employers place on learning outcomes which trainers (who may or may not be adult educators) use as the basis of development of curricula. The narrow, uncritical application of outcomes based approaches to workplace training places the emphasis on learning *to* work as if learning does indeed take place within a vacuum. In this approach knowledge and skills designed to maximise performance against contextless performance criteria may be transferred from the technically proficient and knowledgeable expert to the learning 'vessel'. Authors argue that learning of standard procedures and best practice through error avoidance supports the organisation in institutionalising knowledge, but not in innovating, developing and securing new knowledge (Kennedy 2004: 182).

Competency based learning practice, with its focus on single-loop learning, continues to be directed at organisational members at operational levels in organisations. The focus on skills development in applying canonical knowledge in operation is fixed in the hierarchy. Training and qualification based on competency based learning strategy dominates lower levels in the hierarchy. As a result, opportunities for the sharing of knowledge generated at the base of the organisation are limited and diversity is restricted.

Learning *for* work, on the other hand, places emphasis on power relationships between employer and learner and situates learning as a tool in the development of the organisation. In this perspective learning is goal oriented, the organisation setting the goal for learning outcomes. This teleological perspective brings with it problems regarding the value of the learning for learners, the role of learners and their responsibility to learn, and the assumption of learning as contributing to organisational well-being. Within this frame issues of empowerment are problematic, freedom geared toward organisational rather than personal benefit and real freedom to question organisational assumptions challenged. Spencer (2001), Schein (1999), and others (Fenwick 2001; Field 2004; Huzzard 2004) in their critical perspectives on learning for work highlight the power organisations hold over the learning opportunities for individuals and the coercive dimensions of learning toward the organisation's benefit.

In other critical discussion, Spencer (2001: 32) describes the tradition in which workplace learning is learning *at* work, the workplace unproblematically a *site* of learning. In this tradition discussion centres on the knowledge and skills that are developed within this site. Inherent in this understanding is an assumption that the learner and workplace are discrete and that the role of the educator is to direct the learner to better performance within the work site as a result of workplace specific training. Rather than providing a perspective in which the institution is seen as a encompassing a learning dimension, which Gonczi (2004: 19) sees as critical to lifelong learning, in the traditional perspective of learning *at* work the focus is on the delivery of training programs at the workplace downplaying the value of the learning inherent in engagement in work.

Recently, a clear shift to a focus on learning *through* work provides a perspective in which the engaged learner is central (Fenwick 2001: 15; 2004) and the interests of employers in directing training toward specific organisational outcomes becomes peripheral. This shift in perspective leads to recognition of issues of the relationship between learning and work for the learner, the structure of work roles and work contexts and their impact on learning, the power relationships inherent in workplaces and their influence on learning as well as the organisational imperative on workplace learning outcomes. In his counter to this shift to 'learnerism' Holmes (2004) concludes that far from being emancipatory, the discourse of learning which puts the onus on the learner for engagement in the learning process leads to perspectives in which any failure to reap the benefits of learning is attributed to the learner.

However, much work is available which supports the notion of learning through work as central in workplace learning experience. Conlon (2003: 283), for example, states '… that only 20% of what employees learn comes from more formalized, structured training.' Sorohan (1993: 53) puts the number at 10%, agreeing with Conlon that employees prefer personal strategies of learning in which they learn through questioning, listening, observing, reading and reflecting on their work environment in the carriage of their everyday work. Employees experience workplaces '...as either restrictive (or non-stimulating) or expansive (or stimulating)' (Evans and Kersh 2004: 63) and for adult learners these expansive workplaces are those which promise opportunities for organisational learning and knowledge development.

These notions of situated, embodied, and co-emergent learning which entwines learning, knowledge and context are evident across the literatures in learning and knowledge management. Complexity theories, too, are informing contemporaneous understandings of the fields and contributing to their convergence, offering new perspectives, new opportunities for research and a new language for their consideration.

2.2   COMPLEXITY THEORIES

The value of the new sciences in understanding organisations is emerging in a range of disciplines. Chaos theory, quantum mechanics, self-organising systems, complexity theory, nonlinear systems and fractals are all being used to rethink organisation and learning. A complexity perspective provides a clear divergence from the engineering approach to organisations that has dominated management thinking and practice for the past hundred years. The complexity sciences provide an important source for analogies with human action (Stacey 2003b: 360).

That organisations are complex systems is broadly assumed (for example, Frank and Fahrback 1999; Wheatley 1999; McElroy 2000; Kurtz and Snowden 2003; Stacey 2003b), organisations are now '...routinely viewed as dynamic systems of adaptation and evolution that contain multiple parts which interact with one another and the environment' (Morel and Ramanujam 1999: 278).

While assumptions about the complex nature of organisation are frequent, the control paradigm that has dominated management discourse persists in practice. Dooley and Van de Ven (1999: 369) attribute the dominance of control to a preference for the simple and linear – mechanisms for control are easier to implement and manipulate if organisational dynamics are assumed to be linear. Organisations are built to support linear behaviour and these structures endure.

Increasingly, and across disciplines, however, researchers are explicitly working with the characteristics of complex systems in their attempts to develop and enrich organisational theory. The well worn basics familiar to those interested in organisational dynamics are rooted in traditional, linear approaches; organisational structures, behavioural change, and communication (Stacey 2001: 26) are backgrounded in a perspective informed by complexity theory.

The review of the literature that follows outlines the breadth of application of complexity across disciplines and discusses its use in organisational learning, knowledge management and workplace learning discourses. It provides a brief overview of the application of the complexity theories, focusing on complex adaptive systems theory, and illustrates their emergence as analytical and sense-making devices in organisation studies. The value of the complex adaptive systems theory as an integrating framework is also developed.

2.2.1   DEFINITIONS OF COMPLEXITY

Like organisational learning and knowledge management, a definition for complexity is evasive. Literature attempting to summarise complexity typically begins with phrases like, 'there are a variety of interpretations' (Cohen 1999: 373), or 'one unified theory does not exist' (Anderson 1999: 217), or 'there is no universally accepted or clearly articulated definition' (Morel and Ramanujam 1999: 278). Even representatives from the home of complexity, the Santa Fe Institute, state that within the organisation 'there is no established definition... if you were to ask ten different people... you'd get ten different – and likely ten very distinct – responses (Ellen Goldberg presenting to the first Conference on Complexity Science and Educational Research in Davis, Phelps et al. (2004: 2)).

Rather than adhering to a single definition or presenting a single theory, the field of complexity is described as highlighting a set of basic characteristics (Morel and Ramanujam 1999: 278). Underpinning terms such as Complexity Science (Kurtz and Snowden 2003), Complexity Theory (Anderson 1999) Complex Systems Theory (Schroeder 1990 in Cohen 1999; Schroeder 1990 in Morel and Ramanujam 1999), Complex Adaptive Systems Theory (Holland 1995; Anderson 1999; McElroy 2000;

Rhodes and MacKechnie 2003), Complex Responsive Processes (Stacey 2001) or Complex Organizational Dynamics (Dooley and Van de Ven 1999) is a core set of understandings represented in a variety of ways in the literature.

Complexivists focus on this fairly consistent set of characteristics in relation to complex phenomena. The following review of characteristics is derived primarily from management literatures, although the features presented are reflected across broad ranging disciplines.

Table 2 Features of complex phenomena

Author	Features
Morel and Manujam (1999: 281)	1. A large number of diverse and interacting elements associated with feedback mechanisms and introducing nonlinearities in the system 2. Emergent properties resulting from the collective behaviour of elements within the system.
Davis, Phelps and Wells (2004)	1. Nonlinear dynamics 2. Emergence 3. Self organisation
Anderson (1999: 216) (focusing on complex adaptive systems - a 'class' (Morel and Ramanujam 1999: 281) of complexity)	1. Agents with schemata 2. Self-organizing networks sustained by importing energy 3. Coevolution to the edge of chaos 4. System evolution based on recombination

Rhodes and MacKenchnie (2003)	1. Agents
	2. Schemata made up of inputs and filtering tools
	3. Fitness function or desired outcome
	4. Connections among agents
	5. The state of the system
Holland (1995) states that there are seven basic elements in complex adaptive systems and that any other feature of complex adaptive systems identified can be reduced to or derived from these seven. Holland describes each characteristic as either a property or mechanisms and stresses that adaptation is the 'sine qua non' of complexity, not presented as a property or mechanism but inherent to complex adaptive systems.	1. Aggregation
	2. Tagging
	3. Nonlinearity
	4. Flows
	5. Diversity
	6. Internal models
	7. Building blocks

The characteristics of complex adaptive systems described by Holland (1995) align in many ways with Stacey's (2003b) representation of complex responsive processes, a model developed to highlight complexity in knowledge processes within organisations and a model widely cited in knowledge management literatures. In Stacey's discussion of Holland's work, however, he differentiates his own work on the basis of Holland's explicitly cognitivist perspective and his work's assimilation of systems-based management thinking. Stacey's interpretation posits a perspective of complexity within which microdiversity, radical unpredictability, self-organisation, nonlinear interaction, agency at the level of interacting individual, and dynamic at the edge of chaos are stressed.

In summary, complexity theories are based in a strongly shared set of core characteristics that focus on the nonlinear interaction of diverse agents through rules and feedback loops from which emerge patterns of collective behaviour that are unable to be anticipated.

2.2.2   DEVELOPING THEORY AND PRACTICE

Complexity theories are applied across an broad range of fields. A brief sweep of the literatures uncovers complexivist approaches to art and architecture (Benjamin 1995), medicine (Petty and Petty, 2005), physics (Hubler 2005), globalisation (Urry, 2003) global development practice (Rihani 2002) and literature (Hayles 1990; 1991; 1999)

The application of complexity theories to work organisations provides a similarly diverse range of perspectives. Within this body of literature complexity can be found in application to the study of organisation itself (Anderson 1999), self-organising teams (Anderson and McMillan 2003), aberrant behaviour in organisations (Bella, King et al. 2003; Geisler and Ritter 2003), leadership (Wheatley 1999; Morrison 2002; Snowden 2003b) organisational learning (McElroy 2000; Stacey 2003b), and knowledge management (Choo 1998; Stacey 2001). Complexity also informs discussions of innovation and learning (Harkema 2005), public sector processes (Rhodes and MacKechnie 2003), and human resource development (Garavan, Morley et al. 2002; Critten 2003).

Seminal materials published with the lay reader in mind include Holland's (1995) 'Hidden Order', Waldrop's (1994) 'Complexity', and Kaufman's (1993; 1995) 'The origins of order' and 'At home in the universe'. These texts provide insight into the 'emerging science at the edge of order and chaos' (Waldrop 1994) and a backdrop for paradigmatic turn (Kuhn 1970: 34) from the '...linear, reductionist thinking that has dominated science since the time of Newton' (Waldrop 1994: 13).

Theorists published on the relevance of complexity to understanding organisation as early as 1962 (Simon 1962; Cilliers 2005), but while work on complexity grew significantly in depth and breadth from the mid-1980s, and a group at the Santa Fe Institute was developing organisational theory through complexity in 1995 (Cohen, Burkhart et al. 1995), awareness of emergent order had little impact on organisational theory until a special edition of 'Organization Science' featured complexity and its relationship to organisational theory in 1999.

In this special edition important complexivists including Cohen (1999) and Anderson (1999) contribute to the burgeoning interest in complexity within understandings of organisation. Cohen attributes a number of trends to the growing interest, including globalisation, workforce diversity, quality improvement, information revolution, and the availability of technology to exploit information and increase responsiveness. He situates these trends within '…an environment that seems to be changing, organizations want to be more adaptable and better able to learn from experience or in order to reconfigure themselves in the face of new demands' (1999: 373). The coherence with stated impetuses for organisational learning and knowledge management are clear.

Attempts to bring together the diverse fields of organisational learning, knowledge management and complexity theory suggest a new perspective for the consideration of the emergent, complex and organic nature of knowledge in organisations. Important work continues in knowledge management by theorists and practitioners looking to understand better the nature of knowledge in organisations through complexity (Stacey 2001; Firestone and McElroy 2003).

In learning, interest is generated by such groups as the American Education Research Association whose 'Complexity Special Interest Group' met at conference for the first time in October 2003. The ensuing journal 'Complicity' offers a source for targeted enquiry in complexity and education and provides a forum for researchers and practitioners with

> '… an interest to understand learning, teaching and education from nonlinear perspectives, drawing on the emphasis complexity places on variation as a source and outcome of thinking and the important role of interaction, diversity and redundancy on processes of cognition' (Davis, Phelps et al. 2004: 3).

The intersection between knowledge management and organisational learning is informed by educational perspectives developed through complexity. Learning and knowledge themselves are shown in relief against the distinct and separate fields of praxis

(Cavaleri 2004) and research progresses in the quest to develop a fuller understanding of both the discipline fields and complexity.

2.2.3   TWO PARADIGMS FOR RESEARCH

The organisational complexity literatures tend to occupy themselves with two research paradigms. The first is concerned with modelling complex systems using algorithms and computer simulations to investigate the relationship between their properties and mechanisms and emergent outcomes, the second with developing and applying metaphors arising from complexity. Both approaches inform new perspectives on organisational processes and outcomes.

2.2.3.1   Modelling

The work of Cohen and Axelrod (1984) provides an early example of the investigation of adaptive phenomena through modelling and simulation. Their research highlights a 'common fascination' (Morel and Ramanujam 1999: 279) held by complexivists with the possibilities provided by improved computer power and the possibility of modelling more complex behaviours within systems. The power of such systems lies in the problem inherent in studying complex systems, that one aspect of the system may not be held still for investigation against other components of the system. It is not so much the patterns of emergent collective behaviour that are the target of study as the process of interaction between those components.

Morel and Ramanujam (1999) demonstrate the contribution of complex systems theory to organisational theory particularly in relation to self-organisation using random graph theory applied to analysis of social networks. Frank and Fahrback, too, use 'tools of dynamic systems' (1999: 253) to investigate organisational culture in a school setting and illustrate the complex system underlying it. In so doing, the authors explore a single sentiment and study the interaction around that sentiment, mapping its trajectories and using these maps to draw conclusions about the system and the impact of its environment as well as behaviours of individual agents. This study and the one above demonstrate the movement of researchers beyond the use of metaphors of complex systems to empirical investigation through modelling and complex system simulation. Through this approach researchers limit the breadth of their research to a narrow set of system components that may be mathematically modelled and manipulated within a simulation. This research domain is positivistic, experimental work that sets up and tests propositions about the behaviour of the system (Dooley and Van de Ven 1999: 358). From the earliest days of modelling researchers have questioned the veracity of such models, recognising their 'weak isomorphism' and have sought to understand the conditions under which patterns in models might be said to capture something relevant to learning individuals and organisations (Cohen, Burkhart et al. 1995: 28).

2.2.3.2 Metaphor

Other research draws on metaphors derived from complexity and tends to approach organisational phenomena in a more holistic way. Researchers draw on complexity metaphors to develop new perspectives on organisation and reframe individual and organisational behaviour. In the organisational learning and knowledge management literatures the work of Stacey (2001; 2003a; 2003b) sits firmly within this camp, as does the discussion provided by Snowden (2002; Kurtz and Snowden 2003; Snowden 2003a; 2003b), McElroy (2000; Firestone and McElroy 2002; 2003), and Anderson (1999; Anderson and McMillan 2003). Within this discourse area there is some disagreement, particularly in relation to the 'what is knowledge?' question, and as a result metaphor development varies between authors.

Metaphors from complex adaptive systems are developed with differing emphases depending on the discipline of the authors. For example, Davis, Phelps and Wells (2004: 2) focus on the adaptive nature of these systems and discuss 'learning systems'; Anderson and McMillan (2003) are interested in the self-organising capacity of complex systems and discuss the implications for self-organised teams in organisations, Anderson (1999) looks at the ways in which they behave and develops suggestions for management and influence on organisational behaviour. Snowden (2003b) seeks to develop (among a range of other foci) leadership approaches based on the recognition of organisations as complex adaptive systems, and the list extends.

In a straightforward example of the use of metaphor in organisational analysis, Rhodes and MacKechnie (2003: 58) describe and then apply a complex adaptive systems framework in an attempt to resolve '…outstanding issues in public administration theory and practice' in a case study of a public service system. Phelps (2004: 254) uses the metaphor of complexity more broadly to 'enrich our understandings and practices at all levels of contemporary education'. In so doing, she identifies a set of characteristics of complexity and structures a case narrative around discussion of the features.

As illustrated above, research in this domain is largely (though by no means exclusively) non-positivistic, focused on 'retrospective coherence' (Snowden 2002: 106) utilises narrative, and the discourse is largely theoretical.

2.2.3.3   Model and Metaphor

Holland's (1995) work provides a broad illustration of the use of complexity across the two domains of metaphor and model, using complexity in a descriptive way as well as in the development and application of a simulation model. It appears that both approaches can provide important insight into organisational discourses. As Morel and Ramanujam (1999: 278) state,

> 'the immediate benefits of [complex systems theory] may be as a framework that facilitates conceptual elaborations and encourages formal modelling: both activities may provide fresh and deep insights into organizational phenomena'.

2.3   CONCLUSION

Across the literatures in organisational learning, knowledge management and workplace learning growing attention is paid to the relationship between the individual and the organisational in the development of knowledge; the nature of this knowledge, particularly its situatedness, its elusiveness and its creation in action and interaction; and the role that individual and collective cognition and internal schema play in its development, sharing and institutionalisation.

Complexity theories are shown here to provide fresh perspectives on organisations and throw some light on the questions that are central to the converging themes across the literatures reviewed. In the following chapter complexity is linked to key themes at the point of confluence of learning and knowledge in organisations and the opportunity for novel research, of the type provided by this study, is claimed.

3   CONVERGENCE

In the literature presented above, organisational learning, knowledge management and workplace learning are shown to be mutually informing, the themes across the discourses coalescing in increasingly complex notions of learning and knowledge. It is argued that these converging themes are congruent with central themes in complexity theories and complexity is identified as an integrating device across the traditionally discrete fields.

In this study learning is recognised as an active process of individual and collective development within a specific context through engagement with it and through interaction. Although the individual can be seen to learn individually, this learning occurs within a social context within which the collective of individuals can also be seen to learn; learning in this perspective is at once individual and collective. The knowledge that emerges from the interaction with work is situated in that context and practice, constructed in the active engagement of individual, collective and context.

Links between organisational learning, knowledge management and complexity are illustrated as occurring in three main themes: Firstly, the relationship between the learning individual, collective, and organisation; secondly, the nature of knowledge as complex, situated and active; and finally, the role of mental models in adaptation and generative learning. These themes are developed in support of the claim that the links provide an important opportunity for research and the development of new contributions to theory. In support of this argument, and leading to demand for research of the type offered here, available research is critiqued and calls for research in this area presented.

3.1.1   CONVERGING DISCOURSES THROUGH COMPLEXITY

Interdisciplinarity and complexity are closely linked (Thompson Klein 2004: 2). Complexity theory is currently used to support integration across the fields of enquiry of knowledge management and organisational learning in the work of McElroy (2000) and across knowledge management, organisational learning and workplace learning theory in the work of Critten (2003), Stacey (2003b), and Kennedy (2004).   Complexity offers a way of thinking about knowledge and learning that promises fresh considerations of the issues that have divided knowledge and learning in organisations.

3.1.2   CONVERGENT THEMES

Early iterations of knowledge management, while linked to organisational learning (or more obviously, to 'the learning organisation') differed from it, not only in focus but also in form. Convergence across the contemporary literatures of knowledge management and learning, however, are increasingly clear. Theorists and practitioners alike are recognising and acting on the understanding that the two are entwined and not so much mutually dependent as indiscrete, sharing the same purpose (Cavaleri 2004: 159). Gloet and Berrell (2003: 79) go as far as to equate organisational learning with the humanist paradigm in knowledge management and Koopmans (2005: 180) agrees with Cavaleri (2004: 159) that learning and knowledge management can be seen as different sides of the same coin.

Insights from the organisational learning literature draw on the social construction of knowledge and, in developing knowledge management theories, this notion has become an important one for influential writers such as Wenger (2004). The influence of educational theory on constructions of learning and knowledge in both knowledge management and organisational learning theory is illustrated in work that highlights the 'social embeddedness' of knowledge (Scarbrough 2003: 501). Vygotsky's (1962: 20) assertion that '…the true direction of the development of thinking is not from the individual to the socialised, but from the social to the individual' infers that '… all cognitive learning occurs at a social level before occurring at individual level' (Ghosh 2004: 306). Spender (2006b: 18) also draws on Vygotsky (1978) in his statement that "…prior knowledge evolves within the field of possibility dictated by the social'. Work of this nature is guiding focus to the iterative influence of socialization on individual learning and knowledge. Growing attention to Vygotsky's work points to the importance of socially embedded activity in the development of individual consciousness.

Discussion across the literatures about the construction of knowledge addresses a paradoxical notion which has at its roots epistemological debate about the nature of knowledge and the individuality of the social being.

'Habermas ... rejects this purely monological view of rationality and meaning and proposes a more dialogic, self-reflective and intersubjective view where meaning must be understood as something created between people...This discourse-theoretic approach is complemented by Vygotsky's ... affirmation of the 'philosophical and political power of the ontological socialness of human beings". (O'Donnell 1999: 252).

The growing focus on the complexity of knowledge is apparent too in the workplace learning literatures, where organisational learning, knowledge management and workplace learning are linked as they look to the

'...Vygotskian school of developmental psychology ... in insisting that development occurs as much by interaction with others and the social and cultural aspects of the environment as by internal mental, affective and physical processes.' (O'Donnell 1999: 257).

Fenwick (2004) also stresses that

'The context of these new learning encounters – their cultural, political, physical-environmental and social dynamics – are entangled with individuals' actions, emotional responses, identity performances and meanings...'

In an example of the ways in which complexity supports their convergence, and in support of arguments for their consideration within a single frame, the table below illustrates the historical progress of themes in the learning organisation, first generation knowledge management, second generation knowledge management and organisational learning. The progression of themes through time and across fields highlights their increasing alignment with features of complexity theories and suggests an opportunity for further investigation in a less segmented way, and through strategies that align with complexity thinking.

Table 3 Learning and knowledge converging through complexity

Learning Organisation	KM1	KM2	Organisational Learning II	Convergence through complexity theories
Practice-driven	Practice-driven	Theory and practice-driven	Theory-driven	Theory-driven
Positivist	Positivist	Constructivist	Constructivist	Constructionist
Broad focus	Narrow focus	Broad focus	Broad focus	Broad focus
Main fields: Strategy, organisation theory, organisation design, human resource strategy, marketing, library studies	Main fields: IS/IT strategy, business strategy, operations management, accounting, library studies	Main fields: Cognitive psychology, network analysis, learning, 'new science', IS/IT integration	Main fields: Education, leadership, connectionism, creativity, human resource strategy, communication and development	Main fields: Education, workplace learning, communication, human resource development, change management, connectionism
Systems-based view of the firm	Resource-based view of the firm	Innovation-based view of the firm	Learning-based view of the firm	Emergence-based view of the firm
Mostly abstract/global	Mostly concrete/local	Mostly abstract/global	Mostly abstract/global	Mostly abstract/local
Intangible gains	Tangible performance improvement	Qualitative measures of knowledge capacity	Qualitative evaluation of learning capacity	Qualitative investigation through narrative
Acquisition metaphor	*Mining* metaphor	*Ecology* metaphor	Participation, adaptation and generation metaphors	*Complexity* metaphor set – interactivity, emergence, self-organisation
Emphasis on culture management and organisation design	Emphasis on information systems management and systems design	Emphasis on inclusivity and self-organisation	Emphasis on distributed leadership	Emphasis on self-organisation
Emphasis on maintaining and managing tacit knowledge embedded as organisation culture and values systems	Emphasis on changing tacit knowledge into explicit knowledge	Emphasis on creativity	Emphasis on creativity and valuing, managing and enhancing individual development	Emphasis on emergence of knowledge through interactivity
Strategic/HR managers responsible for change	IS/IT managers and CKO responsible for change	Strategic core leads with entire organisation responsible for change	Leader acts as catalyst for change which is sustained through continuous reflection	Leader observes changes that emerge from interactivity in environment
Sensitive to context (multiple practice techniques)	Independent of context ('best practice' techniques)	Sensitive to context (adaptive)	Sensitive to context (adaptive, proactive)	Reliant on context

Learning Organisation	KM1	KM2	Organisational Learning II	Convergence through complexity theories
Planned culture change strategy	Planned IT change strategy	Flexibly planned probes to facilitate sensitivity to futures	Collectively planned flexible approaches continually revisited	Responsive to change emerging from interaction within environment
Mostly intra-organisational knowledge emphasised	Intra- and inter-organisational knowledge emphasised	Cross-boundary knowledge aimed to increase diversity emphasised	Cross-boundary collective learning and knowledge creation emphasised	Cross-boundary collective learning, diversity, context and knowledge creation emphasised
Major investment in people and management development	Major investment in systems and user training	Major investment in innovation IT/human integration	Major investment in time for collaboration, networking, reflection, innovation	Major investment in opportunity for interaction and exploration through work
Emphasis on 'internalisation' and 'socialisation'	Emphasis on 'externalisation' and 'combination'	Emphasis on 'collectivity' and creation	Emphasis on 'collectivity' and creation	Emphasis on 'construction', 'collectivity' and sense-making
Knowledge as cognition and action	Knowledge as cognition and raw material (resources)	Knowledge as dynamic and constructed	Knowledge as constructed and social	Knowledge as active, constructed, situated, social and emergent
Confronting mental models for generative change	Making explicit mental models for sharing	Making explicit mental models for development of heuristics	Confronting mental models and theories in use	Internal models prominent in agent interaction, broken down and restructured in response to environment
Integrates strategic management theory	Integrates strategic management theory	Integrates 'complexity theory'	Integrates 'complexity theory'	Integrates range of perspectives within complexity theories

Building from Scarbrough, Swan et al. (1999), Malhotra (2002), Wang and Ahmed (2003).

Illustrated in this table is a trend toward convergence of traditionally disparate fields as they each focus more closely on a shared set of themes. These themes are at the centre of this research activity which is designed to enable better understanding of the learning experiences of organisational members and the relationship of this learning to organisational learning and knowledge outcomes.

The convergence above can be summarised as occurring in three main themes: the relationship between the individual, collective and organisation; the nature of knowledge and its growing problematisation; and the role of mental models in adaptation and learning.

Through a complexity perspective the debate surrounding the relationship between individual and organisational learning is resolved as '… a paradox in which individual and group/organisation are aspects of the same processes of interaction between people' (Stacey 2003b: 326). Learning is understood as '…shifts in meaning and it is simultaneously individual and social.' (Stacey 2003b: 330). Knowledge in complex systems is seen to emerge from the self-organising iterative interaction of agents situated in context, nonlinear interactions which result in novelty and which both increase and are increased by diversity.

Adaptation is inherent in complex systems and each discussion of complex adaptive systems includes reference to change as a result of nonlinear interaction within a context. Indeed, complex systems are, by nature, learning systems (Davis, Phelps et al. 2004: 2).

3.1.2.1   Individual and Collective Learning and Knowledge

Recent learning and knowledge management theory strongly emphasises the collectivity of human learning and knowledge, its social nature, its priority in the development of individual consciousness, collective thinking and communication.

The conceptualisation of a collective mind is apparent, too, in more recent knowledge management perspectives in which dynamic sense-making at the collective level is linked to organisational knowledge outcomes (Snowden 2002: 106). Scarbrough (2003: 502), in his discussion of innovation, focuses on knowledge management's role in '…making knowledge a directly productive force … by collectivizing knowledge and learning' and Tsoukas and Vladimirou (2001: 973) attempt to reconcile individual and organisational knowledge through combination of '…Polanyi's profound insight concerning the personal character of knowledge [and] Wittgenstein's claim that all knowledge is, in a fundamental way, collective…'. Their empirical exploration demonstrates a continuing grappling with the relationship between the individuality and collectivity of organisational knowledge.

Manturana and Varela's (1992: 18) seminal work on knowledge and human understanding describes knowledge in terms of cognitive experiences of the knower, '…experience of certainty is an individual phenomenon blind to the cognitive acts of others, in a solitude which… is transcended only in a world created with those others'. Their work informs biological perspectives on leaning and knowledge and highlights the enduring debate in which the individual is seen as primary and prior in constructions of knowledge and learning.

The *process* of this individual and collective learning is explicitly addressed as a focus for discussion through complexity for some literatures. The perspective allows for consideration of mind as both 'inside' and 'outside' the person, '…the mind is thought of as a whole or system of interacting parts contained within a boundary' (Stacey 2003b: 237). This resonates with Lakomski's (2001) concepts through connectionism of the mind as supported by the organisation, the organisation developed to underpin the connections between its members.

Learning, through this perspective, is understood as '…shifts in meaning and it is simultaneously individual and social' (Stacey 2003b: 330). The debate in the discourse surrounding the relationship between individual and organisational learning is resolved as '… a paradox in which individual and group/organisation are aspects of the same processes of interaction between people' (Stacey 2003b: 326).

The individual or the organisation as the base unit for analysis in learning is seen as redundant from a complexivist perspective. For some theorists, rather, the *initiative* (Stacey 2001: 5; Rhodes and MacKechnie 2003: 62) or the *activity* (Sanchez and Heene 2000: 30) provides a more appropriate basic unit for inspection. Backstrom's (2004: 472) research utilises the 'common competence that emerges in interaction between the individuals' as the unit of analysis, describing collective learning as '…neither the sum of the learning of the individuals nor the learning of the formal organization separated from the individuals'. Holland (1995: 11) focuses discussion on the aggregate as the adaptive, intelligent level of analysis, complex, large-scale behaviour emerging from aggregate interactions of less complex agents. In complexity, learning and knowledge are at once both individual and collective.

3.1.2.2   Knowledge as Complex, Situated and Active

Notions of knowledge as existing between individual and collective highlights the growing recognition of its complex nature and investigation of its emergence, just one aspect of '...the increasing complexity of the knowledge system that accumulates within human endeavour' (Geisler and Ritter 2003: 47). Knowledge in complexity occurs through the connectedness of diverse agents and evolves in novel ways. It is situated in its emergence through the partial connection of agents with other elements in the system – that is, agents act in response to their immediate environment through their connections with others within it (Anderson 1999: 222). Cohen and his colleagues (Cohen, Burkhart et al. 1995: 8) describe this situatedness as knowledge which is tightly coupled to a specific context, distributed not just among individuals, but also among individuals and context.

Knowledge through the complexity lens is also about the shared understandings that emerge in the absence of any plan or programme for outcomes. Through complexity, knowledge self-organises through the interaction of diverse agents and the amplification of difference through 'nonlinear iteration' (Stacey 2003b: 316) into new and novel patterns of understanding.

Complexity problematises positivist perspectives within which a clear relationship between cause and effect can be anticipated and mapped. Similarly, deterministic organisational action assumed in organisational theory is challenged, knowledge seen instead as perpetually constructed, restructured and transformed through conversation in context (Morrison 2002: 12).

In complex adaptive systems knowledge emerges from the participative problem solving of its agents in distributed knowledge processing environments (Firestone and McElroy 2004: 182). Inherent in complexity theory is sensitivity to initial conditions, the learning behaviour of complex systems, embodied mind and enacted cognition (Baets 2005: 17), characteristics which underline the fact that knowledge is '...indeed a tricky concept' (Tsoukas and Vladimirou 2001: 975).

The problematisation of knowledge across the literatures is increasingly clear. As exemplified by definitions of knowledge in knowledge management, knowledge and its development in individuals and organisations has shifted from a focus on transfer and acquisition to construction, embodiment and embeddedness in social activity and emergence through interaction within context. Knowledge is recognised as interpreted data becoming meaningful in the process of iteration (Cilliers 2002: 81).

3.1.2.3   Mental Models, Adaptation and Generative Learning

Cognitivist constructions of learning and knowledge dominate both organisational learning and knowledge management literatures. Increasingly, however, recognition of the complexity of learning, knowledge and organisation are impacting on understandings of the role of mental models (schema, or internal models) in the adaptation and learning of individuals and knowledge in organisations.

Mental models, their formation, challenge and disruption provide a clear, though contested theme across the literatures of organisational learning, workplace learning and knowledge management. Mental models are obvious in the organisational learning discourse in Argyris and Schon's (1978) notions of single- and double-loop learning which they use to illustrate their conception of adaptive and generative learning. Within this framework adaptive learning results from instrumental learning which leaves underlying values about 'theory of action' unchanged. In double-loop learning, however, the paradigm through which the world is understood shifts, disrupting values and norms. Schein (1999: 168), too, discusses cognitive redefinition, as the '...essence of generative learning to distinguish it from merely adaptive learning'.

In workplace learning, discussion of challenging mental models is found in cognitive learning discourse where schema organise knowledge in a way which guides thought and behaviour in order to reduce cognitive complexity. Karakowsky and McBey (1999: 196) describe these schema or scripts as discouraging individuals from critically evaluating new situations as they arise. Mezirow's (2000) work on transformational learning also looks to critical reflectivity to bring schema to the fore so that they may be critiqued in order to bring about generative change.

In knowledge management literature Snowden (2002: 107) speaks of disruption, of breaking pattern entrainment, the habit of acting on '...past or perceived future patterns' in order to bring about radical change. Adaptation is inherent to complex systems, changing rule sets and internal models emerging from experience. Complex adaptive systems theory (in Holland's 1995 construction (Stacey 2003: 248)) is inherently cognitivist, the focus for learning on the internal models that agents build to guide behaviour and facilitate lookahead. Holland describes agents as distilling experience into *tacit* and *overt* internal models. These internal models are used to anticipate future events, a tacit internal model '...prescribes a current action, under an implicit prediction of some desired future state', while an overt internal model '...is used as a basis for *explicit*, but internal, explorations of alternatives, a process called *lookahead*' (Holland 1995: 33).

Waldrop's discussion of connectionism describes exploitative and exploratory learning as the difference between improving current knowledge by small changes to the strength of association between activity and reward, and effecting major shifts in knowledge by taking apart the current model, taking large risks and finding a '...whole new realm' of new rules (1994: 291). This discussion is analogous with Argyris and Schon's (1978), single- and double-loop learning, Fiol and Lyles' (1985) lower- and higher-order learning and Senge's (1995) adaptive and generative learning. In using Holland's node-and-connector structure for discussion of emergent mental models Waldrop focuses on the lesson that '...the power really does lie in the connections' (1994: 291).

The emergence of mental models in Holland's (1995) work highlights knowledge as naturally emergent in a complex adaptive system and focuses theory and practice on the search for knowledge 'levers', those triggers within the knowledge ecosystem which lead to generative, rather than adaptive, change - the focus being on innovation rather than replication of knowledge.

Complex adaptive systems' '...retention of a cognitivist perspective on human knowing' reduces complexity to simplicity in Stacey's (2003b: 249) critique. For Stacey, the preoccupation with modelling complex processes provides a context within which complexity is seen to emerge from interaction which is devoid of diversity, noise and fluctuation. Stacey sees learning as far more messy where agents are simultaneously formed and forming, simultaneously individual and collective, learning not deterministic but evolving through language. Hence Stacey's (2003b: 309) strongly worded and italicised statement, '...*there is no analogy between the programmer of the complex adaptive system model and anything in human interaction*'.

Cognitivist constructions of learning like those inherent in discussion of adaptation through developing mental models, in Stacey's view, do not address the reality of human learning. For Stacey, rather than learning progressing through accumulative shifts in mental models in the individual mind, it occurs in their iterative interaction.

Between these two diametrically opposed views lies a continuum of theory which draws on complexity and on notions of adaptation and learning through mental models. Even in the modelling paradigm notions of 'interpretative frameworks' are illustrated as only imperfectly linked to adaptation. Through modelling, the multiplicity of subjectivities in a social context influence and are influenced by imperfect understandings of what is expected and what actually happens (Allen and Strathern 2003: 31). Anderson's (1999: 219) work, too, calls into question notions of schemata that stress learning as the simplistic structuring and restructuring of rule sets in schema. Anderson is sensitive to an agent's interpretation of the landscape as being influenced by managerial control and social cues.

A little further along the continuum, Rhodes and MacKechnie (2003) move toward a new basic unit for analysis while maintaining a focus on schema. Their contribution highlights the essentially transient processes in which agents engage and evolve and introduces issues of economic, social, political and innovative pressures on and in the system.

Further along again, van Eijnatten (2004; van Eijnatten and Putnik 2004) focuses on the holonic characteristic of a complexity perspective where internal models are part of a system upon which people act and from which they are inseparable. The models are both acted on and used in action. Harkema's (2005) interest in complexity and learning provides another step along the continuum, his development of a model which attempts to merge learning and complex adaptive systems theory nodding to internal models as part of a more complex construction of emergent learning. Harkema draws attention to emotion in combination with the rules and routines of organisational culture and structure.

As illustrated in the previous chapter, Stacey's work problematises the perspectives so available in knowledge management, organisational learning and workplace learning theories which place focus on the individual as '…primary and prior to the group' (Stacey 2003b: 49). For Stacey, this focus is in conflict with theories of knowledge as interactivity and in contrast offers perspectives on knowledge and learning influenced by complexity theory.

3.1.3 CONTEMPORARY PERSPECTIVES ON COMPLEXITY AND ORGANISATION

The increasing recognition of complexity in learning and knowledge in organisation points to opportunities for integration across discourses. Complexity is used with some frequency in attempts to bridge both theory and practice divides.

The implications for organisation theory and complexity theory are reciprocal; just as organisations can benefit from the emphasis for attention placed on characteristics of complex systems, complex adaptive systems theory can benefit from its elaboration through application in organisations. As Morel and Ramanujam (1999: 290) state, 'The bridge between the two fields goes both ways'.

As notions of complexity become mainstream in organisational and educational theory interdisciplinary perspectives are invited and pondered. Such discussions highlight the volume and complexity of knowledge generated in work environments and the need for organisations to grow, adapt and survive (Geisler and Ritter 2003: 42). The deeper investigation of notions of knowledge and of learning through complexity contributes to understandings developing in the learning and knowledge management discourses and points to new avenues for research and theory development.

3.2 OPPORTUNITY FOR NEW PERSPECTIVES

The emerging shared themes around the indistinctness of the learning individual, collective and organisation; the situatedness and complexity of knowledge; and the role of mental models in adaptation and learning, demand investigation through integrative means.

Three common ways of establishing a gap in past research are described by Easterby-Smith, Antonacopoulou et al. (2004: 372) to involve '...claims that past research is: *incomplete* and hence new data, settings or problems are required; *inadequate* and hence new theories, perspectives and concepts are required; or that it is *incommensurate* and hence new research designs and methods are required' [emphases in original]. In this dissertation, it is argued that a gap exists in past research on all three claims.

Extant research is *incomplete*, having taken place in discourse-specific fields, defined by the arguments of discrete theories; *inadequate* in its investigation of learning and knowledge through the lens of complexity, and; *incommensurate*, no organisational research design derived explicitly from notions of complexity with the intention of accessing the complex is available.

The literature review across organisational learning, knowledge management and complexity supplied in Chapter 2 highlights the changing perspectives in the fields and Chapter 3 highlights their convergence. The literature points to gaps in each of the fields and gaps in research in their integration. The table at Appendix C highlights the research that has been undertaken in the current decade which relates to these emergent themes and the converging fields. In so doing, it points to the significant absence of research of the type provided by this study.

The research visited here reflects a growing interest in nonlinearity and complexity. Constructions of knowledge that underpin the research are broad, but increasingly epistemology is addressed explicitly and research progressed through sophisticated methodologies aligned with epistemological stance. Culture, technology, training, tacit knowledge, competence, network development and human resource development are examples of the discrete foci of research in the sample provided above.

Little of the available research attempts to represent the experience of organisational members within the moment and context of their work in an exploration of the relationship between their learning, the organisation's knowledge and complexity. There is little evidence of research which attempts a more holistic perspective through the design of a methodological approach that allows for the emergence of new perspectives through interactivity and sensitivity to complexity.

Such research, however, is needed to bridge the gap between discourse areas and to inform fuller, less granulated understandings of what it is to learn in an organisation and how this learning contributes to organisational knowledge.

3.2.1 CALLS FOR RESEARCH

The theoretical perspectives advanced in organisational learning and knowledge management literatures are sometimes overwhelmingly optimistic and simplistically reductionist. Authors continually call for empirical study to investigate the theory advanced. The call for research of the type provided by this study is clear. The following table details the recent research and theory which includes calls for research of the problems this study addresses.

Table 5 Calls for research

Author (date)	Focus of research	Call for research
Mirvis (1996)	Review of theory and research on organisations as social, information processing, interpretive and inquiring systems	On how people interpret prior experiences and improve collective learning
Applebaum and Goransson (1997)	Transformational and adaptive learning	On how organisations learn
Karakowsky and McBey (1999)	Organisation as a facilitator or inhibitor of adult learning	On relationship between individual and organisational learning

Author (date)	Focus of research	Call for research
Anderson (1999)	The relationship between complexity theory and organisation science	For exploration of the ways in which ideas, initiatives and interpretations form an internal ecology within organisations
Chaston, Badger and Sadler-Smith (2000)	Organisational learning style and competences	On how learning occurs in relationship oriented firms Leading to detailed understanding of learning process not possible through classic positivist, survey-based approach
Garavan et al. (2000)	HRD research and theoretical perspectives	On resolving the learning-performance dichotomy
McElroy (2000)	Integrating complexity theory, knowledge management and organisational learning	On cross disciplinary approaches to understanding the nature of organisational knowledge, how it is generated, diffused and the development of knowledge-based strategies
Bontis, Crossan and Hulland (2002)	Managing organisational learning system by aligning stocks and flows	On how to improve learning flows
Garavan et al. (2002)	Emerging theoretical perspectives and organisational practices in workplace learning	On the evolving organisational and individual practices in workplace learning
Hurley (2002)	Human dimensions of organisational learning	On redirecting research to the human dimension of learning in organisational learning
Spencer (2002)	Research and the pedagogics of work and learning	On the pedagogics of work and learning that do not contribute to new forms of oppression and control in the workplace
Yeo (2002)	Linking theoretical and empirical perspectives on learning within organisations	On how organisational learning is developed On identifying the factors that influence organisational learning at various stages

Author (date)	Focus of research	Call for research
Burnes, Cooper and West (2003)	Organisational learning as a management paradigm	On organisational learning in a range of sectors
Critten (2003)	HRD and emergence	On making the link between individual and organisational learning through complexity theory
Moffett (2003)	Empirical analysis of knowledge management applications	On rigorous theory-building/theory testing research to informal organisational application and to contribute to the body of knowledge within the knowledge management spectrum
Muscatello (2003)	Use of knowledge management for training	On the merging of traits of knowledge management and training in the development of new theory
Shelton and Darling (2003)	Use of new science concepts in organisational learning	On discovering new ways to design and lead learning organisations through the new sciences
Rhodes and MacKechnie (2003)	Using complex adaptive systems to better understand public service systems	To provide empirical verification of the claims of complex adaptive systems theory and to generate novel hypotheses through its application
Van Eijnatten (2004)	Suggestions for a complexity framework to inform a learning organisation	To validate the new lens of complexity and to specify the circumstances in which is can add value to learning organisations

The calls for research cited above underscore the gaps in the literature which this study aims to close. In its empirical investigation of organisational learning and knowledge experiences, and its aim to provide a more holistic understanding of workplace experience through sensitivity to complexity theory from which to build practice, this study responds to the calls effectively.

3.3 CONCLUSION

This chapter argues that the convergence of themes across organisational learning and knowledge management provides fresh ground for more holistic organisational research into learning and knowledge. Important implications for workplace learning approaches are suggested in the convergence and a broad sample of literatures are presented to illustrate the need for research of this type.

The convergence of themes across the literatures is presented as occurring in three main discourses and complexity is presented as an integrating device which promises new perspectives in the fields. This chapter develops an argument in which more holistic perspectives of learning and knowledge at work are posited as critical to better understandings of, and practices in, learning and organisational knowledge development.

This chapter provides an overview of the theoretical and practical context in which this research is conceived. It shows the separation of learning and knowledge in organisations to be problematic, and more importantly, inappropriate in the context of converging theory. The discussion highlights the ways in which the complexity metaphor set provides a new opportunity for more holistic understandings of the ways in which organisational members learn and the contribution this learning makes to the knowledge of the organisation. The literature supports an investigation of learning and knowledge experiences at work, and yet there is silence in the field. It is a silence into which researchers and theorists alike are making calls for research specifically of the type provided in this study.

'But is sensory experience fixed and neutral? Are theories simply man-made interpretations of given data? The epistemological viewpoint that has most often guided Western philosophy for three centuries dictates an immediate and unequivocal, Yes! In the absence of a developed alternative, I find it impossible to relinquish entirely that viewpoint. Yet it no longer functions effectively, and the attempts to make it do so through the introduction of a neutral language of observations now seem to me hopeless.' (Kuhn 1970: 126)

This chapter provides the theoretical background for the development of methodology in this study. It highlights the critical role the theoretical frame plays in the selection of methodology and methods in this dissertation where learning and knowledge are subject content as well as research outcome.

Epistemology and empiricism are intricately intertwined in any research about learning and knowledge. The researcher's understandings of knowledge inform not only the research question, but also the research approach. Pears' (1971) question, 'What is knowledge?' is core to any investigation of the emergence, development, dissemination and institutionalisation of knowledge and learning in organisations.

It is not only the question of the nature of knowledge, however, that confounds researchers in organisational learning and knowledge, the theory that emerges from the literatures and underpins the research question also has impact on the research approach. The focusing of debate on the diverse, yet overlapping and interacting, aspects of knowledge and learning is illustrated as convergence in the key themes described in the previous chapter. Aligning the research approach with the theoretical interest in collectivity and interactivity, notions of knowledge as complex, emergent and situated, and sophisticated discussion of the role of mental models in learning and knowledge is critical to the integrity of this study.

This chapter builds a rationale for the selection of methodology. It does so by highlighting the alignment of theoretical discussion in the fields of organisational learning and knowledge management with epistemological, theoretical and methodological assumptions in research approach.

4.1 DEVELOPING A RESEARCH APPROACH

The influence of developing perspectives in science and organisation reflected in the literatures present opportunity for more holistic research and novel insights into organisational experience. These new perspectives point to interpretative systems of understanding and mutable research designs. Simultaneously, however, they challenge traditional perspectives of rigorous research and demand careful attention to process to ensure the validity of research outcomes.

This challenge and the ensuing demand are well recognised in literatures in qualitative research (Strauss and Corbin 1998a: 34; Sturman 1999: 110; Denzin and Lincoln 2000b: 11). Developments in the new sciences provide support for the observation of emergent phenomena as an appropriate way to investigate and make sense of features of complex systems.

In this research project the theory, more than inviting, actually directed the methodological approach. Crotty's (1998: 4) four elements model illustrates the relationship between epistemology, theory, methodology and methods and was used in this research to facilitate development of a research approach aligned with the thesis content.

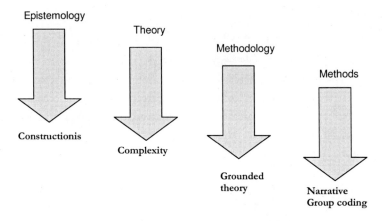

Figure 4 Developing a research approach

Epistemology

Theory

Methodology

Methods

Constructionis

Complexity

Grounded theory

Narrative Group coding

Following Crotty (1998)

This chapter concerns itself with the first three of these four elements, presenting the ways in which the epistemological base of the research emerges from the literature and resonates with the researcher's personal conception of the nature of knowledge. Complexity is presented as an important informing theory and reference is made to theoretical discussion in the literature that supports a complexivist approach. Common themes in developing complexity theories of interaction, emergence, novelty, self-organisation and diversity underpin the methodology in this study.

4.1.1   EPISTEMOLOGY

Given the broad review in the previous chapters on the range of perspectives on the nature of knowledge in the informing literatures, discussion here is brief. Without attempting to debate further on the meaning of knowledge (less still of trying to resolve it) it is, however, important here to summarise the nature of knowledge as it is conceived in this study. In this research knowledge does not accord with Maddox's (1993: 3) representation, where knowledge is both true and verifiable, corresponding to observed fact, consistent with the general body of established facts and substantiated to others by the knower. Rather, the epistemology that underpins this research is focused on the view that objectivity and subjectivity are concurrently engaged in knowledge, and that

'... all knowledge, and therefore all meaningful reality as such, is contingent upon human practices, being constructed in and out of interaction between human beings and their world, and developed and transmitted within an essentially social context' (Crotty 1998: 42).

It is from this epistemological stance that the methodology progresses.

In the findings of this study the participants' own constructions of 'knowledge' are illustrated through their narratives. It is the researcher's intention that these constructions are legitimised in the research, and that these constructions guide discussion about the experience of learning and knowledge in later chapters.

4.1.2   THEORY

The literature review illustrates the increasing propensity of theorists and practitioners to represent knowledge as problematic. The development of the research described here is strongly influenced by Spender's (1996) work in exploring this problematic through integration of theories of organisational knowledge, learning and memory. In his pursuit of such integration, Spender rejects positivist approaches to organisational analysis, asserting that 'In an uncertain, non-positivistic world, where there is no privileged access to truth, there are always problems of meaning' (Spender 1996: 65) and advocates the exploration of 'richer' epistemologies which '...can address more complex notions of uncertainty than are admissible in a positivist framework' (Spender 1996: 67).

In developing agreement between the themes of interdisciplinary convergence and methodological approach, this research looks to a range of authors and overlapping theories. In particular, and briefly reviewed below, the methodological approach is sensitive to theoretical discussion of complexity (Waldrop 1994; Holland 1995; Anderson 1999), constructivism (Schwandt 2003) and constructionism (Crotty 1998), the collective mind (Weick 1995; Spender 1996; Lakomski 2001; Weick 2001), and knowledge as an activity of interdependent people (Stacey 2003a). Aligned with this discussion, and in recognition of the influence of the theory on the approach, this research rejects atomisation and objectivity in support of a fresh perspective on the lived experience of organisational members.

4.1.2.1 *Complexity*

New perspectives on the nature of the physical world through the investigation of new science provide researchers with the opportunity to rethink the distinctions between observer and observed, subject and object. Through the recognition of the limitations of Newtonian science in explaining quantum gravity, chaos and self-organising systems new research perspectives are advanced which recognise the problems inherent in modernist scientific method. Ackermann (1976: 63) argues that 'Where relativistic phenomena are involved,... Newton's theory isn't even viable'. The new sciences demand a fresh perspective in which theory is about developing metaphor rather than accurate descriptions of reality and where description is deeply complex and problematising.

As perspectives from the physical sciences domain transfer to studies of human experience, the researcher is prompted to consider the interdependence of all phenomena; biological, psychological, social and environmental, and ponder the embeddedness of individuals and societies in the patterns of nature (Capra 1983: xviii). Such perspectives suggest the research look at wholes rather than reducing the world to its constitute parts, focusing on the interrelationships, dynamics and interactions in which phenomena reside. Insights from the new sciences contribute to an approach which recognises uncertainty, complementarity, discontinuity, and wholism as profoundly impacting on our understandings of research and observation.

This research assumes that within set boundaries, the setting of research 'attractants' (Snowden 2003b) or foci will lead to the organic emergence of themes and concepts that are meaningful to the research. Complexity theories suggests that some phenomena only become clear in retrospect and that the self-organising capacity of complex systems requires the freedom of agents to interact in ways which are undirected. The flexibility of this research design facilitates this freedom and attempts to find 'retrospective coherence' (Kurtz and Snowden 2003: 9) in the phenomena which emerge in its findings.

4.1.2.2   Constructivism and constructionism

The literatures frequently cite the work of Polanyi (1967; 1969) in explaining or exploring knowledge and its nature in individuals, collectives and organisations (Nonaka 1994: 16; Spender 1996: 67; Snowden 2002: 101; Stacey 2003a: 159). The humanist paradigm in knowledge management is strongly influenced by this work and the research discussed here also draws heavily on Polanyi's representation of knowledge. For Polanyi, knowledge is not so much about fixed and objective truth as it is about understanding and meaning. He describes knowledge as rooted in acts of comprehension rather than based on verifiable fact (Maddox 1993: 13).

Polanyi's definition of knowledge highlights its embeddedness within human beings and its existence in human meaning-making and has the timbre of a constructivist epistemological approach. A simple representation of the constructivist viewpoint is offered by Schwantdt (2003: 305),

> *'Most of us would agree that knowing is not passive – a simple imprinting of sense data on the mind – but active; that is, mind does something with these impressions...in this sense, constructivism means that human beings do not find or discover knowledge so much as we construct or make it.'*

These constructions occur within a context and are developed through shared language, activity and understanding (Weick and Roberts 1993: 358).

Constructivism, according to Crotty (1998: 58) is '...an individualist understanding of the constructionist position' maintaining focus on the sense-making activity of individual minds. Keeves (1999: 6) further illustrates the focus on the individual in constructivism, 'Wisdom is unique to individuals, is slow to form, and is applied by individuals critically and practically. It is this individual knowledge that constructivist research is investigating'. This individual focus, however, is one which is problematised in the literature and in this study, and the investigation of the role of the individual in the knowledge of the organisation is an important foundation theme in the theoretical framework of this research.

A constructionist focus, in comparison to a constructivist one, looks to '...the collective generation [and transmission] of meaning' (Crotty 1998: 58), this meaning-making constructed primarily through conversation (Stacey 2003b: 8). Jun (2005: 86) describes constructionism as providing a focus on the ways in which identity is formed through the contexts and relationships in which individuals interact to make sense of the world. This collective meaning making is an important theme in the knowledge management literatures and has some resonance with the work of Stacey (2001; 2003b; 2003a) in his theory of knowledge as an activity of interdependent people

4.1.2.3 Knowledge as an activity of interdependent people

Stacey's (2001; 2003b; 2003a) discussion about knowledge in organisations is important to the development of the theoretical framework for this research project. Stacey's work bridges knowledge management, organisational learning and workplace learning through a focus on the actions of human beings in creating patterns of meaning in their iterated interaction with each other. As people interact, '...coherent patterns of meaning, of knowledge, are perpetually iterated.' (Stacey 2003a: 328), knowledge is an activity, held in the ether of relational processes.

Stacey's work resonates in some ways with Vygotsky's work in early childhood education on activity theory. Vygotsky's focus on 'gradual individualisation' (1962: 133), the shift from social to individual is one Stacey may disavow, given his rejection of the primacy of the individual in distinctions between individual and group. However, Vygotsky's focus on understanding arising from the interaction of the social and the individual in the development of consciousness provides a bridge across the theories of constructivism and knowledge as interactivity and invites consideration of what has been termed the 'collective mind'.

4.1.2.4 Collective mind

The concept of 'collective mind' directs focus to the space between individuals where knowledge is negotiated and exercised through a social, rather than individual, identity. '...[T]he social implicit element of the individual's knowledge processes is typically called collective' (Spender 1996: 71) and the relationship between the social and individual is interdependent, '...the mind of consciousness is manifested in social institutions, that is, ways of life, which give identities, self concepts, to individuals' (Stacey 2003a: 328).

In knowledge management and organisational learning this theory provides an important node of intersection in the literatures and informs a central argument in the organisational learning literatures about the relationship between individual and organisational knowledge (Easterby-Smith, Crossan et al. 2000: 787). As highlighted in Chapter 3, the focus on collectivity of mind and knowledge reduces what has been presented as a dichotomy to a phenomenon where '…the individual is the singular and the social is the plural of interdependent people' (Stacey 2003a: 327).

Introduction of the concept of the collective mind by Weick (Weick and Roberts 1993; Weick 2001) in concert with discussion by Spender and Stacey leads to consideration of the relationship between organisational learning, knowledge and culture, where 'Collective knowledge comprises both meaning (cognitive, affective, symbolic and cultural) and praxis (behaviours, rituals and organizational routines)' (Spender 1996: 73), and

> 'External, symbolic features, traditionally believed to represent culture, and internal non-symbolic ones such as beliefs, values and meanings, usually taken to be the property of the individual mind, are no longer seen to represent separate worlds but one world' (Lakomski 2001: 69).

These notions introduce paradox in understandings of knowledge and learning in organisations. Paradox is accommodated by perspectives offered by the 'new sciences', perspectives which demand fresh approaches to investigation unfettered by traditional assumptions and which invite more holistic views.

4.2 METHODOLOGY

The methodology developed for this exploration of experience is one which blends a number of recognised methodologies. It is inspired by grounded theory, influenced by theory elaboration and is sensitive to complexity. The methodology lays out the theoretical approach to investigation, stressing the mutability inherent in the design and the opportunity for emergence of phenomena through this flexibility.

4.2.1   GROUNDED THEORY

Grounded theory provides for emergence of phenomena from the interaction of the researcher with the data, the data with themes that emerge from their investigation, and these themes with other themes and other data. The complex connections and interconnections that emerge in the checking and rechecking of data against developing theory results in a web of interlinking concepts, each of which informs and is informed by the other.

Complexity theories, with their focus on emergence of novel phenomena from the interactivity of agents, suggest a parallel with grounded theory use in research. Complexity thinking rejects a teleological approach, discrete and directed steps toward a defined outcome, where a master controls progress toward a goal, informed by the segmentation of components for their individual observation and manipulation. Instead, complexity insists that the researcher consider connections in an interactive system, focusing on the emergence of phenomena from the interconnection of the components. The underlying principles of complexity theory are accommodated in a grounded approach to research, and in this research, the influence of complexity is obvious in the research design.

Discussions about grounded theory predictably reveal grounded theory purists who advocate a strict adherence to the very early work of Glaser and Strauss' (1967) and their prescriptions for qualitative research. However, more recent discussion frames grounded theory as a 'way of thinking about and studying social reality' (Strauss and Corbin 1998b: 4) which allows '...much latitude for ingenuity' rather than a set of commandments to follow in process. Central to the methodological approach, however, and unequivocally essential in grounded approaches for Strauss and Corbin (1998b: 46) are the '... procedures of making comparisons, asking questions, and sampling based on evolving theoretical concepts'. It is this understanding that inspires the hybrid approach in the methodology of this study, and which allows the research to follow emergent findings as the study progresses.

Strauss and Corbin (1998b) describe grounded theory as theory grounded in the data collected rather than from theory generated from logical deduction. It is at once about critical and creative thinking. They argue that this approach can allow more useful hypotheses to arise than inductively developed hypotheses. Others argue that even if it were an intention to begin investigation without a guiding theory, it is 'impossible to start with pure observation, that is, without anything in the nature of a theory' (Sturman 1999: 104). Indeed, Ragin (1992: 5) states that 'It is impossible to do research in a conceptual vacuum' and asserts the need for reducing the infinite scope of phenomena through the use of theoretical principles. In doing so, he claims, we structure our descriptions of the empirical by '...the application of constraining ideas to infinite evidence'.

In 1970 Strauss '...suggested in detail how a grounded substantive theory could be greatly extended, leading either to a more elaborated substantive theory or to formal theories developed in conjunction with multiarea data' (Strauss and Corbin 1998a: 176). This variation on the 'point-of-viewless' (Bruner 1991: 3) basis for a grounded theory has led others to investigate opportunities for grounded theory research based in substantive theory. Vaughan (1992: 195), a thoughtful and celebrated grounded theorist (Strauss and Corbin 1998a: 176), for example, uses grounded theory beginning from substantive theory in an approach she calls 'theory elaboration'. Vaughan recognises the limitations of theory while advocating their use in assisting researchers to understand research phenomena;

> 'The paradox of theory is that at the same time it tells us where to look, it can keep us from seeing. Glaser and Strauss argue against initiating qualitative analysis with any preconceived theory that dictates relevances in concepts and hypotheses prior to the research... but this method of elaboration relies upon comparing data with some sensitising theory, concept, or model. It rests on the assumption that a researcher never begins with a clean slate.' (Vaughan 1992: 194).

In this present study, the researcher explicitly explores the relationship between complexity theory and workplace learning experience in relation to organisational knowledge. Following Vaughan the researcher begins research by using '... theories, models and concepts as sensitising devices, rather than translating them into formalized propositions that are tested.' (Vaughan 1992: 196). In this way, she takes '...intuitive practice – using theories about the world to organize and understand it – and make the practice overt so we can better direct our analysis of social situations' (Vaughan 1992: 196).

While Vaughan's approach '...directly contradicts Glaser and Strauss's position that verification and discovery cannot go on simultaneously' (1992: 194), Strauss and Corbin's (1998b: 176) work supports Vaughan's interpretation of grounded theory methodology. In their description of means for stimulating thinking about the properties and dimensions of a phenomenon they point to using comparison to understand better the similarities and differences between the comparison concept or object and the phenomenon. They suggest that such an approach leads to clearer insights into the nature of the phenomenon.

Vaughan's theory elaboration is a 'method for developing general theories of particular phenomena... refining a theory, model or concept in order to specify more carefully the circumstances in which it does or does not offer potential for explanation' (Vaughan 1992: 196). The methodological approach in this study differs from Vaughan's in that it does not apply a theory across, and within, a range of organisational forms, but rather takes a theory from one domain and uses it to sensitise understanding of one other. Unlike Vaughan's work, the research described here does not systematically compare one case against another; instead, it takes one case and systematically analyses the properties and dimensions of the data against the theory. In this way, both theory of the phenomena and the substantive theory co-emerge.

The constructionist posture of this research accords with the grounded theory methodology used by Charmaz (2000: 522) which fosters '...the development of qualitative traditions through the study of experience from the standpoint of those who live it'. This is an important concern in this study. Strauss and Corbin (1998a: 178) suggest that adaptation of grounded theory will include its combination with other methodologies. This research is designed to collect data in a natural setting to 'get in deep' (Schostak 2002: 75) in order to create 'thick interpretations' (Denzin and Lincoln 1998: 92) through 'lived experience' elicited through narrative.

4.3   ETHICAL CONSIDERATIONS

This research places the researcher within a human organisational context and allows her the opportunity to observe and engage with trusting individuals and groups. This opportunity carries with it responsibilities to protect the rights of organisational members, especially in relation to the confidentiality with which their experience is observed and reported. It is the researcher's responsibility to ensure that the trust organisational members place in the researcher's confidence is protected at all times and this is achieved through the careful stripping of all identifying features of individuals, organisation and position from transcripts and the dissertation itself.

This research does not attempt to critique the experience of organisational members as it does to understand it. It is the responsibility of the researcher to ensure that the experience of organisational members is accurately represented and that these members have access to all records that pertain to their experience. In the carriage of this responsibility the researcher has ensured that participants approved stripped transcripts, contributed to the analysis of the data and discussed developing theory with each other and with the researcher.

Ethical considerations are highlighted in any study that may enable recognition of its participants (Sturman 1999: 106). According to Charles and Mertler (2002: 13) the researcher's ethical responsibility relates to beneficence, honesty and accurate disclosure. This research adheres to these principles throughout the research process through a clear and focused intention to contribute to the body of knowledge of organisational learning and knowledge, maintaining integrity in data collection and interpretation and through familiarising each research participant with the intention and design of the research.

The researcher is responsible to the participants of this study in making moral choices about representing their voice accurately, providing their stories in ways that reflect their reality (Charmaz 2000: 521). The researcher is also bound to share with them what she has learned, and how their stories have been interpreted (Strauss and Corbin 1998a: 174). This is achieved by the preparation and provision of transcripts for participants' approval, meetings to discuss developing theory and reporting on findings as well as implications for practice.

Confidentiality and protection of individuals are not at any time be threatened by this research. The participants are assured that no harm will come to them as a result of the research and sensitive areas of discussion that may have resulted in discomfort were not breached. The research received formal ethics approval through the University of Canberra.

4.4   LIMITATIONS AND DELIMITATIONS

This study, while aspiring to reflect the experiences of participants honestly, is limited by the very nature of research and delimited by the need to maintain focus on the research question and eliminate some aspects of experience from exploration.

The study is limited in its exploration of a very narrow slice of organisational experience. It artificially bounds the experience at the edge of the organisation, where the boundary in reality is shown to be difficult to define. It does not propose to be generalisable, exploring as it does a experiences in a very limited sample, instead it aims to better understand the experience of a few organisational members in an attempt to better understand learning and knowledge within it.

This study does not claim to represent any objective truth, but it does claim to have verisimilitude, offering participant voice and story in the reality they are offered. It constrains itself in its use of the complexity metaphor set, but attempts to counter this limitation through critical reflection on its use. The methodology is one which may be challenged by researchers looking for reliability, given this study's recognition of the role of the researcher in the analysis of the data and the understanding that initial conditions (the context of the original study) may not be replicated.

4.4.1   THE BOUNDARY OF THE CASE

Complexity draws attention to the boundarilessness of interaction, problematising notions of subject and context. For the purposes of this study, the research is artificially bounded by the organisation itself, although the organisation's context impinges on the learning and knowledge experiences of the participants. Questions about the role of the organisation, its relationship with community and environment, and the pressures which contribute to its internal processing are raised by

Halligan (2004) in reference to organisations of the case type. They are not addressed in this study in order to guarantee the anonymity of participants and maintain focus on a manageable set of themes emerging from the data.

4.4.2   GENERALISABILITY

This research does not attempt to provide an objective description of the processes of knowledge creation, development and dissemination in a generalisable context. This research limits itself to understanding the experience of three groups of organisational members within a specific organisation. It recognises that the understanding is that of the organisational members, developed between them through narrative and discussion and interpreted through the researcher's understandings of the participants' analysis.

4.4.3   TRUTH AND VERISIMILITUDE

Bruner (1991: 4) addresses issues of truth in this way,

> *'Unlike the constructions generated by logical and scientific procedures that can be weeded out by falsification, narrative constructions can only achieve 'verisimilitude'. Narratives, then, are a version of reality whose acceptability is governed by convention and 'narrative necessity' rather than by empirical verification'.*

This researcher assumes the value of the themes emerging from narrative on the basis of verisimilitude and attempts understanding of the narrative as if it were true. In a constructionist account, '…objectivity and subjectivity need to be brought together and held together indissolubly' (Crotty 1998: 44) and in this research narrative description provides the research some dependability (Denzin and Lincoln 2000a: 21) through interactive story-telling within a known group and context. This researcher takes the view that every narrative contributes some important consideration to the field although she recognises that narrative is always a construction which is embedded in cultural discourses and narrative performance. Narrative is recognised as individually constructed within social and cultural contexts which mediate it's accuracy in reflecting experience.

4.4.4   MODELS, INSIGHT AND BLINKERS

A dilemma is posed in this study in its quest for new, unconstrained perspectives through participant experience and its sensitivity to complexity. While the metaphors contributed by complexity provide novel points of view through which to consider organisational experience they also confine discussion to the features of complexity. Gough (1999: 59) describes concerns about the use of metaphors and models that are shared by this researcher, 'Metaphors and other concepts have complex histories that endure in the form of conceptual baggage that accompanies their circulation and reproduction in contemporary discourses.' This researcher attempts to limit this effect through the maintenance of a personal journal in which the she records her reflection on the use of the heuristic, a process which resulted in a number of challenges to its application. The researcher's critical appraisal of the metaphor set in relation to the findings led to the analysis and representation of themes in the experience of these participants which are not well served by complexity. This limitation is discussed further in Chapter 10.

4.4.5   METHODOLOGY, EMERGENCE AND FLUIDITY

The research design is centred on flexibility, accommodating emergent findings and allowing narrative to drive investigation. This flexibility, however, is in conflict with traditional assumptions about the scientific method and rigorous research. Notions of replicability become redundant in research of this kind, the implications of complexity and the inability to accurately define initial conditions confounding attempts to replicate research outcomes. The research is not apologetic in this regard; the opportunity for exploration of novel phenomena that is accommodated by such a flexible research approach is a valuable one.

4.5   CONCLUSION

This chapter describes the role of complexity in the development of methodological approach. It frames complexity as conversant with important theoretical discussion across the fields of organisational learning and knowledge describes how it prompts a grounded approach to the study. It illustrates the ways in which the literature's growing preoccupation with notions of constructionism, constructivism, collective mind, and knowledge as an activity of interdependent people leads to a methodological approach that is mutable, iterative and unbounded by hypotheses.

In the following chapter the methods are described. The chapter illustrates how the theory leads to research techniques that draw on diversity, allow for the emergence of themes, provide a base for 'retrospective coherence' and accommodate the construction of knowledge in a social context. The methods are shown to provide for analysis of the ways in which organisational members make sense of their experience and in so doing, lead to outcomes which reflect truth as it is constructed by the participants.

5 METHOD

This chapter illustrates the process of working through the aims and objectives of the research to methods of inquiry, selection of population and study site. It describes the tools and techniques chosen for inquiry in this study and justifies their selection through reflection on the theoretical frame. It goes on to explain the actual process of collecting and making sense of experience through narrative. The flexibility of the process and its responsiveness to developments in the research as it progressed is also outlined.

This chapter introduces the categories revealed in analysis which led to the adoption of the complex adaptive systems metaphor set. These metaphors then provided a base for further analysis. The chapter closes with an evaluation of the methodological approach.

5.1 OVERVIEW OF METHOD

21 individuals from a large public sector organisation worked in 3 narrative groups to share their experiences of learning in the organisation. 7 participants from across the three groups then worked with the researcher to analyse and categorise the main themes that emerged from narrative. Table 7 below summarises the method.

Table 7 Data collection and analysis through phases

	Phase 1	Phase 2	Phase 3	Phase 4	Phase 5
Activity	Group narrative workshop	Group sense-making and category development	Group connection-making	Category saturation and theoretical sampling	Theoretical integration and grounding the theory
Participant involvement	Three groups of six to eight individuals share stories relating to experience of learning and knowledge in the organisation.	Group of seven volunteers from the original three groups uses metanarrative to make sense of experience elicited through the narrative workshop. Researcher facilitates discussion to draw out main themes in group and develop categories	Group of seven clusters categories into conceptual clusters		Group of six members of the connection-making group critically discusses emergent theoretical structure.
Researcher tasks	Researcher . audio-tapes interaction for full transcription, further analysis and summary . selectively transcribes narratives for analysis and from these records metanarrative for group use in phase 2 . develops preliminary codes against data.	Researcher . audio-tapes interaction for further analysis and summary . selectively transcribes group discussion for analysis in phase 3.	Researcher . recognises parallels between group-developed categories and properties of complex adaptive systems . develops formal definition of properties and dimensions of categories . adds group developed theoretical memos to those accumulated through open coding . selects narratives to test and further develop categories for phase 4.	Researcher . explores further examples through transcripts until no new categories emerge.	Researcher . compares emergent theoretical framework to existing theoretical models . grounds emergent theory through validation against text.

5.2   AIM OF THE RESEARCH

The aim of this research is to develop a holistic perspective on learning and knowledge in organisations through exploration of workplace experience.

5.2.1   OBJECTIVES

The objectives of the research are to:

- Describe the themes arising from learning and organisational knowledge development experiences

- Illustrate the relationships among emergent themes

- Apply research methodology aligned with complexity theory

- Use research findings to develop learning and knowledge facilitation strategies.

Allowing organisational members to relate their experiences and discuss these experiences as a collective gives the researcher an opportunity to explore learning and knowledge in organisations in a way which accommodates novel perspectives. It provides for more holistic views, unlimited by defined and discrete areas of inquiry and unencumbered by theoretically derived hypotheses.

Themes arising from this study are developed by participants collectively and refined by the researcher. The objective of their description is to understand better the ways in which organisational members make sense of their learning experiences and the relationship of these to organisational knowledge. In describing the themes that emerge, the researcher attempts to identify fresh points of view and alternative meanings of the phenomena (Strauss and Corbin 1998b: 105) and to develop a fuller understanding of the relationship between learning experience and organisational knowledge.

Following Strauss and Corbin (1998b: 15), the researcher looks to relate emergent concepts to one another in search of an integrating theory. In this research the participant organisational members join the researcher in discussing the ways in which themes cluster in their experience and in the stories told. The researcher uses the insights of the participants to help make sense of the ways the themes interact.

The development of a methodology that aligns with the theoretical framework of the study is a major consideration in the research. The methodology allows for the emergence of novel outcomes through the interaction of organisational members with diverse perspectives and experience. Similarly, the grounded nature of the approach accommodates the self-organisation of ideas and the recognition of the role of the researcher in the research. While the methods employed are derived from tested methodological approaches, their combination in this research is an innovation designed to provide a parallel between theoretical frame and means of investigation.

Complexity theory is highlighted in this research as a sensitising device for the researcher, informing the development of methodological approach and methods selected. Complexity's focus on the interaction of diverse agents in the development of emergent aggregate properties also offers a lens through which to scrutinise the experiences elicited and explore them in a novel way. The integration of learning and knowledge management within a perspective which focuses on the whole experience and the interdependence of its parts is a key objective of this study, complexity theory providing a set of concepts which support the goal.

Investigating experiences of learning and knowledge in the organisation in relation to perceived enablers and limiters provides the researcher with the chance to identify strategies that support learning experiences that lead to organisational knowledge. Emergent patterns in stories and discussion of learning experiences that lead to better organisational knowledge outcomes inform the development of facilitators of such learning.

5.3   DEFINITIONS

In this research participants' constructions of meaning around core terms are critical to discussion of the findings, and these constructions are presented in the first of the Findings chapters. However, a number of definitions emerge from the literature that are useful in providing a background against which participants' use of terms can be discussed.

Learning: 'The activity of interdependent people [that] can only be understood in terms of self-organising communicative interaction and power relating in which identities are potentially transformed' (Stacey 2003a: 331).

Training: '...the acquisition of a relatively narrow band of employment-related or job-specific skills and competencies' (Anderson, Brown et al. 2004: 234).

Organisational learning: A problematic term, described as learning by groups of people with common political and ontological interests (Field 2004: 211-212).

Knowledge: Constructivist definition provided in 3.2.1 Epistemology.

Organisational knowledge: '...the capability [that] members of an organisation have developed to draw distinctions in the process of carrying out their work, in particular concrete contexts, by enacting sets of generalizations (propositional statements) whose application depends on historically evolved collective understandings and experiences' (Tsoukas and Vladimirou 2001: 983).

Knowledge management: A problematic term, described as impossible, ' ... it is not only impossible to manage knowledge, even asking the question makes no sense' (Stacey 2001: 220).

5.4   ASSUMPTIONS

The following assumptions are made in addressing the research aim:

- Organisations recognise the value of a knowledgeable and skilled workforce and the value of an organisation's knowledge as an organisational asset

The prevalence of discourse about the value of organisational knowledge to organisational success is remarkable. As illustrated in the literature review, knowledge is increasingly cited as central to the organisation's advantage. The rhetoric in management theory by authors such as Limerick, Cunnington and Crowther (1998), and Baets (2005), in organisational strategy (Von Krogh 2001), human resource management (Scarbrough 2003; Steyn 2003) and professional development (Marquardt 1999) (as just a few examples) is ubiquitous.

- The literature shows a convergence of theory in organisational learning and knowledge management

Chapter 3 of this dissertation explored the convergence of the theory in the fields of organisational learning and knowledge management through complexity. As knowledge management has shifted from a technological focus to one of individual and collective knowledge, from practice-driven to theory- and practice-driven, from positivist to constructivist, it has aligned itself more closely to the organisational learning literature.

- Learning and knowledge management are commonly treated as separate human/technical systems in organisations

This assumption derives from the literature over the past decade, and is evidenced in the discussion of authors such as Scarbrough, Swan and Preston (1999), Malhotra (2002), Gloet and Berrell (2003) and Vera and Crossan (2003). While an extensive shift from a technological focus in knowledge management to a human focus is apparent, the two separate foci have led to division of practice; learning and knowledge management practiced as separate and discrete organisational functions. Where knowledge management has been implicated in learning practice, it is typically in its information technology dimension – the facilitation of e-learning (Lytras, Pouloudi et al. 2002), information sharing and communication support, as described the work of Alavi and Tiwana (2003), for example. Even as organisational learning and knowledge management literatures converge to focus on individual and collective learning, the nature of knowledge and the role of schema in its development, they remain fixed in separate paradigms with different foci, both of which largely neglect the *experience* of learning and knowledge of individuals and collectives within organisations.

- Complexity theory is an appropriate lens through which to consider organisational issues

Given that complexity theory is used broadly in theory of organisation (as described in detail Chapter 2), the researcher assumes that its application to an empirical study in an organisational context is appropriate. While application of complexity to the analysis of organisational members' experiences of learning and knowledge in organisation is novel, theorising about its appropriateness for analysis is well documented (Anderson 1999; Morel and Ramanujam 1999; Miller, McDaniel et al. 2001).

- A grounded methodology aligns the research with complexity theory

The ways in which the grounded theory approach parallels the mechanisms and properties of complex systems is argued in Chapter 4.

5.5   RESEARCH QUESTION

The guiding question for this study *What is the relationship between workplace learning experience and organisational knowledge?* reflects the convergence of themes across research strands in organisational learning, knowledge management, and implicates workplace learning. The question is a broad one, designed to accommodate new perspectives as they emerge from the study. It is geared toward integration, aiming to inform an understanding across the fields and demonstrate the relationships between them.

The loosely bounded question emerged over time and in reference to the literatures. In early review of the literature the trend in knowledge management toward more human interests prompted consideration of how the shift might be aligned with a learning perspective on organisational knowledge. Further review invited exploration of the nature of both learning and knowledge in organisations, and the growing representation of complexivist perspectives suggested an opportunity to discover how learning and knowledge might be empirically investigated through complexivist sensitivity. The table below outlines the development of the question through investigation of the literature.

Table 6 Research question development

Does the literature on knowledge management from 1998 – 2003 continue to show a trend away from information systems and information technology toward personalised and learning/social knowledge systems illustrated in Scarbrough and Swan's (1999) 1993 – 1998 examination? How is this trend explained? What is the significance of the realignment of organisational learning and knowledge management	↓
What are the inherent limitations of early conceptualisations of knowledge management? How have these changed over time? What challenges to current practice did early conceptions contribute?	↓

How does current practice reflect the shift in understanding over time?	↓
What perceptions of knowledge and learning exist to support current practice?	↓
How does learning practice relate to knowledge management? What understandings of the role of workplace learning currently exist to support workplace learning strategy? What limits the organisation's ability to implement learning strategies to support organisational learning and knowledge management? In what ways can traditional workplace learning strategy influence organisational learning and knowledge management? What understandings of the role of knowledge in organisations currently support knowledge management strategy?	↓
What is the relationship between knowledge and learning systems?	↓
What learning strategies and policies can facilitate knowledge creation and transfer to promote organisational effectiveness?	↓
In what ways do individuals and collectives develop and share knowledge	↓
What workplace learning experiences support organisational knowledge?	↓
In what ways does the complexity metaphor provide insight into organisational learning and knowledge?	

This study recognises that in defining the question for research the researcher assumes some knowledge of the answer, and so in this study the question remains open to enrichment through the research. Following Taft (1999: 114) the researcher works from her understanding of the theory but does not aim to prove certain hypotheses.

The researcher, however, recognises the role of preunderstanding, prejudice and prejudgement (Schwandt 2003: 195) in her engagement with the phenomenon being explored and explicitly admits the role of complexity theory in sensitising the question and its exploration. The researcher situates herself within the study, recognising that 'Analysis is the interplay between researchers and data' (Strauss and Corbin 1998b: 13) and the role she plays in the sense-making process in this iterative and fluid research approach. The researcher maintains research rigour through 'disciplined subjectivity' (Sturman 1999: 108) including her maintenance of a critical stance through reflection in a personal journal, a 'rigorous' research tool (Janesick 2000: 392) used to reflect on data and on progress.

5.5.1 QUALITATIVE RESEARCH

The subject of this research and its epistemological underpinnings align it with a qualitative approach. Qualitative methods are useful in explorations of understandings, for uncovering novel insights and for accessing intricate details, thought processes and emotions (Strauss and Corbin 1998b: 11).

Credibility of subjective research techniques is an express concern in qualitative research (Sturman 1999: 109). This concern arises from the scientific focus on objectivity and is countered in much qualitative research by the claim that all observation demands personal judgement and the assertion that credibility and precision may be obtained in this methodology through disciplined subjectivity. This precision requires that evidence is available for scrutiny, conveys credibility, and is trustworthy.

Sturman (1999: 110) lists strategies for achieving credibility in qualitative research:

- Procedures for data collection should be explained.

- Data collected should be displayed and ready for re-analysis.

- Negative instances should be reported.

- Biases should be acknowledged.

- Fieldwork analyses need to be documented.

- The relationship between assertion and evidence should be clarified.

- Primary evidence should be distinguished from secondary and description from interpretation

- Diaries or logs should track what was actually done during different stages of the study.

- Methods should be devised to check to quality of data.

This study adheres to these strategies in an attempt to deliver disciplined and credible research outcomes. The ways in which this study meets the requirements for credibility are available in this chapter's discussion of methods and data analysis.

5.5.2   POPULATION

5.5.2.1   Organisation

The population for the research is drawn from a large Federal government department with its head office in Canberra, Australia. This government department is in an unusual position in the Australian public sector in that while it enjoys the stability of the national public sector framework, it competes with non-government organisations for work and subsequent funding. As a service delivery department it is very close to the environment within which it operates. Changes in the social, political and physical environment in Australia impact immediately and forcefully upon the organisation and its business.

Learning is a primary focus for this organisation. It has set up an award winning Registered Training Organisation [these awards are not cited to protect the anonymity of the organisation] within its boundaries and the organisational structure is supported by a learning and qualification structure. The organisation's leadership group is committed to the learning of its members, and the value of learning is overtly discussed at all levels of the organisation.

This organisation is at the forefront in Federal public sector organisations in its development of knowledge management strategies that integrate latest knowledge management theory [Awards provided by international knowledge management organisations are not cited to protect the anonymity of the organisation]. Diverse knowledge management initiatives can be observed throughout the organisation, and knowledge management is formally recognised as a strategic business issue.

The organisation is geographically dispersed and diverse in its membership in terms of educational background, cultural background, age and role. Varying workplace cultures exist, providing breadth in organisational understandings, practices, and values. Access to diversity is critical to the emergence of novel phenomena in complex adaptive systems, and as such, critical to the emergence of themes through the research methodology.

5.5.2.2 *Participants*

The study drew on the experience of a total of twenty-one volunteer participants from three different working groups within the study site. The three groups operate within three discrete parts of the organisation; the learning and development centre, the information and communication technology centre and a client service centre.

These twenty-one participants contributed to the narrative workshops and from these participants, seven volunteers contributed to an analysis activity, one from the learning and development centre, four from the information and communication technology centre and two from the client service centre. While the representation in this sense-making group was not faithful to the composition of the three initial groups, the selected narrative from which they worked was equally drawn from each of the groups and discussion accommodated the varying perspectives of the participants.

While the participants were diverse in age, experience, background and gender as well as in occupational specialisation demographic data were not collected nor used in analysis as this exploration of individual and collective experience did not seek to categorise individual difference.

5.6 METHODS

This research is designed to maximise emergence of new theory from interactions between participants. It is designed to access participants' own insight into their lived experience and profit from their sense-making in collectively analysing the experience. For these reasons, this research collects narrative in undirected group contexts and relies upon the participants' collective analysis of the themes that emerge from the narratives. Participants' clustering of themes is used as the basis for categorising and theoretical sampling, and their feedback on the developing theory contributes to the researcher's development of a theory of learning and knowledge in this organisation. The literature that supports the selection of these methods is detailed below.

The methods developed for this study are geared toward meeting the theoretical and epistemological challenges set out by the literature, and in so doing also minimise the prominent criticisms of grounded theory. Charmaz (2000: 520) summarises these criticisms as assumptions that grounded theory

'(a) limits entry into subjects' worlds and thus reduces understanding of their experience;

(b) curtails representation of both the social world and subjective experience;

(c) relies upon the viewer's authority as expert observer; and

(d) posits a set of objective procedures on which the analysis rests'.

The methods in this study address (a) and (b) by opening access to the participants' worlds through undirected narrative and by providing a social setting for their discussion of subjective experience, (c) by asking participants to make sense of the stories collected, and (d) recognising the role of the researcher within the research and the construction of knowledge within and between participants and researcher.

5.6.1   NARRATIVE

Narrative is used extensively in this research following the work of theorists and of knowledge management researchers and practitioners (Snowden 2002; Callahan, Rixon et al. 2006).

Organisational narrative process is also framed in the metaphor of complex systems in the work of Luhman (2005: 15). The alignment between narrative and complexity is evident in his discussion,

> '*As humans we tell stories, and make drama, we attempt to make our narratives meaningful to the listener, to help them see connections and to participate. In each telling, or dramatic performance, the narrative may change as we respond to the reactions of participants. We may draw on other stories as comparisons, embellishments, to situate our narrative in a broader discursive space, or orient the listener by linking our story to theirs. In other words, our narratives are ongoing linguistic formulations, composed in the moment, and responsive to the circumstances of a particular time and space. This is not necessarily a linear or cyclical process, but a responsive one.*'

Narratives, according to Stacey (2001: 124), rather than facts, '…make experience meaningful and are the privileged mode of sense-making'. This study is designed to draw on that sense-making in order to better understand knowledge and learning. Bruner (1991: 3) refers to Vygotsky (1962) in linking narrative to constructivism, describing how cultural products like language mediate thought and impinge on the ways in which we represent our world. Narrative achieves verisimilitude by '…not only representing but of constituting reality' (Bruner 1991: 5). Narrative allows the researcher to abandon '…the attempt to treat respondents' accounts as potentially 'true' pictures of 'reality'', instead allowing analysis to generate accounts of the world which are 'true' to the participant's world (Silverman 2000: 823).

Narrative in this study ensures that it is not the mere skeleton of the experience of learning and contribution to organisational knowledge which informs the investigation, but also (in Bruner's terms (1991: 6-8)) diachronicity (an account of events over time), particularity (specific happenings), intentional state (their beliefs, desires, theories, values and their interpretations of intention), and hermeneutic composability (an account of the meaning of the experience). The richness of the narrative account in providing depth and glimpses of participants' constructions of meaning around experience are vitally important to this study.

5.6.2   COLLECTIVE NARRATIVE

For similar reasons, methods draw on collectives of individuals in order to access the social construction of meaning in the organisational context. Weick (1995) regards sense-making as both individual and social and highlights the way it affects the construction and interpretation of text. Crotty (1998: 64) concurs, 'When we describe something we are…reporting how something is seen and reacted to, and thereby meaningfully constructed, within a given community or set of communities'. Collecting narrative in groups facilitates the interplay between personal narratives and provides for the iterative development of narratives through interaction.

5.6.3 GROUP ANALYSIS

This study draws on interactions of collectives in both the development and analysis of narratives. While individual stories are told, they are told within a social context and subject to sense-making at the collective level.

The group analysis is important to the verisimilitude of the data. The theoretical frame on which the study is based rejects a universal truth in favour of an understanding in which truth '… and any agreement regarding what is valid knowledge – arises from the relationship between members of some stakeholding community' (Lincoln and Guba 2000: 177). The group analysis of narrative and the clustering of codes are designed to capture the group's negotiated agreement on the validity of the findings.

5.6.4 PERSONAL JOURNAL

Record of this sense-making and the progress of the research was maintained over the period of research in a personal journal which assists in surfacing retrospective coherence and provides a tool for continuous critical reflection on the research process and the emerging findings. The journal provided an important outlet for the uncertainty that emerges in human research, and a critical opportunity for voicing theoretical musings. A sample of journal reflection is available at Appendix D.

5.7   DATA COLLECTION AND ANALYSIS

Data collection and analysis progressed alongside the process developed and tested by Strauss and Corbin (1990). As stressed in the previous chapter, Strauss and Corbin emphasise that the methods described in their grounded theory process need not be applied rigidly. The progress through a standard grounded theory approach (Bartlett and Payne 1997: 183) follows:

1.   Collect data

2.   Transcribe data

3.   Develop categories

4.   Saturate categories

5.   Abstract definition

6. Theoretical sampling

7. Axial coding

8. Theoretical integration

9. Grounding the theory

10. Filling the gaps

Each of these stages is important in the grounded theory approach, but they do not sit discretely, rather than a linear process grounded theory approach is an iterative, unpredictable one. In this particular study several steps are combined within phases.

This research deviates from the process described by Bartlett and Payne (1997) in its use of collectives of research participants in the coding of data and in its elaboration of theory from grounded data. In this study themes induced from the data reflected features of complex adaptive systems (as described by Holland 1995), and so his model was then used in the deductive phase of the research. The use of definitions from a general theory is a mode of interpretation recognised by Strauss and Corbin (1998a: 168) as valid, grounded as it is '…in the interplay with data and developed through the course of actual research'. This deviation and its justification follow in discussion of data collection and analysis.

5.7.1.1   Narrative workshop

Three workshops of two to three hours' duration took place between October and November 2004. The researcher made contact with individuals within each of three organisational areas through the Dean of the learning and development centre. The Dean provided a contact person within each of the areas, and the researcher worked through this contact person to gather volunteers and schedule the workshops.

Prior to each workshop volunteers were forwarded a detailed information pack outlining the research, its purpose and aims and their role as a participant (included at Appendix A). The pack also included contact information for the researcher and her supervisor as well as information about ethics clearance. At each workshop the volunteers completed and signed consent forms, stating their understanding of the research process and their rights as participants.

Each workshop included six to eight participants and was recorded using digital and analogue recorders. The researcher did not take notes, focusing instead on the interaction of the group and the stories shared.

Each workshop began with an introduction of the research purpose and process. When introducing the purpose of the workshop, the researcher took some time stressing that the words used in the research question should be interpreted at their broadest. The researcher worked from notes to ensure that participants understood that the terms 'learning' and 'organisational knowledge' were to be interpreted in their broadest sense, participants should not feel limited to any particular construction of the terms.

In this way, the introduction provided a context within which participants were free to use their own interpretations, and in so doing, construct, through stories and discussion, a socially mediated understanding of the words' meanings. Some analysis of these meanings is available at the beginning of the Introduction to Findings Chapter.

In each workshop the participants were asked to share stories about their learning experiences and how these contributed to organisational knowledge. The researcher used sentences such as, 'I'm really interested in the stories that you have about the learning processes that led to a change in the knowledge of the organisation… a change in the way the organisation knows something', or '…does anybody have a story about something they've learned that has contributed to organisation's knowledge?' to prompt discussion.

The participants began hesitantly in each workshop, and in each case the first narrative was prefixed by a qualifier, for example, *What we learn every day or what we do every day doesn't really have an impact, sorry'* (Participant 2.1). As the workshop progressed, though, participants became more confident in sharing experiences, perhaps encouraged by the stories told by peers.

Each workshop ran over the two hours allocated. Once discussion began, participants became involved with the topic and on two of the three occasions the researcher was unsuccessful in winding up discussion until well after the allocated period. Participants' engagement with the process highlighted its value not just a data collection tool, but also in facilitating organisational discourse.

Throughout the workshops the researcher joined the participants in probing stories and relating experiences to one another. While the researcher was involved in this discussion, she did not share her own experiences. Workshop participants, on the other hand, worked together in constructing and developing stories about experience, building from or finding contrast to the experience shared.

5.7.1.2 Transcribing data

The researcher transcribed each workshop in full and verbatim, including pauses and inaccuracies in speech and overlaps of utterances. Identifying characteristics (including workplace specific terms) were removed from the transcript. On completion of each transcript, it was forwarded to the representative from each work area and checked for accuracy and anonymity.

5.7.1.3   Developing a metanarrative

When transcripts were returned and changes made the researcher developed a metanarrative from the three transcripts, selecting complete stories from each transcript and presenting them in one 20 page document. This document and the three confirmed workshop transcriptions were placed in an NVivo project file for later analysis.

The metanarrative sampled from the 50 thousand words gathered in the three narrative workshops. It could not, and did not aim to be completely representative of the complete data set, rather it provided a range of experiences across the three work areas for exploration in the development of codes for use in Phase 2. The researcher again looked to Strauss and Corbin (1990: 88) for direction in the selection of text, choosing interesting stories and narratives that stood out as being repeated, contrary to others, or very rich. For example, a detailed narrative which told of a high-energy self-organising group at the edge of chaos which exhibited great learning was included, as was another story of friction and tension in which the local learning of the office was protected from outside scrutiny. A range of narratives were used in the metanarrative which crossed the breadth of perspectives offered by participants.

5.7.1.4   Preliminary coding

In preparation for phase 2 and the facilitation of the coding instruction session, the researcher developed codes against the metanarrative. These codes were not intended to be, and were not used in the group coding activity, but the process of development assisted the researcher in attempting to make her own sense of the narratives prior to meeting with participants. The researcher identified 27 open codes from this brief exploration of the data.

Table 8 Codes developed prior to group sense-making

Project: Learning and knowledge 090205		NODE LISTING	
1	accountability	15	letting go
2	change	16	memory of the organisation
3	consistency	17	organisational learning
4	cost of learning	18	ownership
5	customer focus	19	professionalism
6	disconnection	20	real world
7	diversity	21	reinventing
8	effectiveness	22	role perspective
9	expert	23	skills
10	finding solutions	24	structure
11	identity	25	tools
12	job design	26	training
13	learning from mistakes	27	work around
14	learning strategy		

While the development of these codes was not a required activity from a methodological point of view, it aided the researcher in later comparison against group-developed codes. The value of the group coding was apparent in the comparison where the participants' collective identification of themes differed substantially from the researcher's individual coding. A strength of this research approach is recognised in its accommodation and valuing of participants' sense-making.

5.7.2   PHASE 2

5.7.2.1   Group sense-making and category development

A group of seven participants drawn from the three narrative workshops met in February 2005 to work with the metanarrative. The group developed emerging themes and categories through questioning of the narrative and discussion about emergent concepts.

This phase of the research focused on breaking down the narratives and looking closely at the underlying concepts, comparing and contrasting stories and themes. In Strauss and Corbin's (1998b: 102) words, in order to '…uncover, name, and develop concepts, we must open up the text and expose the thoughts, ideas, and meanings contained therein'.

Having introduced briefly the concept of coding in grounded methodology the researcher provided each participant with the 20 page metanarrative and asked them to read it in full.

5.7.2.2   The coding exercise

Once participants had finished reading, the researcher facilitated a coding exercise, using a single passage of transcript to illustrate the method following the direction of Strauss and Corbin (1998b: 102 - 106). In this exercise, participants worked as a group word by word, line by line to develop codes against the transcript, using, 'What's happening here?' 'How does this relate to what else is going on?' 'What's this person really saying here?' 'What's the underlying concept?' and similar questions to investigate the text. The researcher encouraged the use of participants' own words in the development of codes and described the nature of *'in vivo'* codes (Glaser and Strauss 1967).

As codes were identified they were written on sticky paper and presented on a large wall. At the conclusion of this initial exercise, the group was comfortable with the process and over 20 codes had been generated. In the first few minutes of discussion the term 'disconnection' was coined and its in discussion the codes 'valuing the work', 'sphere of responsibility' and 'capturing the learning' were developed. Participants linked narratives and codes, comments such as, 'it goes to that later story about recognition' (participant 3.1) illustrating their iterative development.

The group then progressed to broader text derived from the three workshops. Participants frequently diverged from the text to develop ideas generated by it and, as the discussion progressed, the researcher continued to record codes and display them on the wall.

After working in detail with three sections of text, the number of new codes being developed dwindled. At the completion of the session the group had identified 99 raw codes.

Table 9 Codes developed in workshop

Project: Learning and knowledge 210205 NODE LISTING

1 'I didn't become it, I came that way'
2 accountability
3 baptism by fire
4 blame
5 blockers
6 brain space
7 capturing the learning
8 care factor
9 career
10 challenge
11 change
12 Chinese whispers
13 commitment
14 compartmentalise
15 concern for the organisation
16 confidence
17 consistency
18 control
19 cost of learning
20 courage
21 crisis
22 customer focus
23 customer responsibility
24 danger
25 developing people
26 direction
27 disconnection
28 discretion
29 diversity
30 dynamic of group
31 effectiveness
32 encouraged to explore
33 expert
34 fear
35 finding solutions
36 flexibility
37 frustration
38 glory seeking
39 good faith
40 hiding
41 honesty
42 identity
43 in the book
44 individuality of customer
45 inequity
46 isolation
47 ivory tower
48 job design
49 knowing why

50 knowledge seeking
51 learning from mistakes
52 learning strategy
53 letting go
54 limiting factors
55 localisation
56 make it work
57 measurement
58 memory of the organisation
59 motivation
60 narrow focus
61 organisational learning
62 ownership
63 perfect world
64 permission
65 politics
66 power
67 professionalism
68 ramifications
69 real world
70 recognition
71 reinventing
72 relationship
73 resources
74 rhetoric
75 risk
76 risk taking
77 role modelling
78 role perspective
79 secrecy
80 sharing
81 shifts the outcome
82 skills
83 source of innovation
84 specialisation
85 sphere of inclusion
86 sphere of responsibility
87 structure
88 support
89 survival
90 time
91 tools
92 training
93 trust
94 usefulness
95 valuing people
96 valuing the work
97 what I know
98 what you can't do
99 work around

5.7.3.1 Grouping codes (categorisation)

The participants then formally discussed the relationship between the codes. They worked at grouping of codes, rather than the naming of categories, and the researcher worked with the group to gather codes to the participants' instruction. Participants often disagreed on placement of concepts and negotiated consensus, working through the basis for categorisation and inclusion of codes within each cluster. In gathering one cluster, for example,

Researcher   Perhaps something to do a little bit with all of this, um "what you can't do"?

3.2   Process stuff

Researcher   OK, and that's about the issues around how learning isn't shared…?

3.4   No, that's the other end of it

Researcher   Here, maybe?

1.1   *No.*

3.4   No. Not really… It's kind of the victim end of it

Researcher   Yeah. Feeling no power, feeling under threat…

The participants engaged with this process of clustering without any intention of naming the categories, rather loosely gather themes and concepts into groups.

5.7.3.2 Early categories

On completion of the workshop six quite loose clusters of concepts had emerged. These clusters centred around:

Trust, ownership, care factor, secrecy, finding solutions

Localisation, knowledge seeking, customer focus

Real world, crisis, risk

Disconnect, ivory tower, perfect world, intention, measurement

Diversity, individuality of customer

Role modelling, structure, blockers, what you can't do

Again, this session was audio taped and a full transcript made and provided to participants for review and confirmation. On confirmation the transcript was placed in the NVivo project file along with the codes (or nodes in NVivo).

5.7.4   PHASE 4

5.7.4.1   Category saturation and theoretical sampling

At this stage in a traditional grounded theory approach the researcher would return to the site to collect additional data to refine codes. In this case, however, the researcher sampled from the full narrative transcripts in development of the evolving theory. Strauss and Corbin (1998b: 212) highlight the value of sampling previously collected data, as the data reveals more to the researcher as researcher sensitivity to concepts grows. The narratives lent themselves effectively to further sampling, and through further sampling the category saturation apparent in the workshop was tested.

The researcher analysed full transcripts of each of the three narrative workshops as well as to the sense-making workshop transcript, applying the codes developed in the sense-making workshop and developing new codes as an occasional new concept emerged or as a number of concepts merged. While coding the stories the researcher made memos on the text, highlighting emergent themes, new insights, references to literature or references to other stories in the texts. These memos were also coded for future cross-reference.

The impact of the group-developed codes on the analysis of the data was crucial to the researcher's understanding of the narratives. The researcher's ability to reflect on the participants' justification of categories and codes assisted with further analysis of data and of connection-making between codes and categories. The researcher's journal reflects the value of the participant developed codes, the researcher reflecting that 'I keep thinking as I'm coding, of what the group talked about as they talked about the code, and it makes the code much richer for me' (Journal entry 19 February 2005). This richness led to important connections between concepts and categories in the narratives.

Beginning from the groupings developed in the sense-making workshop, the researcher worked with node reports (summaries of all text coded to each node) to develop the nodes further, working to define their boundaries, properties and dimensions. Category development progressed in an organic, iterative way; the researcher studying the stories and discussion closely, identifying themes that appeared to emerge from the data. The process led again to the merging of some nodes identified as repeated concepts and selected examples in text. In this iterative way, the researcher moved between text, nodes and trees (groupings or categories of nodes) to develop a structure of categories within which nodes and text sat.

5.7.5   PHASE 5

5.7.5.1   Theoretical integration and grounding the theory

In analysis, the researcher recognised that the nodes, *in vivo* codes and early categorisation reflected aspects of a complex adaptive system (Holland 1995). While the research was sensitive to complexity theoretical frame and in its design, the emergence of the model in the categories developed by the participants was very surprising. The researcher's journal of 23 February 2005 describes her sudden recognition of features of complex adaptive systems in the categories. The recognition of an extant theory in the emerging data posed enormous difficulty for the researcher as she attempted to reconcile the use of a formal theory in a grounded investigation. While the theory elaboration approach developed by Vaughan (1992) accommodates the application of previously developed theory in a grounded approach, her use is of substantive (that is, previously grounded) theory in elaboration, not of formal theory. Vaughan also uses theory as a sensitising device, not a testing device, and so the emergence of a theoretical frame not previously grounded provided a seemingly improper turn in the research.

Closer reading of the later work of Strauss and Corbin (1998a; 1998b), however, provided some agreement with the use of the formal theory in the deductive phases of a grounded approach, and given that the framework emerged from grounded data, the analysis progressed alongside the definitions provided by Holland's (1995) model of complex adaptive systems.

5.7.5.2 *Complex adaptive systems model as an organising device*

Settling on the model of a complex adaptive system focused analysis on the elaboration of a model within a new context, following Vaughan (1992). More than providing a sensitising device, however, the model provided definitions of the properties and dimensions of categories and a base for the theoretical sampling of data. Moreover, it provided for the development of the model within this research context.

Theoretical sampling at this stage involved the researcher selecting narratives coded to each node in the model and comparing them against descriptions of properties and mechanisms of complex adaptive systems developed from Holland's work. Holland (1995: 10) describes complex adaptive systems in terms of their properties (or characteristics) and mechanisms. His model includes seven basics of complex adaptive systems. Definitions were developed from Holland's theory and used in analysis of the findings.

Table 10 Definitions derived from Holland's (1995) theory of complex adaptive systems

Aggregation	A property of complex systems, aggregation is referred to in two ways, firstly, the grouping of similar things within categories (what complex adaptive systems do) and secondly the emergence of collective behaviour from the interactions of individuals (Holland 1995: 11) within the system. 'Emergent aggregate outcomes', patterns of aggregate or collective behaviour which is complex but which arises from quite simple rules that agents within the system follow. One of the important emergent outcomes of aggregate behaviour (and a particular focus in organisational studies) is self-organisation.

Tagging	Tagging is the mechanism that facilitates 'selective interaction' (Holland 1995: 14), tags providing 'banners' or distinguishing features in each agent's environment which attract agents' attention and through which agents define a basis for cooperation. Through tagging agents identify around what or with whom they will aggregate. As a result, tagging facilitates the development of hierarchies in complex adaptive systems.
Nonlinearity	Interactions within complex systems result in outcomes which do not result in 'a sum of the parts', complex outcomes which cannot be predicted and which cannot be anticipated from individual behaviour. In nonlinear systems agents interacting with each other interfere with the outputs of the system, and as a result the system must be approached holistically – an analysis of each part will not provide a picture of the whole.
Flows	Movement over a network through nodes (agents) and connectors. Examples of flows in organisations may be flows of information, physical resources, or sentiment. In complex adaptive systems these flows change in response to the success or failure of agents, their role as nodes and possible connections shifting with the adapting system.
Diversity	A property of complex adaptive systems, diversity arises from ongoing adaptation, and each adaptation gives rise to the opportunity for further change through new interactions and new niches in the system. A single agent will not have the aggregate properties or capabilities of a complex adaptive system, but the aggregation of diverse agents provides a distributed base.
Internal models	Built to form filtering rules that agents apply in decision-making, internal models are a mechanism of complex adaptive systems otherwise known as schema or schemata and used as an anticipatory device; these internal models comprise a set of inputs which includes: all possible action/decisions that agents are capable of taking, combined with all possible pairings of current and future states, and the concept of desired outcome or 'fitness function' (Rhodes and MacKechnie 2003: 59)
Building blocks	The component parts of which internal models are built. Internal models may be deconstructed and its building blocks recombined to apply to new situations. Holland (1995: 34) describes the process that individuals use when exposed to a complex and unfamiliar scene, we 'parse' (in the computer science sense of the word, to separate into more easily processed components) the situation looking for building blocks with which we are familiar and can use in the new context.

While working with codes, the researcher simultaneously transcribed the sense-making workshop and worked between the model, categorisation, the narratives and the sense-making in an iterative way, finding the investigation of each informing understanding of the other.

Strauss and Corbin (1990: 206) describe this experience as a feature of the process of sampling, 'The more sensitive the researcher is to the theoretical relevance of certain concepts, the more likely he or she is to recognize indicators of those concepts in the data'.

This iterative process of analysis meant that boundaries were placed around categories of nodes through reference to descriptions provided in the literature. Using the NVivo Node Explorer tool, the researcher generated reports on all codes in each node. The table in Appendix B illustrates the categorisation of codes developed with participants and further development of these codes and categories through theoretical integration.

5.7.5.3 Testing and filling gaps

Testing and filling gaps in the theory was both simplified and made more difficult by the presence of a theory to work from. The complex adaptive systems framework was greatly helpful in illustrating the ways in which the stories the participants told reflected aspects of complex systems, but also highlighted gaps in the theory. Indeed, it was the inconsistencies between the theory and the data that provided the greatest insight into the data and the theory of complex adaptive systems. At this stage, the researcher spent a a significant amount of time in both the literatures and the data, identifying ways in which one informed the other and developing a tight network of relationships between theory, concepts and categories.

5.7.5.4 Laying out of theory and validation with data

The process was never a linear one. The researcher moved continually between theory, data, coding and categorization. In the iterative process of testing the theory against the data a number of insights developed, particularly in relation to the characteristic of 'building blocks'.

In Holland's (1995) model there are seven properties and mechanisms, and in the emergent categories of this study only six. Holland's 'building blocks' did not emerge as a well developed, discrete category in the data although reference to reconstruction of mental models was made. Such references, however, were discussed in relation to the mental models category and pointed to what later became a central issue in discussion of the organisation as a complex adaptive system.

The researcher maintained a critical perspective on the model and the data, continually comparing the data with the descriptors and identifying examples which contributed some new understanding to the model as well and to the data. For example, in comparing the data coded to 'tagging' to the definition, the stories of participants clearly illustrated their selection of others which whom to interact based on fairly clear standards about the ability to assist in the local environment. Tagging also suggests, however, that hierarchies build through these selections and interactions, and this defining feature of tagging (and indeed of complex adaptive systems) was vivdly absent in the narratives of these participants.

5.7.5.5 Introducing a model to participants

Taking the model to the participants at the earliest stages of development was a critically important event in the progress of the research. A group of six participants from the sense-making workshop met and talked through the overview of the findings. The researcher described the way the clusters that they had developed in the workshop reflected features of complexity. The group discussed the notions that underpin complexity and the participants made further links from the narratives and their experience to the properties and mechanisms as they were discussed. Participants discussed the appropriateness of terms like 'nonlinearity', 'tagging' and 'aggregation', using the words to further develop their discussion of 'real world' issues in their interaction and the development of 'spheres of inclusion'.

The group responded positively to the model, the terms and their descriptors provided a new language through which they could discuss and analyse the experience. The language provided a new way to develop the themes that emerged as central to their experiences of learning and knowledge in the organisation.

5.7.5.6 And so on, in an iterative process

The more time spent in the stories and in the literature, the more the researcher adjusted the theory in response to the data, and the more insight she gained on the data as a result of better understanding the theory. This process of comparison and connection continued until the connections held firmly in the developing model.

The research reflected the phenomenon identified by Strauss and Corbin (1990: 214), where '…sampling often continues right into the writing because it often is at these times when persons discover that certain categories are not fully developed'. This was certainly the case in this research, the iterative process of sampling data, working with developing theory, investigating descriptions and dimensions of concepts continued into (and beyond) writing up of findings.

What became important at this stage of analysis, given the researcher's use of the complex adaptive systems model, was the developing 'what sits outside' document. The researcher developed the document to use in analysis of the limitations of Holland's (1995) model in understanding the experiences being explored. Particularly important, too, was the researcher's reflection on her own role in the construction of the thesis story, her self-critique and focus on authenticity.

5.8 EVALUATING THE RESEARCH PROCESS

The methodology employed in this study was fluid, following the findings of the research in its attempts to authentically reflect the experiences of participants. This fluidity resulted in the opportunity to systematically check data grounded in the research findings against the developing theory of complex adaptive systems. In order to satisfy herself to the adequacy and quality of the process, the researcher again looked to Strauss and Corbin (1998b: 269), addressing their criteria for quality theory building research:

Criterion 1: How was the original sample selected? On what grounds?

The original sample was selected on the basis of the researcher's sensitivity to the case, her interest in accessing a range of perspectives and the organisation's identification as one focused on learning and on building knowledge.

Criterion 2: What major categories emerged?

Categories emerged through group analysis in six main themes as described above. The researcher recognised these themes as aligned to the properties and mechanisms of complex adaptive systems.

Criterion 3: What were some of the events, incidents, or actions (indicators) that pointed to some of these major categories?

Chapter 6 provides the participants' narrative accounts of these events, incidents and actions. Some central categories are briefly offered here to illustrate some of the pointers. *Disconnect*, for example, emerged as a central category, participants describing events in which knowledge was developed locally and held near. *Real world* was another important category, incidents of customer interaction that involved crisis, uncertainty and innovation portrayed. The category *self-organisation*, too, was developed from narratives about aggregate behaviour that was undirected and improved the fitness of the group.

Criterion 4: On the basis of what categories did theoretical sampling proceed? That is, how did theoretical formulations guide some of the data collection? After the theoretical sampling was done, how representative of the data did the categories prove to be?

Once the clusters of themes were seen to reflect the complex adaptive systems model, the descriptions provided by the model were used for further sampling of data. The sampling progressed in the previously collected narratives rather than in new data, the theory driving a search for examples which aligned with, disconfirmed or added some insight to the theory as it developed within this context. As theoretical sampling progressed, the model proved to be largely representative of the experiences of the participants, although there were several important disagreements between the findings and the theory.

Criterion 5: What were some of the hypotheses pertaining to conceptual relations (i.e., among categories), and on what grounds were they formulated and validated?

As categories developed, there were important connections between them as the models in Chapter 9 illustrate. For example, narratives suggested links between aggregate behaviour (*support, stretch*, and *protect*) and flows (*disconnect*) in which emergent aggregate behaviour impacted on flows of information between aggregate levels in the organisation's hierarchy. Similarly, narratives revealed a connection between aggregate behaviour and tagging based on localisation which implied an important relationship between knowledge sharing and physical proximity. Again, the emergent categories pointed to a relationship between internal models at individual, collective and organisational levels and the constriction of innovative practice. These connections were formulated and investigated through the searching for, and sampling of, data for comparison and confirmation or contrast. In this research the formulation and investigation also developed through reference to theory. The theory remained grounded in the data, but added sensitivity to the data was provided by the theory while the data reciprocally contributed to the developing theory.

Criterion 6: Were there instances in which hypotheses did not explain what was happening in the data? How were these discrepancies accounted for? Were hypotheses modified?

The hypotheses that emerged from the connections between categories and from complexity were helpful in explaining many aspects of the data, but there were some areas in which the theory did not effectively support analysis of the participants' experiences. One notable example is in the category *internal models*. Other minor themes that appeared in participants' narratives were not adequately represented by the theory and these were used to highlight gaps in the complex adaptive systems theory application to this setting and to contribute to its development. These themes and the ways in which they conform or deviate from the complex adaptive systems theory are addressed explicitly in Chapter 10.

Modifications to hypotheses are reflected in contributions to complex adaptive systems theory in its application to this organisation. The theory is a developing one, and grounded as it is in this data, it accommodated some important variation to the theory provided by Holland (1995).

Criterion 7: How and why was the core category selected? Was this collection sudden or gradual, and was it difficult or easy? On what grounds were the final analytical decisions made?

Originally, the loose *clusters* were developed by a group of participants on the basis of their understandings of codes that 'seemed to go together'. This clustering was valuable to the researcher because it provided access to the group's sense-making and some insight into the codes themselves based on the features the participants used to group them. These clusters formed the base for core category development and were described and analysed by the researcher based on the complex adaptive systems model (as described above) as they reflected for her the models to which she was already sensitive. The model was validated by participants once it had been developed to a working level.

The collection of codes into clusters by the participants was quite swift, the loose grouping taking less than one hour. The recognition of the collection's resonance with complexity for the researcher took some weeks, and confirmation of the model as a categorising tool took some weeks longer. The actual realisation, however, of the alignment of the categories and the model was abrupt, occurring in a flash and in a moment.

Recognising the alignment of the clusters with the model complex adaptive systems, however, brought with it some adjustment to the anticipated mode of inquiry. The researcher at first attempted to reject the model, looking for alternative readings and emergent themes. Finally, however, alongside a shift which looked to elaborate theory in a new setting, the analysis progressed through iterative analysis of the data and theory, resulting in further insight into the data and contribution to the theory.

5.9   CONCLUSION

This chapter illustrates the evolution of the research alongside emerging themes in the data. It highlights the blending of a constructivist grounded theory approach with one of theory elaboration and underlines the complexity of a research task committed to portraying the participants' lived experience. Participants' contribution not just through their shared narrative, but also in making sense of the narratives is an important feature of this method which allows the researcher some insight into their understandings of the experiences being explored.

The heuristic used to make sense of the stories is described in some detail, and the emerging patterns of concepts, categories and properties briefly identified. This introduction to the model is designed to provide an introduction to the concepts that underpin the following chapters. These chapters present the findings through participant narrative.

6 INTRODUCTION TO FINDINGS

This chapter introduces the findings of the research. It is a brief introduction, focusing initially on the ways in which participants construct meaning around the words *learning* and *knowledge* and associated phrases. Participants' use of the terms is presented here to ground the findings and discussion in the participants' own meanings. In this early focus on defining terms through participant use, some discussion of the literature is progressed. Later in the chapter an introduction to the findings of the study is presented, outlining the categorisation of narrative themes alongside the heuristic of complex adaptive systems.

Throughout this, and the following findings chapters, narratives are presented alongside dissertation prose. While it is not intended to separate the participants' voices from the findings, the structure allows the reader to follow the research through its findings in a more coherent way, the narratives and prose working together to illustrate participants' experience.

6.1 CONCEPTIONS OF LEARNING AND KNOWLEDGE

The ways in which participants make sense of the terms learning and knowledge is central to analysis of the narratives offered in this study. Participants were given no definitions for *learning* and *knowledge* from which to proceed, indeed, as illustrated in the method chapter, they were asked to treat these words in their 'broadest sense'. The researcher's goal was to gain some understanding of the ways in which meaning is constructed around the words within the groups. Participants' representations of the words and associated phrases as they emerged from narrative and discussion add depth to the research data and better insight for the researcher in analysis.

These paragraphs identify the major themes that emerged from participants' discussions about learning and knowledge in this organisation. They do so with some reference to definitions available in the literature, but it is the participants' definitions that frame this study's use of the terms in analysis and discussion. While individual definitions varied, there were clear and strong themes which are represented below.

6.1.1 LEARNING

For these participants, learning is primarily related to problem solving within a context and in response to immediate and pressing problems. Learning is presented as participative, something naturally emergent from the process of engaging in work, related to risk and anxiety, and valued by its relevance to the whole person and the collective.

Participants told of the naturalness of learning and the engagement of active individuals in its pursuit.

1.1 ...when you learn something new, you move outside your comfort zone, there's a, you know, that's a total person experience, it's the full person, it's not only just in your head, it's, it's being prepared to take a risk, to try something different, to almost to fail, to grow and develop, and that's intrinsic to people. You can't do that, um, in a clinical way, you do that as a holistic thing.

Learning occurring naturally as a result of engagement in work is prominent in contemporary workplace learning literatures (Fenwick 2003; Fenwick and Tennant 2004; Field 2004). The narratives from this study support Oval's (2003: 7) finding that 'Learning through work is what most workers nominate as the most important contribution to their learning' (a finding further supported by Chappell, Hawke et al. 2003: vii).

Participants talked about the learning that results from their interaction with a widely diverse and often difficult customer group.

In this example, learning is constructed as an activity toward preparation – the learning seen as emerging from interaction with the environment and supporting further interaction. From this participant's perspective, the diversity of the environment contributes to the richness of the learning.

2.4 There must be no amount of learning you could do, say if you were working in another customer place and role, that, you know, that, you wouldn't be prepared in the same way you are here. Because here you are seeing society. And it ain't the society that just comes and borrows money, or the society that just comes and buys new cars or just buys new clothes at David Jones, this is warts and all. This is the whole gambit...

Learning from mistakes is a central theme in narratives that related to a range of important concepts in this study including *deviance* and *protection* as well as *innovation*. Many participants describe their learning through mistake-making and the serendipitous outcomes that emerge through error. They often frame this discussion however, in terms of their inability to risk making mistakes for fear of organisational reprisal.

Participants spoke, too, of the influence of role models on learning.

Role models are seen to provide a frame of reference from which learning progresses. Learning with and from others in work is illustrated in this participant's words.

3.2 Whatever role model you have, whether it be your team leader, or your manager, or peers, or whatever it is, that's the person you learn from, whether you are consciously learning or not. And so, if that modelling is negative, then that's what you learn, if it's positive then that's what you learn.

The comment of this organisational member introduces another common concept in narratives of learning, that of the cognisance of learning. The relationship between learning, reflection and action is a seminal issue in some learning literatures (see, for example, Daudelin 2000; Mezirow 2000) and is illustrated here as one which is only loosely linked, that is, learning and action are tied together without reference to reflective practice.

In this example about attitudes to work, learning is described as a non-conscious process, seen as a flow, a naturally emergent process.

3.2 Yeah, I don't think you even consciously, I mean, attitudinal stuff is not something you consciously learn, it's something that just kind of

3.3 It flows

3.2 picks up and it happens …

Overwhelmingly, learning is discussed in terms of interaction within a work context or problem. The narratives illustrate a conception of learning that is not narrowly focused in any one dimension be it cognitive, behavioural, social, or political. Participants' constructions of learning, rather, represent a melding of a plethora of phenomena including these as well as inspiration, synergy, energy, group dynamic, freedom to test and tolerance of failure, exploration and innovation which may result in both positive and negative outcomes for the organisation, but occurs as a result of improving individual and collective performance at the local level.

1.1 Yeah, yeah it did, but by the same token, all the people that were there were really inspired to do something, whatever it was, and that synergy was clearly there

3.2 But again, because no one was saying they couldn't they took it to say that they could, because no one had actually come along to say, 'actually, no, that's not how we do things around here' so, they were actually allowed to do that and as they got further into it and nobody said no the energy just kept growing and growing

1.1 They self-destructed

3.4 Then they went to meltdown

3.2 Then they went, well, that's done

3.4 Well, they did what they, they accomplished their purpose

3.2 What the story doesn't say, that would have been good to see is whether those people, when they dispersed into new teams were able to carry that with them and you would assume that they would, because that was their learning from that environment.

6.1.2   WORKPLACE TRAINING

Given that the narrative workshop asked participants to tell of their learning experiences in relation to their organisation, it is surprising that very few stories include reference to workplace training approaches. Learning for these participants is only tangentially related to training, but when training is mentioned it is exclusively discussed in relation to technical skill development and participants are critical of its effectiveness in assisting them in developing skills to deal with *the real world*.

This participant highlights the insufficiency of training for complex interactions in their ever-changing and challenging workplace.

3.2 ...it gets back to what we were saying before. We train people to do process, not...

1.1 not, no to, yeah. We don't have the...

3.2 so we train for process, not people

The word *training* is used by participants in a very limited sense in this study, reflecting a notion somewhat discrete from that of learning, a stripped-down, narrower meaning relating exclusively to directed opportunities for job-related skills development based on others' interpretation of worker needs.

6.1.3   ORGANISATIONAL LEARNING

The term *organisational learning* appears infrequently in narratives, used by one participant familiar with organisational theory and used in its theoretical sense. Its use is tied to development of institutional knowledge.

This example, from the sense-making workshop, illustrates a participant's sense-making around the relationship between individual and organisational knowledge.

> *3.4 It's also a bit about organisation learning, I think, because it's saying, I've learnt a different way to fix this and I've learnt a different way to deal with this difficult customer, that potentially lots of people could benefit from, but there's no way that that can move.*

6.1.4   KNOWLEDGE

For these participants, knowledge is most commonly represented in stories about ideas, solutions and activity. This representation conforms to Nonaka and Takeuchi's assertion that 'knowledge is essentially related to human action' (1995: 59) and Polanyi's ideas about knowledge as related to the 'groping that constitutes the recognition of a problem' (Marjorie Grene in her introduction to Polanyi's collected essays Polanyi 1969: ix). The narratives, however also reflect an understanding of knowledge that seems richer than pure human problem solving, broader and more entangled with individual, collective and organisational identity.

Ideas and innovations are primary in participants' narratives. This form of knowledge is often spoken of in individual terms, and is treated as personal and owned by the individual.

3.4 ... because you've got the idea and it's not really, you know, and they perceive it to be their job, it shows them up. You know, your, your good idea, your innovation shows up their lack of that quality.

At other times, and using very similar language, participants also spoke about collectively developed and owned knowledge.

1.1 And this is about that idea of 'we know what works for us', that kind of stuff...

In this study, solutions to work problems in the form of *workarounds* is also a major theme. Workarounds are seen to represent knowledge outcomes developed at the operational level of the organisation and are identified as important contributions to the group's knowledge.

In this example of workarounds as crucial knowledge, the participants' discussion reveals the interweaving of learning and knowledge and the influence of problem-solving in the everyday work of meeting customer needs.

1.2 The workarounds, you know, we just, we are so proficient at it. And if we could capture that, that flexibility and resilience is something that we're not as good at, but flexibility...

1.1 And problem solving is what it is...

1.2 Exactly. And we don't capture that learning. We don't capture that learning.

Connected to discussion of knowledge is some consideration of the knowledgeable. The term *expert* is used with some frequency in discussion of the knowledge of the organisation.

Discussion of the role of the expert reveals some fascinating concepts around the nature of knowledge in contemporary organisation as this excerpt highlights.

3.4 And, and, I think it's part of our, um, notion of what an expert is, you know, we're still back on that old [structural] hang up about how do you remember it? You know, if you're an expert then you've been doing it so long you remember all the legislation and you can quote it without reference and the procedures.

1.1 because they never changed.

3.4 Yeah, that's right, but people haven't moved to the new paradigm of accessing information, you know, I've got someone there, I'll look it up, and probably as an organisation we don't support that as well as we should.

The construction of a knowledgeable person in this example shifts from one who holds knowledge to one who is able to develop knowledge through interaction.

6.1.5   COLLECTIVE KNOWLEDGE

One of the most interesting insights into the participants' understandings of learning and knowledge for this researcher relates to their representation of the levels of ownership of knowledge, that is, where participants see knowledge as being held.

This excerpt illustrates a participant's description of knowledge held within collectives in the organisation.

1.3 And it brought home to me that [each part of the organisation] would have their own ideas about their part …well, this is the best, no, this is the best, and really, it doesn't matter where [the customers] are…

Discussion about consistency of knowledge and action in the organisation is seen to relate to the level of knowledge ownership in the organisation. Individual and collective knowledge are assumed to exist and while the two are discussed jointly, the mutuality of the individual/collective is not apparent in the organisational.

6.1.6   ORGANISATIONAL KNOWLEDGE

Organisational knowledge is a problematic concept for these participants. Perhaps as a result of a described disconnect between the local and the organisational, participants do not perceive knowledge developed or held at the team level to contribute to organisational knowledge.

Discrimination between local and organisational knowledge is a clear theme in many narratives. This comment which was made to clarify an example offered illustrates the participant's discrimination between group level and organisational.

1.1 *It is, but it wasn't organisational knowledge, it was business team knowledge that improved...*

In this example, the participant articulates the notion that organisational knowledge is something that is shared throughout the organisation and differentiates this from localised knowledge which is restricted to the business team.

Tsoukas and Vladimirou (2001), in their extensive exploration of the question 'What is organisational knowledge?', provide a definition which describes it as a capability relying on individual distinction-making within specific contexts, guided by the abstract rules of the organisation and influenced by history and experience in the development of shared understandings of the collective. In the participants' constructions of knowledge, however, the shared understandings of the collective are not clearly linked to organisational capability.

Participants did speak of attempts to transfer workarounds between offices and attempts to feed back outcomes to head office. These attempts are represented as atomistic transfers of innovations rather the emergence of than organisational knowledge from the interaction of individuals and collectives within the abstract rules and history of

146

the organisation. While localised knowledge is described by participants as emergent and dynamic, when discussing organisational knowledge participants use a language which represents knowledge as institutionalised and fixed in policies and procedures. In the words of participant 3.4 as shown above, '... *there's no system for actually capturing that level of knowledge in the organisation and moving it through'*.

6.1.7   KNOWLEDGE FLOW

Knowledge flow is primarily discussed in stories about shifting innovations through the organisation, *escalating* problems and sharing solutions. Reflecting themes in organisational knowledge, knowledge flow is considered problematic, constructions of knowledge flow seen as tied up with issues around group boundaries and hierarchy.

For this participant, knowledge flow *outside* of *the office* (*the office* represented the boundaried entity for knowledge holding in this case) has connotations of directional transfer on a vertical plane. The excerpt portrays knowledge flow between the aggregate and the organisational as transactional and highlights attempts to facilitate movement of knowledge up and down the organisation.

3.4 *Well, yeah, but I'm just trying the think about some offices where they really try to escalate problems for IT and that sort of stuff, and they'll start to bombard particular areas of NSO with, you know, please fix this, there's something wrong with this, or, we've had this great idea about how you might fix this, and they never go anywhere. But, yeah.*

6.1.8   CONCLUSIONS ON CONSTRUCTIONS OF LEARNING AND KNOWLEDGE

This section briefly explored the ways in which research participants constructed meaning around the words *learning* and *knowledge* through their shared narratives and discussion about organisational experience.

Learning in this study is constructed by participants as an active process of engagement with work and with others in the work environment to improve outcomes for organisational members and those they service. It is entwined with notions of innovation and problem-solving, a natural and sometime non-conscious process in the performance of relationships and interaction in context.

Discussion displays themes around knowledge creation, its sharing in localised environments, its disconnection at differing levels and locations in the organisation, its *ownership* and the fear that relates to *deviant* knowledge created to solve localised, complex and individual problems.

Participants construct *knowledge* within a frame of relationships, trust, locality, and effectiveness. It highlights the priority for organisational members of maximising performance in complex environments and the ways that they relate knowledge acquisition, transfer and application to localised *fitness*.

The ways in which participants define the terms learning and knowledge and associated phrases inform the analysis of findings and contribute to the ways in which narrative themes are categorised.

6.2 OVERVIEW OF FINDINGS IN CATEGORIES

The Method chapter discussed the process of coding and categorization and the role of the complex adaptive systems model as a heuristic (as described in 5.7.5). In the following paragraphs, the heuristic is presented and the main categories described. There is some development in this section of the descriptors used for each category as well as some illustration of the ways in which the data points to categorisation. This section aims to lay bare the sense-making paradigm and uses the language of complex adaptive systems to illustrate its relevance to the experience of the participants in this study.

6.2.1   OVERVIEW OF CATEGORIES

As described above, categories emerged through group analysis that broadly reflect the properties and mechanisms of complex adaptive systems (Holland 1995) and provide a framework for analysis of data. The framework is used as a heuristic device, the categories used broadly as metaphors rather than specifically as prescriptors. These categories served as 'building blocks' for combination and recombination in relation to other theories of complexity and complex adaptive systems.

As with any model, the complex adaptive system model provides a framework for focusing attention on some aspects of the data and obscures others, in Holland's words, 'We decide which details are irrelevant for the questions of interest and ignore them' (1995: 11). In using the metaphors provided by Holland (1995) the researcher recognises that frameworks and models constrain discussion, focusing it only on those characteristics provided by the model. This effect can be moderated by attempts to critique thoroughly the model's application in this field and the data itself. As Vaughan stresses,

'It is the 'loose ends,' the stuff we neither expect nor can explain, that pushes us toward theoretical breakthroughs. If the guiding theoretical notion truly is used heuristically, case analyses should raise additional questions relevant to understanding the concept, model, and/or the theory being considered.' (Vaughan 1992: 176).

Analysis in this case was undertaken in the hope of providing new insights on organisation through the application of complex adaptive systems theory as well as providing new insights into the theory itself. The findings are explored through reference to what Holland (1995) describes as the characteristics (or properties) and mechanisms (or processes) of complex adaptive systems just as the theory is explored and developed through the findings.

6.2.2   CHARACTERISTICS AND MECHANISMS OF COMPLEX ADAPTIVE SYSTEMS

In this study, the characteristics of complex adaptive systems prompt the question, 'What are the characteristics of organisational members' experiences of learning and knowledge development?' Mechanisms prompt the question, 'What are the mechanisms by which organisational members learn and develop organisational knowledge?'

The introduction to the findings is presented here under three headings which combine characteristics of experiences of learning and knowledge with mechanisms for learning and knowledge experience. The first heading includes findings that relate to aggregation and tagging, the second to nonlinearity and flows, the third to diversity, internal models and building blocks. While these concepts are represented separately, the characteristics and mechanisms work together in a system of learning and knowledge development, sharing and institutionalization, their interaction described and discussed in later chapters.

Throughout the overview and in later chapters the participants' *in vivo* terms and categories used in analysis of the data are italicised to assist in their reading as specific terms in this study.

6.2.3   AGGREGATION AND TAGGING

Organisational members' narratives feature *aggregation* and the mechanism for forming knowledge developing and sharing groups, or *tagging*, in their description of experience. In this study, and in *in vivo* terms, the concept *aggregation* describes a group's ability to *find its own order*, in *meeting the need* of the environment, and adaptive responses through *work around*. This cluster of themes reflects the experience of learning and novelty that arises from group (*aggregate*) behaviour.

A related set of themes that describes the ways in which organisational members identify with others by means of an attractant and form boundaries around these aggregates is *tagging*.   Again, in *in vivo* terms, and for these participants, tags for interactivity contribute to and result in *sphere of inclusion, sphere of responsibility, localisation,* and *concern for the organisation.*

6.2.3.1   Aggregation

The concept *aggregate* was first identified (though not named) by the sense-making workshop group as a cluster of themes around the *in vivo* code *care factor* and the related outcome theme, *effectiveness*. Throughout the workshop the group struggled with a concept that crossed over (1) the dynamic of the localised group and its properties and (2) the ways in which group members solve problems and develop knowledge as a collective.

For this research, *aggregation* in this first sense also includes the form and impact of aggregation on individual agents as well as on their behaviour as an aggregate. In this node, narrative that relates to the emergence of 'complex large-scale behaviours from aggregate interactions of less complex agents' (Holland 1995: 11) is presented. This concept, *aggregation* provides a descriptor which allows for consideration of groups as interacting, connected collection of self-organising agents. It focuses attention on the outcomes of the dynamic group in broader, complex and coherent learning and knowledge outcomes.

The emergence of a category of aggregation *self-organisation* developed through the grouping of *group dynamics* codes, for example, *support, commitment* and *trust*. This category relates to the undirected gathering of individual members into aggregate and the ways in which the group works and individuals benefit from inclusion..

The second category under the aggregate concept, *improving fitness* grew from the gathering of themes around individual and collective attempts to *meet the need* of the organisation's environment, *find solutions* to problems encountered and *cut it* as an effective organisational member.

Table 11 below illustrates the properties of the group dynamic highlighting three attributes of the dynamic - supporting behaviours such as *care factor, sharing, trust, commitment* and *confidence;* stretch behaviours such as *motivation* and *challenge;* and protective behaviours relating to *secrecy* and *ownership*.

The concept *aggregation,* then, includes the categories *self-organisation* which has the properties, *support, stretch* and *protect,* and *fitness function* which has the properties *change, effectiveness* and *innovation*.

Table 11 Categories and properties of the concept 'aggregate'

Category	Property	Description
Self-organisation	Support	Commitment of organisational members to other aggregate members and the aggregate
	Stretch	Encouragement by aggregate members to maximise performance within the environment
	Protect	Individual and aggregate claims on both individual and aggregate outcomes
Fitness function	Effectiveness	Outcomes of aggregate's attempts to provide 'fitness function' to effectively solve problems at aggregate level
	Innovation	Novel outcomes resulting from aggregate behaviour
	Change	Impact on individual, collective or organisation as a result of aggregate behaviour

6.2.3.2 Tagging

Related to *aggregation* is the concept *tagging* which gathers together themes around the ways in which organisational members identify others with whom to develop solutions to workplace problems, increase *fitness function*, and *shift the outcome* for the organisation in facilitating continuing change. This concept accommodates narrative and discussion about how organisational members find each other, what foci attract them to each other, how they create boundaries around their aggregate, and how these aggregates build hierarchies.

This was an important concept in the findings, providing for participants a language for discussion of the nebulous *sphere of inclusion* theme developed in the sense-making workshop. For participants, this category brought together themes about the influence of members' perceptions of work role on the ways in which they learnt from and shared knowledge with others, as well as the prominent theme of *localisation*.

Table 12 Categories and Properties of the concept 'tagging'

Category	Property	Description
Sphere of inclusion	Localisation	Aggregate inclusion based on co-location and focus on localised issues
	Knowledge seeking	Aggregate inclusion developed through seeking out knowledge that facilitates improvements in fitness function.
Concern for the organisation	Valuing people	Identification with others as a result of their commitment to people within the organisation
	Valuing the work	Identification with others as a result of the importance they place on the work

6.2.4   NONLINEARITY AND FLOWS

The relationship between inputs and outputs in this organisation can be seen as *nonlinear*, as a result of interaction between members and between members and others in the organisation's environment. This *nonlinearity* impacts on *flows* through connections among members, whether through information exchange, learning and sharing, innovation and knowledge development or limiting access.

Participants spoke at length about the impact of nonlinearity on *flows*, telling stories about the learning that occurs at the edge of the organisation in finding solutions to very individual problems and the difficulty of sharing the resulting knowledge with organisational members outside of the aggregate. The flows were interrupted in all directions at connection points in the hierarchy – supervisors and managers as well as subordinates and peers in other organisational areas.

6.2.4.1 Nonlinearity

This was a strong theme in narrative and discussion revolved around the tension that emerges in the conflict between the nonlinearity of participants' interactions and the processes of delivering service (and maintaining effectiveness), and the formal structure and linear processes defined by the organisation. The property of *nonlinearity* in this learning and knowledge sharing system relates to the *in vivo* terms *real-world* and *interdependency* and associated themes resulting from the disconnection between participants' experience of *real-world* and the organisation's need for consistency, its assumption of *perfect world*.

The following table presents the main themes articulated through participant stories and discussion that relates to their experiences of learning, and organisational knowledge development within a nonlinear system.

Table 13 Categories and properties of the concept 'nonlinearity'

Category	Property	Description
Real world	Flexibility	Participants' need for process which allows for individuality of customer and context need
	Discretion	Participants' need for flexibility in decision making to improve effectiveness in organisational outcome
	Crisis	Members operating at edge of chaos
Perfect world	Consistency	The organisation's requirement for consistent application of policy
	Control	The exertion of control over process and outputs

6.2.4.2 Flows

The nature of *flows* of information through the organisation and the paths for knowledge sharing through interaction are represented by themes in narrative around power, *permission, structure* and *what we do with information.*

The characteristic, *flows* represents participants' experiences that relate to the nodes and connectors (Holland 1995: 23) described as providing access to knowledge or opportunities for innovation and learning. These are the points at which transfer is facilitated or inhibited. *Direction* is an important category which illustrates the manifestation of control in *risk, blame* and *rhetoric* and highlights themes that gather around the impact of *permission* and *exploration* on *flows* through the organisation. *Disconnection* highlights structures and processes which interfere with flows between nodes and connectors.

Table 14 Categories and properties of the concept 'flows'

Category	Property	Description
Direction	Permission	The extent to which organisational members are allowed to make mistakes in seeking solutions to workplace problems
	Exploration	The extent to which organisational members are encouraged to explore options and develop innovative solutions maintaining effectiveness
	Risk	Participants' perception of the negative personal repercussions resulting from breaking organisational rules
	Blame	Repercussions of making mistakes or breaking the rules of the organisation
	Rhetoric	Perceived gap between what the organisation espouses in learning and knowledge sharing and what occurs

Disconnection	Structure	Formal organisation
	Measurement	Control over the behaviour and outcomes of organisational members through systematic evaluation
	What we do with information	Patterns of behaviour around information sharing

6.2.5   DIVERSITY, INTERNAL MODELS AND BUILDING BLOCKS

As the listing of categories, properties and sub-categories earlier in this chapter illustrates, this group represents fewer themes identified in narrative and discussion than other codes. These three concepts relate to the makeup of aggregates and the ways in which the individuality of each member, their sense-making and anticipation system (or schemata (Anderson 1999; Rhodes and MacKechnie 2003)) and the ways in which these schemata are constructed and recombined to impact on the aggregate and its outcomes.

6.2.5.1   Diversity

Diversity emerges in participants' narratives about the makeup of aggregates and the impact on organisational outcomes, especially in relation to the survival of the group in its environment and in the novelty of solutions it develops in improving effectiveness. Participants' stories illustrate the range of individuals working in the organisation and the ways in which they fill niches within aggregates. The stories also underline the dynamic interaction of these diverse members and the impact of the context provided by other members on each other individual member (Holland 1995: 27). In this case, *diversity* is an *in vivo* code and narrative is coded to the concept directly, it is both a concept and a category and its only child theme relates to novelty.

Table 15 Categories and properties of the concept 'diversity'

Concept/Category	Property	Description
Diversity	Novelty	Innovative outcomes attributed to the individuality of aggregate members

6.2.5.2   Internal models

Participants spoke about the ways in which individual and aggregate learning was influenced by set *internal models* – in participants' own terms *the normal confines*, *the right thing* and *what I know*. Narrative that relates to assumptions about dealing with organisational problems and rules for anticipating appropriate behaviour is coded to this node. In many instances discussion coded to this node relates to inhibitors of innovation and learning, participants claiming that the *memory of the organisation*, held within individuals' and aggregates' internal models restricts organisational members' ability to *let go*, and the flexibility of the organisation in meeting the needs of a changing environment.

Table 16 Categories and properties of 'internal models' (incorporating 'building blocks')

Category	Property	Description
The normal confines (tacit organisational)	Make it work	The perception that organisational developments, products and processes should be supported rather than questioned
	Letting go	Shifting frames of reference to accommodate new ideas and practices
The right thing (tacit personal/collective)	Good faith	Organisational members attempts to put in place solutions that are based on perception of 'the right thing'
	What I know	The knowledge that I have as a result of my experience of life and the organisation that allow me to do what is right

The component parts of *internal models* are described by Holland (1995) as *building blocks*. In this study narrative and discussion reveals building blocks of internal models through themes around *repetition* and *recombination*, reflected in participants' reflections on shifts in understandings resulting in satisfaction of *real learning needs*. As indicated earlier this category is problematic. There are few excerpts coded to this mechanism directly, although they were recognised as inherent in participants' discussion of internal models. For this reason, building blocks is represented with internal models and discussion of both mechanisms is integrated in analysis and discussion.

6.3   CONCLUSION

This chapter introduces participants' constructions of learning and knowledge in order to frame the use of these terms throughout analysis and discussion. It also provides an overview of the heuristic utilised in analysis of narratives, developing the characteristics and mechanisms of complex adaptive systems as outlined by Holland (1995) in order to provide some context for the presentation of findings in the following chapters. The concepts, categories, properties and descriptors used to make sense of the findings are introduced along with some reference to participant narratives.

The following chapters develop these findings in each concept, painting cameos of workplace experience coloured by complex adaptive systems theory.

7   FINDINGS – AGGREGATION AND TAGGING

In this, and the following chapters on findings, the concepts described in the Overview of Findings in Categories are developed and their categories and properties illustrated using participant narrative and discussion. This chapter details the experiences of participants in forming collectives and the ways in which knowledge emerges from their interaction in these collectives. The ways in which organisational members identify others with whom to interact, and the relationship between this interaction and learning and knowledge outcomes for the collective and the organisation are highlighted.

This chapter begins with the concept *aggregation*, presenting its categories *self-organisation* and *fitness function*, these categories are then more specifically discussed in terms of their properties. *Tagging* follows *aggregation*, and its categories *sphere of inclusion* and *concern for the organisation* are similarly illustrated through the data.

7.1   AGGREGATION

'I see the organisation as my office, as our team' (Participant 2.1)

Individuals work within organisations through 'Different patterns of relationships [that] constitute ways of coping with informational complexity' (Rhodes and MacKechnie 2003: 64). In this study, the ways in which aggregates of these individual, adaptive agents combine to deal with the complexity of their context is fascinating. The concept *aggregation* focuses attention on features of the group that relate to

1.   the responses of groups to their environment,

2.   the nature and form of that grouping,

3.   and to the outcomes of aggregation.

Participants had a keen sense of belonging to small, localised, problem-focused groups and discussion around interrupts or disconnects between levels of aggregation were associated with this.

3.4 Well, if you're in the local office, then, then, your whole experience with [this organisation] is what happens in that office, pretty much, if you've never been outside…unless, unless it's got connections to real people and relationships and, and what you sort of perceive as relating to your work. It's not, there's nothing very real about it.

The clear delineation between practice in the local environment which was equated *with real life*, and the rest of the organisation is vividly clear.

Aggregation is a common theme and one that the sense-making group targeted for long and detailed discussion. For example, when coding had moved the group on from this concept, 1.1 interrupted to draw attention back to a segment of text.

1.1 There's another, sorry, for me there's just something else in here that I can't quite pin down. But it's just bugging me in the back of my mind and I'm, but [quoting from the transcript], 'I suppose, from our perspective, or from my perspective, I see the organisation as my office, as our team, I don't see it as…'
[General comments of agreement]
1.1 '…this whole big thing'. That's the, there's something really important in that….
[General. Yes, there is, there is!]

The following segment of text was drawn from the very first comment of the customer service narrative workshop. After the researcher's request for stories about learning experiences and their relationship to organisational knowledge a customer service manager began,

2.1 *'Suppose at this level we're still stuck in what we do every day, I mean at the level that's more grass roots than national, um that all we do is implement, we don't necessarily create ideas or affect the organisation. We don't see what we do every day, whether it be a workaround or finding a different way of dealing with a difficult customer as being any more worthwhile to the organisation than it is to us as an individual and to our office'*

This telling comment is one that framed the group's constructed meaning around the words *learning* and *knowledge* in the organisation and pointed to issues around what constitutes knowledge in this organisation. The customer service manager went on to provide, with her narrative group, an large number of examples of ways in which she and her colleagues learn from interaction with their environment, each other and available information and the ways in which they share (and protect) this valuable knowledge. It also imprints on the researcher the notion of valuing localised learning within the aggregate environment.

Participants' stories reflect their focus at the local aggregate level, their belonging not to an 'organisation' but to a small group.

1.1 So, it comes once again, back to that, there's this thing called [the organisation] and then there's this thing called my office, and they're totally different things.

In complex adaptive systems, '…agents are presumed unable to forecast the system-level consequences of their individual choices, and so they optimize their own fitness, not that of the organisation' (Anderson 1999: 220). Examples of this phenomenon abound in the narratives and participants appear aware of the interaction of the aggregate in their individual pursuit of fitness.

Similarly, participants are aware of their use of others within the aggregate, their payoff related to the behaviour of other agents within the collective's 'adaptive landscape' (Anderson 1999: 200).

1.2 …but we've pushed them out of the mix now because they're not useful.
1.3 … more of a hindrance than a help
1.2 exactly.

161

Overwhelmingly, participants talked about the impact of other individuals on the adaptation of the aggregate to its environment. In contrast to assumptions of linear and formal interaction, these participants talked about their reliance on interaction with other agents within their environment for improving their own individual fitness.

1.1 But it's always been a case of, you know, to be professional, you have to keep a distance. And that's not necessarily true in this type of environment. In fact, to actually get to the end result quicker, to have a good relationship with people who you're working with …

The concept *aggregation* highlights participants' affiliation and sense of belonging to localised groups that are problem focused, interaction with which results in payoff and improving individual and collective fitness in the local context. The ways that individuals identify with others in order to form aggregates is discussed below in tagging, while this section deals with the dynamics within the aggregate and its outcomes.

7.1.1   AGGREGATION - SELF-ORGANISATION

Self-organisation is a concept central to complexity, order emerging from interactivity, coherence observed in the face of change. Anderson (1999: 223) describes self-organisation as a natural outcome of the nonlinear interaction of agents rather than any attempt on their behalf to choose or seek order.

Participants told stories about groups that come together to solve a problem and then develop along their own path.

3.1 I worked in another team doing workforce planning [in another organisation] that was self empowered like that, and was able to find its own order, and to, out of, because people felt so comfortable, and because it sort of was like its own little hothouse, if you like, and it was able to generate all sorts of innovative and different approaches to different things.

Participants, too, talked of group members

3.5 Originally we were operating on the basis of

flexibly assuming roles to 'round out' the group and to make it most effective in solving problems.

'this is the sort of work we do', and now we are operating on a basis of 'well, if there's something new…we'll have a go at evaluating it and seeing if we can find a way to make it more useful and more valuable'.

In many cases, these stories include references to the energy of the group, metaphors like *hothouse* and *high energy levels* reflected the participants' perspectives of *the energy just growing and growing* in self-organising groups. Anderson (1999: 221) describes self-organisation as occurring in systems that import energy from the outside, and draws attention to the ways in which informal structures emerge and persist through the contribution of member energy.

3.2 So when we have diversity and we don't have those barriers, it creates a ball of energy which leads to some really great things.

Similarly, individuals talked about the alignment of *high performing* groups *self organisation*, as in this vignette from 3.4, an individual working within head office developing learning products for customer service staff.

3.4 It was just one of those circumstances where, everything had to, was under review if you like, and so, and not necessarily from a point of view of that management had said, 'It's time to look at everything', but other outside influences, like the training packages were under review… And one of the interesting dynamics we had was that a lot of us were, … we were operating off very high stress levels and so it was almost like our work was our outlet, and we just did some absolutely amazing things, and I think it's because we were all complementary skills, I suppose and that we were working off these very high energy levels…it was a self-leading team, you know, there was no, no one was saying, 'This is what we're doing and this is the role you play in it'.

Interestingly, participants see the environment of the aggregate as simultaneously influencing and being influenced by their interactions in aggregate. The focus is consistently maintained on contact, exchange of information, support, positive reinforcement and self organisation.

3.2 … some of the others that often contact and provide info, and, yeah, so it's really grown its own environment now, where I think people leave that, having learnt, shared something, and that people feel good about being able to do that, so it's given us a real opportunity…

Self-organisation for these participants, organising described as emerging from local group interaction in a non-linear environment, organisational members developing skills and assuming roles to support their own and their collective's local effectiveness.

7.1.1.1   Aggregation - Self-organisation - Support

Support is an important feature of sharing knowledge within the aggregate for many participants. Stories abound about individuals' reliance on the group when attempting to deal with problems that emerge within the organisation and at its edge in interaction with the organisation's clients and customers.

Support is often described in terms of connection with other members, the variety of information available in those connections and the availability of the contact.

3.1 I ask a question, and there's five people behind me, 'Yeah, what do you need?' … but they also go, 'Oh, well, I would do this' and someone else will go, 'Well, no, I would do this' and then another person say, 'I would do this'. So you can then base it on, they all just share their knowledge so well.

Some participants relate the level of support to the level of need in their particular role and in a particular context. 2.6, who works in an office which organisational members describe as 'infamous' for the difficult environment within which it operates, talked about the difficulty of the work environment contributing to the dynamic of the group.

2.6 Making that bit more… helping each other out, and just maybe supporting each other a little bit more than maybe every other site could, because there's always a concern that something may be going to happen.

Participants refer to positional leaders in the organisation either as within the aggregate where they are seen as supporting members…

3.2 So, you know, all this stuff comes back to leadership and allowing people the space to learn and try things
3.4 supporting people, even to learn, god forbid!

…or sitting outside the aggregate, limiting opportunities for members to learn, as this reference to lack of support for an individual's pursuit of formal learning highlights.

1.1 But you can understand why people are so reluctant when there's not that sort of support in the workplace.

Similarly, the knowledge systems of the organisation are not considered important to the aggregate, structures that do not fit with its needs.

1.2 But we are not supported by the knowledge of the organisation. And the knowledge management prerogatives of the organisation.

The support of the aggregate, though, is seen as critical to learning and sharing.

3.4 ...we all knew at the time that we were only ever going to be together for a limited, yeah, but that it was a very unusual and unique, where you have a group of people where you know that you can give something to someone and you know that you are going to get what you expected back.

The local aggregate self-organises to support members, support relating to connections and access to other members.

7.1.1.2 *Aggregation - Self-organisation - Stretch*

Some participants shared stories about the capacity of the aggregate and its individual members to stretch or motivate rather than simply support other members toward aggregate goals.

Aggregate members talked about their learning from others within their local environment through supported problem solving, and setting up boundaries for their personal and professional development. This example highlights the participant's ability to learn through their work and the generosity of knowledge sharing in the local aggregate.

2.4 It's about that sort of, you know, I can remember [a colleague] coming to me and, 'What do you reckon?' and I reckon it took him about twice to get the gist of, 'Whatever you think is best'. And then as soon as he knew he had that permission to do that, that's fine, off he goes, fine, no issues. And the fact is, you've actually increased his compliments and it improves the way we do business, and it makes people willing to learn.

This example, too, shows the encouragement given by aggregate members for development through work.

2.4 She was apprehensive about it and I said, 'No, no, you can do it, come on' and she did it and after that, I said, 'Now that's how I try to deal with things', and she learnt from then and she said 'Oh, OK, um, if I deal with it…' The longer you put it off the more difficult it is to deal with, and even our instance yesterday, she said 'Well, look…' You know, she felt more comfortable in making some decisions because she'd seen a hard decision had been made. So she's learning…

It seems members of the aggregate assist other members to test the environment and fail within a set of fairly loose boundaries or rules, the members learning directly from their environment and through the feedback (negative or positive) of their interaction.

3.2 …you have to do things differently, but there are risks in that in a personal and team level, that you take the courage to try and do things differently.

Stretch was a term that described the localised aggregate's role in supporting problem solving that contributed to the member's learning.

7.1.1.3 Aggregation - Self-organisation - Protect

While the local aggregate is shown to support and stretch it members, it also protects the aggregate and its products from other levels of organisation and the environment. There is a sense of ownership over individual and aggregate outcomes and (perhaps because these are sometimes seen as deviant) members of aggregate keep their learning secret, limiting the sharing of the knowledge that is developed at the local level.

Individual members lament the loss of control over, and recognition for, the work that they do at the local level. Although members believe they should be thinking at an organisational level, their emotional tie to their learning and ideas remains individual and local as this excerpt illustrates.

3.4 ...and a year later back it [my idea] comes with someone else's name on it. And I'm thinking to myself, that's all right, we've achieved what we wanted to as an organisation, but underneath that (and I'm far too professional to say this outside of this room) but, underneath that I was thinking, 'You bastards, you stole my idea!'... So what you can see is, somebody saw what we were up to and thought, 'Well, gee, that's a great idea. I can work that where I am, but we don't need to involve [3.4's previous team] in this'.

Similar examples were offered that underline the sense that locally developed knowledge is owned by the aggregate. Bad feeling arising from lack of recognition for aggregate outcomes is similarly clear.

2.4 The danger is it does create a degree of cynicism and I'm far too corporate to worry about the sort of ramifications of that, but it would have been nice to see some recognition not just for me, but for my team. We invented it...

This local ownership is explained by organisational members as a response to the distance between the local aggregate and other organisational groups.

3.1 ...they don't have the capability themselves to know what you have produced or to know what to do with it.'
3.4 You know, your, your good idea, your innovation shows up their lack of that quality.

Trust within the localised aggregate is also central to participants' discussion of protection.

168

Participants see trust as a characteristic of aggregate behaviour. They also describe this trust being broken outside of the aggregate, especially through *lack of recognition,* and *stealing* of aggregate outcomes.

3.1 There's also a factor of honesty, too, you know, if you come up with um, a solution for a particular problem, and in one of these stories it talks about, well, you just ignored what I had to say and somebody else claimed the credit for it, well, where's the honesty in that? There isn't, that's why people become sceptical.

Trust outside of the group is difficult to nurture as 1.5 (a manager in head office) found when he attempted to gather some understanding of the knowledge that was being developed in another area of the organisation. Met with distrust, 1.5 lamented the loss of opportunity for knowledge sharing.

1.5 When they… then they started saying things like, 'So, if I tell you things are you just going to walk off and leave it? Like, what happens with all my ideas once I give them to you?'

In response to this sense of ownership over ideas initiated at the aggregate level, and their lack of trust of organisational information that conflicts with their experience, organisational members keep secret the solutions they develop in solving workplace problems.

This excerpt illustrates the aggregate's response to the conflict between the local and the organisational and the secrecy that develops around new knowledge developed in response to organisational problems.

2.6 I think something that I'd like to touch on that you're talking about too is corporate information is only of use if it's accurate and I honestly believe that there's an awful lot of people who have a great fear that it isn't. And I certainly am one of them. This works with workarounds as well. We do a lot of workarounds that National would have a fit if they knew we did them. We do things quietly. We do things…

The fear about the consequences of knowledge development at the local level manifests itself in secretive behaviour. Participants' experience of problem solving at the local level highlights anxiety about knowledge sharing outside of the local aggregate.

3.4 …a workaround, which might be the source of a, because I think often in [customer delivery] people are, people are very quiet about owning their innovations and anything new and different, and get into trouble for doing something else, a workaround or whatever, so you just do it and go…

Ownership, trust, fear and secrecy are themes that relate directly to the local aggregate's unwillingness to share locally developed knowledge outside of the immediate group. These themes illustrate some of the barriers to knowledge dissemination that impact on the organisation's access to the knowledge that exists within its bounds.

7.1.2 IMPROVING FITNESS

The second important category within the aggregate concept, *improving fitness*, grew from the gathering of themes around individual and collective attempts to *meet the need* of the organisation's environment, *find solutions* to problems encountered and *cut it* as an effective organisational member. Participants told of their struggles to increase their fitness within their constantly shifting local environment through interaction with it and aggregate members. They are aware, too of their ability to succeed within the environment as reliant on the behaviour of other members.

Examples of problem solving within the *frantic palaver* that is the everyday environment of organisational members is offered most frequently through *workarounds*.

1.2 [this organisation] is better than any organisation I've been a part of, or read about. Anyone. They're the best at workarounds. They are the best. [General laughter] We have such a capability within the organisation to be responsive to workarounds.

In making sense of this term, the researcher asked for clarification.

(Researcher) Someone talk me through an example of a workaround

1.2 Every day

[Energetic laughter]

1.3 An example, OK. And this is at ground level again. People who would [detail of complex problem that customers have with a particular service and the face-to-face worker 'fiddling' the system to make sure that the customer receives the correct service] At the same time, we've got KPIs, we've got key performance indicators that these staff have to be meeting so what they were doing is [detail of the 'fiddle'] ...so the system won't have a conniption [deleted detail] and then another team, they'll just say, 'let's just stockpile, and when we get to this point, we'll work around again'.

So, workarounds are innovations designed at the local level to deal with the conflict between the struggle for the organisational member to maintain effectiveness in their environment and the rules of the organisation.

(Researcher) Is workarounds one of the ways of dealing with that bubbling chaos that you were talking about earlier?

1.2 That's how we combat it, absolutely

1.1 Because you have to. You've still got customers needing [the service].

Participants are well aware of the value of the knowledge that emerges at the edge of the organisation as a result of dealing with this conflict in developing workarounds. Innovation is highlighted under this category as an important source of valued knowledge for organisational members.

7.1.2.1   *Aggregation - Improving fitness - Effectiveness*

Participants' stories reveal a commitment by organisational members to effectively meet the needs of their clients and their environment. Effectiveness is a term used exhaustively in these tales of learning and knowledge, the term most often used in reference to *meeting the need* of clients encountered in the local, everyday work of the participant.

Personal effectiveness in solving immediate problems is often described as more important to organisational members in their everyday work than meeting the rules of the organisation, as this example from a participant working in head office illustrates.

1.3 I have a really strong belief in what I do, and I want to do my very best at it. And so, I'm always putting workarounds into what I do as well. In order to get to that end result. You have to.

Individuals' need to perform and improve performance within the environment is discussed as a tension this drive creates within the organisational context. In contrast, organisational members who adhere to the rules in preference to *meeting the need* are seen as ineffective.

2.4 The complaints are about those people who go, 'Well, technically, this is what we do. And under the legislation…' those sorts of quotes and things like that.

The mismatch between organisational members' attempts at increasing fitness is contrasted with the organisation's constraints on behaviour through key performance measures.

1.1 …and I just found that really odd that [the telephone service area] was saying that because his stats were great he was the best, and yet, from a customer perspective he was awful
1.3 wasn't meeting the need
1.1 wasn't meeting anybody's need and so what I got from all that was just to reinforce just how the reality gap is just gigantic.

Similarly, participants talked about their frustration with the organisation as limiting their attempts at improving fitness by imposing strict rules on members' discretion in dealing with their environment.

2.7 You can't just tie this in a neat little package and say, 'this is what you will do. For every single person that you come across.'

For some participants, the conflict between their personal need for effectiveness in responding to the environment is overwhelmed by their need for survival within the organisation's framework.

2.1 The fear and the cynicism and all of that baggage can stop you from making that right decision.

For one manager, the reluctance to act on knowledge developed in response to her environment resulted from fear, not so much for her survival within the organisation, as fear of futility of action.

3.3 People are a bit reluctant, um, in the context of learning, reluctant to make decisions because of the pressure from others and the fear about, if I make this decision, is so and so going to come over the top and veto that.

For this participant, the futility of her attempts to increase fitness within the organisational context is linked to the organisation's structures and difficulty with change.

3.2 Or well, if I try something new, well who is going to be upset that I'm not doing it the way it's always been done… But, yeah I think that's been a big problem for the work that I do is that you're always trying to find new and exciting ways of doing things, but the pressure on you to do things in a way that is already accepted, generally tends to override the benefits of trying to do things in a new way.

The frustration plays itself out in a perceived disconnect between aggregate levels in the organisation, participants repeatedly describing gaps between local aggregate and head office. *Cutting it* at the local level means remaining effective within the *bubbling chaos* of the changing environment.

This customer service officer spoke of the local aggregate as working to *meet the need* of customers, while administrators in head office weren't able to *cut it* in the complex service environment. His frustration is apparent in his story.

2.2 'And the group that has cut it and done their hardest work here don't say anything because the view from National [office] (National as a general…) is from these people who just give up and can't cut it out here, so go for the little hidey-hole and they're so, we're so convenient a target for them.

Ultimately, for these participants, the issue of effectiveness sits with the individual's capacity to recognise the nature of the issue at the local level and their ability to utilise a rule set around the organisation's policy requirements and their personal sense of *the right thing*. As a result, members report a need for learning opportunities to develop this capacity in organisational members at all levels.

2.4 …there are other ways around things. That. How we teach people that. How we get that through to people.

Effectiveness, for these participants, was centred on *meeting the need* of the direct environment in the every day work of the organisational member. Learning occurred as a result of this pursuit of effectiveness, and knowledge which provided timely and appropriate local solutions held great valence.

7.1.2.2 Aggregation - Improving fitness - Innovation

Innovation is another important property of participants' narratives about learning and knowledge development and sharing in pursuit of increased fitness. Indeed, innovation is used synonymously with knowledge creation through problem-solving, and frequently linked to *workaround*.

For many participants, innovation is highlighted as attempts to improve performance within the environment in a conscious way, associated with replacement of an outdated or unworkable organisational strategy or product.

3.1 And I decided I wouldn't, that wasn't a really good idea, I mean, if you're going to have an opportunity like that, then you might as well use the opportunity you've got to see what you can do to drive some change and to get a better result.

Participants are keenly aware of the value of innovation to improving their fitness, referring to the difference between what the organisation would accept as adequate performance and performance for improvement in interaction with the local work context.

This is common theme, drawing attention to the conflict between the individual or local aggregate attempts to innovate and the organisation's preference for consistency and reluctance to allow innovation at these levels.

3.2 But, yeah I think that's been a big problem for the work that I do is that you're always trying to find new and exciting ways of doing things, but the pressure on you to do things in a way that is already accepted, generally tends to override the benefits of trying to do things in a new way.
3.3 It's playing that political game that I find quite frustrating as well, so you come up with innovative ideas and then, 'no, no, no, no, it doesn't quite fit the mould'.

Getting caught is a significant factor in stories about innovation, innovation associated with risk, and risk with blame.

3.1 There's also the stuff around the blame culture there as well, there are people within our team who have had, actually, lots of ideas in the last week or so who've never had the opportunity to contribute those, haven't been taken seriously, have been told to keep on that little old treadmill.

In discussion around a head office narrative, the researcher attempts to clarify a point in the story about innovation as this exchange illustrates,

(Researcher) …you started to say was that we get people who are innovative and they learn to…
1.2 quench that, quell it
1.5 and it's about survival techniques.

In this example, *not* to innovate is an adaptive response to the organisation, resulting in consistency and stagnation of behaviour.

In contrast, in one narrative about the experiences of a highly innovative, successful and growing team within the organisation, the participant describes the innovation as related to the level of autonomy the group is awarded as well as the freedom of direction the group enjoys in finding its niche within the organisation.

3.6 …we were given a lot of scope because nobody really knew had much idea where it was going or what it was going to do.

The team was set up to stimulate innovative practice in evaluation in the organisation and the team has managed to flex with changing requirements of the organisation and the environment by maintaining an acceptance of, even encouragement of innovative practice.

3.6 …we'll have a go at evaluating it and seeing if we can find a way to make it more useful and more valuable to the users.

In a similar story about the success of a high performing team in innovative practice, one participant describes innovation as arising from lack of tight restriction on outcome.

3.4 I can remember at one point, I wasn't really quite sure where it was going to end, but there wasn't any, do you know what I mean? There was no pressure, it didn't matter because I knew that it was going to end somewhere. I just wasn't quite sure just how it was all going to fit together.

This particular story of organisationally endorsed and supported innovation continued, providing a rare example of innovation that moved well beyond the aggregate to alter understanding throughout the organisation.

3.4 The complete change around to the way that we developed that program was a huge change in [the organisation] as well as for what had been traditionally done, I mean, from the [central learning unit in the organisation] all the way through to the [end users]. It was a very different way of doing it in [this organisation]. And the sort of, the thinking, you know, that has led to an enormous change in the thinking within [the organisation].

In this short conversation, building from a participant's story of her experience at head office, innovation is presented as an important opportunity for positive feedback. When she was involved in developing new ideas, implementing them and receiving feedback on their success she described the feeling as *wonderful* and the outcomes as important to the organisation's ongoing development.

1.4 But, you see, I also get to start and finish something. I start at its infancy and I get to the end result and I see it through...

1.2 That's so wonderful

1.4 That's something that so many people in the organisation never get to have

1.2 Nobody gets involved in the birthing and ideas...

1.5 But you also have different barriers in [your] team. You have those wins, those constant wins, it's a bit like training, isn't it, in that you come out, you have your, you have your immediate feedback

1.4 You do, yeah, you do. Instant gratification. It's a long process to get there, but you can get that. You can have that satisfaction at the end. And you can feel good.

1.2 ...Because as you say, you're involved in the birth, the evolution...

1.4 ...And that final outcome.

1.2 Yeah. I think that's fantastic and I think we can do that much more than we do. And I mean organisationally speaking.

[General comments of agreement]

Innovation is illustrated here as a localised response to pressing problems in the performance of work. It is described by participants as positive, necessary for survival on a day-to-day basis. The tension between this innovation and organisational requirements for consistent behaviour is highlighted here as an important issue for knowledge development in the organisation.

7.1.2.3 Aggregation - Improving fitness - Change

Narratives describe change as occurring as a result of interaction between individual agents and between individuals and aggregates within their environment. Participants talked about the inevitability of change and its ubiquity in the work environment.

In discussion about a story of changing relationships in the organisation this one participant reflects on change.

1.4 ...these are things that happen all the time, isn't it? That there is always something, not always something leaving, but something always happens that shifts the outcome...

The perception at head office is reflected in discussion about the organisation's willingness to change. In this example a head office participant discusses the reluctance for following through on change directives from management by the operational areas of the organisation, claiming that it is difficult to drive change. The participant is answered by another.

1.5 I don't know that they don't want change. I think that a lot of areas have great ideas and a lot of them implement them...

In the example above, the recognition by head office of new knowledge developed at the edge of the organisation by local aggregates is apparent, as is the assumption of the role of head office in permitting change to be instigated at this level.

Experiences of the local aggregate that hints at opportunities for change are described by participants as frustrating.

This excerpt from a narrative about a new approach to recruitment that earned external praise and reward shows the participants' perception of the futility of innovating at the local level in an attempt to bring about organisational change.

3.1 Nothing actually changed within the organisation. I mean, they all thought it was good, but, they didn't... there's no recognition or... not that we were looking for rewards, sort of thing, but ... there's nothing, there's no groundswell, nobody says, 'Oh gee. That was really good [deleted] that you put that up on the webpage after the last couple of years where nothing's happened' or whatever... It's always s the reasons why you can't... It's quite a negative sort of a culture, oftentimes.

Participants talked about the pressure of change within the environment in contrast to the flexibility of the organisation to change, relating the sharing of knowledge as a change issue inhibited by organisational structure.

2.4 Because there's a lot we can get pick up off each other, um, isn't going to come from the sort of structure we've got now, the sort of involvement we've got now. The structure, yeah, the environment, no. Because the environment needs to change. And in order to do that, there's a lot of work to be done.

This sentiment is reflected within aggregates throughout the organisational groups interviewed, this example from head office about an attempt by 1.1 to instigate change at a broader than local level.

1.3 It did change very slightly, though...
1.1 But not because of anything I was able to achieve, and that was one of the reasons why I actually left [that area of the organisation] because I was so frustrated with their wanting to please the executive. And that's the bottom line. My [most senior manager] wouldn't go to the CEO and say 'look, we've made a mistake here, we need to look at a way to rejig it' that wouldn't happen
1.2 And I don't think it generally does.

Frustration at lack of autonomy to bring about change at the organisational level is continually highlighted.

1.4 Because it just continues to happen. It just amazes me that you can put in so much work towards something, and have this belief that its, that something wonderful, and it can work, and it just falls, like a pancake, you know?...

1.2 ...And the sad truth is in my first few months I began to sense this exact thing that you're...

1.4 Just splatter on the ground...

1.2 ...touching on right now, and I thought to myself, 'I can't do this. I cannot be a part of an organisation like this. I can't'. And here I am, a year on, almost a year later, figuring it to be an intrinsic part of the environment that I can't change. I have lost my energy to overcome the inertia.

The concept *aggregation* in this study provides a device for analysis and discussion of findings that relates to the way individual interaction leads to group characteristics and the characteristics that emerge from interaction between organisational members and the environment (however loosely, and by what features *environment* is bounded). The concept is tied up with the pursuit of *fitness* within rugged fitness landscapes (Kauffman 1995; Stacey 2001; Morrison 2002) and illustrates the mutuality of individual and collective in learning and knowledge development in this context.

7.2   TAGGING

'You know, fit for purpose. You know, you can engage in an appropriate level of interaction, according to the circumstances' (Participant 1.2)

Holland (1995: 12) describes *tagging* as a '...mechanism that consistently facilitates the formation of aggregates...and boundary formation in *cas* [complex adaptive systems]'. Because *tags* facilitate selective interaction they are important to agents in establishing groups for specialisation, cooperation and, ultimately, the formation of hierarchies.

In this study, participants spoke about *tags* in relation to aggregation and their stories point out the characteristics of other organisational members (or tags) that they select for in forming problem-solving groups. Overwhelmingly, agents are identified by *localisation* – agents with local knowledge, local experience and who are locally accessible. Participants also told stories that illustrated their selection of others with whom to interact based on their perceptions of role, commitment to the organisation, commitment to role and opportunities for knowledge sharing.

Participants at the customer service level of the organisation describe their aggregation as occurring in response to broad issues emerging from interaction with the *real world*, the tags they use for selective interaction based on accessing a broad range of aptitudes for dealing with a diverse environment. These organisational members contrast their experience of selecting for tags that mediate useful interaction (that is, diverse experience) with that of groups in head office which they see as aggregating along a narrower range of tags.

7.2.1   TAGGING - SPHERE OF INCLUSION

An important theme within *tagging* for these participants gathers around the *in vivo* term *sphere of inclusion*. This code was developed after a lengthy discussion which attempted to clarify the ways in which participants' stories told of boundaries around dynamic groups. This phrase became an important one in the group's development of understanding about the ways that participants select others with whom to interact. The term is intertwined with that of *self-organisation*, and participants use it to describe the boundaries to the aggregate. It provides a frame through which the aggregate can allocate inclusion and exclusion based on useful or unhelpful interaction.

A customer service employee commented on the reasons why people in head office are not useful to the aggregate in solving problems that emerge in day to day interaction.

2.1 They know the technicalities of it, but when it comes to implementing it, the group of people sitting around this table are the people who have to punch the keys and discuss it with the customer.

The *sphere of inclusion* most often forms around a particular issue or problem or, in Snowden's (2003) use of the word, 'attractant'. Participants provide many and varied examples of their gathering in an organic way around a problem.

2.4 ...the problem was very complicated, but the bottom line was, we thought, well why don't we... and we had [clients] complaining, significant numbers of [clients] complaining...so we thought we could look at a number of ways
(Researcher) 'When you say 'we'... I'm sorry to interrupt...
2.4 Oh, me and my team... we did it as a meeting, you know we set up, we said well, OK what are some of the things that we can do, let's set up some hair-brained ideas...

Indeed, some stories suggest that the greater the need, the more urgent and pressing the problem, in this case a very difficult and conflict-ridden environment, the increased concentration of tags for selective coordination. In other words, and for example, the following demonstrates the tighter definition of the aggregate as a function of the difficulty of the environment.

2.4 ...but it is probably one of the better environments to work in. It's the most team work, the most people tend to pull together.
2.1 ...The feeling when you walk in just different
2.2 ...It's different to every other site.

In contrast, one manager's attempts to form a group to facilitate knowledge sharing were frustrating, the group having no need, no pressing concern around which to form and respond.

3.2 Well, it wasn't, it wasn't bad, but it was just the first meeting and I think there was that, you know, all right, well what are we all here for, we've got nothing in common.
3.3 And it didn't go anywhere, did it?

Thinking about identifiers for selective interaction highlights the different issues of priority for different aggregates within the organisation. Some of the frustration experienced at the operational level with head office assistance in the solution of local problems can be considered issues of tagging.

If head office selects for tags that facilitate its own adaptive process it may well be that these tags differ from those represented in members at operational levels of the organisation. This example would support this view.

3.1 Well, yeah, but I'm just trying the think about some offices where they really try to escalate problems for IT and that sort of stuff, and they'll start to bombard particular areas of Head Office with, you know, please fix this, there's something wrong with this, or, we've had this great idea about how you might fix this, and they never go anywhere.

Similarly, a participant working in head office having moved from an operational area describes the impact on her focus as a result of shifting priorities and shifting targets for interaction.

1.5 So, the urgency, the urgencies you would have felt back in [the operational areas], thinking 'Why doesn't [central administration] do something about these?', and then you get into [central administration] and they're not... you can still feel them, you can still empathise with them, but they're not..., but the priorities aren't the same. Your priorities then are trying to get your team together.

Organisational members form boundaries around their localised groups through selection of useful others for interaction and problem-solving. This selective coordination is a self-organising process which facilitates the group's adaptive process.

7.2.1.1 Tagging - Sphere of inclusion - Localisation

Localisation emerged early as a prominent theme in narratives about learning and knowledge development. It was one of the first codes developed by the participants in the sense-making workshop although the researcher had not identified the theme in preliminary coding. Participants talked about *localisation* in relation to *self-organisation* but also in relation to a second prominent theme *disconnection*. *Disconnection* is dealt with in detail in the findings section *nonlinearity*.

In each of the three narrative groups, participants spoke of the influence of the local context on their interaction and their seeking out of other members of the local environment in the solution of local problems.

For each of the groups, too, this localisation results in a lack of interest in working beyond the boundary of the aggregate, the need emerging from the local environment only influencing formation of aggregates for problems solving at the local level.

2.7 It's also localisation, because you know in your own team who you can rely on, what you can do, and what your work, you know, if you need this done, you can go to get things done. So it's a localisation thing.

2.7 People don't need to care either. It you're doing a good job, and your office is doing a good job and everyone's working as a team, do you really care whether someone, you know, in Perth are short staffed or have a customer complaining, you don't care about that level of detail because if you're doing a good job and the people around you are doing a good job, customers are happy, you're happy. You know what I mean?

For participants working with customers, *localisation* for them is about *real world* issues – their stories highlighting their perceptions of their work environment as interaction with the *real world*, and as a result perceived as far more complex than that of head office.

3.4 I think it's a bit about the reality side of it, too. You know, what I, what I, you know, see here and experience every day here, locally is what's real, and I know that I'm part of something bigger, but that doesn't really, it's not really experienced as real. It's all a bit theoretical.

In the sense-making workshop one participant's view was that a person's position in the organisation influences their perspective on the organisation.

1.1 For me, it's also about where you are in the organisation as to what you see. See, me from [central], I see the organisation as this huge thing that goes right across Australia, but somebody [who deals with customers] and, you know, it's captured in this first paragraph, sees the organisation as a much smaller being...

Yet, examples from the head office narrative group indicate that although this group could consider the organisation as a whole and real entity, their preferred interaction is indeed localised.

1.7 Like the organisation is too big to have a care factor any greater than the environment you work in.

1.1 ...and your, your immediate environment because the organisation's so big that there's that disconnection again.

Similarly, this exchange reinforces this strong theme about localisation and interest in local interaction and success.

3.2 But it's even the same in [central office] as it is out [in regional areas] and outside of our area, really, like, you know,

1.1 ...who knows what's going on in the team that is one floor away from you...

2.7 ...or cares?

There is an apparent conflict between theoretical understanding and the real life working of an individual within his or her environment. Indeed, stories of practice illustrate that the organisation, perceived as a theoretical construct, is often disregarded as irrelevant to localised *real world* operation.

3.1 A good example of that is, like, I find ACT very political, very, you here with National, whatever, you have to use the stuff that comes out, I've worked in country towns, and they look at it and go, 'This is crap, we're not using it' and they don't, because they're not here and they're not being examined, and they're not... so they just go, 'this is crap, not using it'.

This returns to discussion of fitness and survival, priority for problem solving, sharing information and learning from and with others and how these are tied to real, local and pressing issues. Overwhelmingly, and across groups, participants shared similar comments.

3.2 Again, it's only in your environment. You don't care if someone else...

2.7 Yeah, yeah. I don't care about what's going on in another office.

Perhaps because organisational members are focused on the local and select for interaction based on features of other agents in dealing with the local, stories abound about the organisation's attempts at maintaining consistency across its regions and offices being frequently dashed. Practice at the local level is based on local knowledge.

7.2.1.2 Tagging - Sphere of inclusion - Knowledge seeking

Participants also identify others with whom to interact based on their perception of the value of the knowledge an organisational member or collective holds in relation to a particular problem. Participants are keen to share stories about the support they receive in knowledge seeking, and in particular, the breadth of available knowledge types on which to draw.

This example illustrates the features of knowledge seeking most often discussed – a local and immediate problem, a local source of information, a range of perspectives for solution presented by the aggregate, and the individuals' selection of information based on their own expectations and problem-solving preferences.

2.1 Oh, it happens all the time. Um, oh, like today, for example, I had the person that didn't [complete some paperwork] properly, I couldn't figure it out, spoke to someone and they said, 'Well, ring the customer' another person said, 'Oh, no, no, they mean this, they mean this, they mean this' and, like everyone has different ideas on what to do in that specific situation. And it depends on whether they are more customer service based or more technical based as to what the answer is and how you go about it. But no one really kind of minds how you choose to be. If you want to be technical based, well they don't mind as long as you're doing everything properly.

Some participants talked about the way that some individuals become *magnets* for knowledge seeking, and reflected on this *gravitational pull* in terms of the features for which they were selected for interaction.

In this example, a participant describes the preference of individuals to select for features in others that align with their own preferred way of working.

2.6 And people tend to gravitate towards somebody who is like them to ask a question like that. You know, if you go to the person who's technically minded, they'd say, 'well, you got to do, that, and that, and that, and then you've got to go to that screen' and your eyes go crossed and you don't know what they're talking about. What screen's that? This person says 'Ring the customer', you go, yeah, I know that. That I can do.

It seems, though, that while participants believe that they select for certain characteristics in their knowledge sharing, they perhaps are selecting for something other than technical knowledge to assist in problem-solving. One customer service participant spoke about research that had been carried out on the experts that customer service workers gravitated.

2.2 You know, we had these, you know, the person who everyone gravitates to in the site, and something like 45% of the answers they gave were wrong. Both technically, and probably ethically as well. So, you look at that, and you think to yourself 'Whey!'.

While the participants of this study did recognise the organisation as a whole and real entity, their identity is tied up with that of the local environment, local interaction and local effectiveness. The priority for their activity was with local outcomes.

7.2.2   TAGGING - CONCERN FOR THE ORGANISATION

Aside from individuals' tagging for features of their workmates that assist them in immediate problem solving and improving fitness, participants also talked about their experience of identifying with others on the basis of their perception of the organisation and the role they play within it. While many participants described the difficulty members had with relating to the organisation as a whole, they did speak about their relationship with each being influenced by their understanding of the organisation.

In this excerpt, for example, a customer service employee is discussing some organisational members' attitudes that he believes to be disruptive to cooperative behaviour.

2.3 Well, it's a large organisation. 'Oh, well, look I don't really see that I need to do that, so I can flick pass it to someone else'. And they don't really need to ... You know, and what they're forgetting about is that at the end of the day we're here for our customers.

Perception of others' *concern for the organisation* provides tags for selective interaction and the converse also appears true; the lack of interest in the organisation is illustrated as blocking information flow for some participants.

2.4 ... you know, you look at that, and you say to yourself, 'well there was a lot of information that wasn't transferred to the right people, and I wonder how much of it was glory seeking and how much of it was real genuine concern for the organisation'.

In the example above, the organisational member describes the tag *concern for the organisation* as a facilitator of interaction and organisational knowledge development, highlighting *glory seeking* as antithetic to these outcomes (*glory seeking* and its associated codes are discussed further in *disconnection*).

In a rare reference to formal training, one organisational member points out with some regret that there is no opportunity for the sharing of learning about the urgencies that arise from organisational members' concern for the organisation and its customers. For this participant, the opportunity to interact with others on the basis of a shared concern for customers is critical. In this example of decision making which impacts on customers, this participant's need is obvious.

2.1 It's heart wrenching to do it, because you think, no, we're here for the customer, we're here for the customer, and you don't get training in how to deal with that situation. And it's not until you have, and [here] how many do you have? One a week? It's not till you have a succession of them and you go, 'Yes, I'm making the right decision for X, Y and Z'.

The apparent paradox described in this section between localisation (and participants' intense concern for the immediate and local) and concern for the organisation is highlighted in narratives as bringing about tension.

3.2 But, it's the, that tension between, you know, the best thing for the customer versus the policy and legislation that we have to work with and often it's a choice of one or the other, you either, you know...'

The tension plays itself out, it appears, in the sense-making that occurs in relation to the role of the organisation and the individual's perspective of their responsibility within that role.

In this study, participants use their own interpretations of the role of the organisation and their responsibility to it as justification for breaking organisational rules. That is, where a rule appears in conflict with the participant's construction of the role of the organisation and their role as an organisational member, the member will privilege their own interpretation to justify breaking rules. It appears too, that participants select others for interaction based on alignment of those others' perception of the value of the organisation and the development of their personal and role identity within it.

The following excerpt highlights selective interaction and the perceived tension between interaction with others based on a shared concern for the organisation and the difficulty posed for those working in delivering services to customers.

1.1 And the customer doesn't give a rat's arse what the political imperative is for this to happen, they want [an immediate tangible outcome]. Achieved through coming in and interacting with us. So, we don't seem to be able to reconcile those two things. Because they should be the same.

Although organisational members appear to be unable to connect their local interest and learning with 'the organisation', their local interactions are based in understandings of the organisation's role and goals. This appears to be a mediating factor on the knowledge that is developed by the aggregate – aggregate members acting on their local understanding of the organisation's role in solving problems and making decisions in local interaction.

7.2.2.1   *Tagging - Concern for the organisation - Valuing people and valuing the work*

Some participants spoke about interaction based upon a shared understanding of the value of the people within the organisation and the work that they perform. These stories and insights arise in discussions about lack of sharing and *disconnection* between members of the organisation who differ in the value they place on these two.

This example illustrates organisational members' need to tag for similar values by providing an example of the difficulty posed when values differ.

3.1 So, he couldn't understand, didn't matter what we did, he couldn't understand what was being proposed, and he didn't see the value of it, and that makes life quite difficult.

Using the ways in which others value the work that they do as a tag for selective interaction is obvious in a range of narratives collected in this study. At the beginning of the sense-making workshop, within the first three sentences exchanged, participants were working through the notion of valuing work as a facilitator of learning. This quite lengthy exchange illustrates the development of the notion within the group and the discussion of nuance around valuing work as a precursor to learning and knowledge exchange.

This excerpt is begins with a participant from head office addressing the first passage in the metanarrative. In the passage under discussion a customer service employee states that they do not see what they do as any more valuable to the organisation than it is to the local office in solving a local problem.

1.1   It's about working with customer as being any more worthwhile to the organisation...

3.1   Isn't that about valuing… and it's also about that disconnection

3.4   …that disconnection that we talked about

1.1   …clearly, yes

Researcher   *So, it's about valuing… difference?*

2.7   No. Valuing the work

3.3   It's about valuing the work, I would have thought

2.7   Or being valued

3.1   Yes…that too.

2.8   Whether it be a workaround or finding a different way of dealing with a difficult customer they don't see it as being of any worth to the organisation

3.1   It goes to that later story about recognition

1.1   Yes.

This exchange illustrates the group's grappling with notions of the value of knowledge that emerges from work, especially work at operational levels. The segregation of what 'counts' as knowledge in the organisation and how sharing is facilitated by tagging for similar values leads to issues around flows across organisational members and aggregates.

7.3   CONCLUSION

This chapter draws attention to the interactions between individuals which result in self-organised groups focused on increasing fitness within a changeable work context. It highlights the ways in which these aggregates reinforce boundaries around themselves and how these boundaries limit learning and the sharing of locally developed knowledge beyond the local context.

The relationship between *aggregation* and *tagging* points to localised learning as a self-reinforcing behaviour that is related to constructions of the role of the organisation and the value of work and its outcomes at different levels of organisation. These concepts focus attention on the ways that individuals and collectives work together in developing knowledge to improve their localised fitness and the lack of connection between this knowledge and the formally endorsed knowledge of the organisation. They highlight the value of knowledge in its local validity and use, pointing to knowledge as active, situated and existing in stock and in flow. These findings prompt questions about the alignment of the formal organisation with the experience of its members. These issues are developed in the following chapter, 'Nonlinearity and Flows'.

8 FINDINGS – NONLINEARITY AND FLOWS

Participants' narratives make frequent reference to the learning that emerges from their engagement with their work. This engagement is described as influenced by the work's changeability, continuous novelty, and participants' subsequent difficulty in finding clear connections between *the rules* of the organisation and the needs of their customer and work colleagues. The uncertainty of the work and its impact on opportunities for new knowledge to flow through the organisation is presented here as critical to participants' experience of learning and knowledge in this workplace.

This chapter presents findings that relate to the characteristics of *nonlinearity* and *flows*. In illustrating *nonlinearity* through the data it highlights the tensions apparent between the *real world* experience of participants and organisational expectations of consistency, *perfect world,* and draws attention to the interruptions this tension causes to the sharing of knowledge in the organisation.

8.1 NONLINEARITY

There's no way in day-to-day that any two situations are going to be the same with the same outcome. (Participant 2.6)

Interactions within complex systems produce outcomes which do not result in 'a sum of the parts' (Waldrop 1994: 65), rather in complex outcomes which cannot be predicted and which cannot be anticipated from individual behaviour. In nonlinear systems agents interacting with each other interfere with the outputs of the system, and as a result the system must be approached holistically – an analysis of each part will not provide a picture of the whole.

Almost every tale gathered about the interaction of organisational members within their environment includes a reference to nonlinear phenomena. In many cases, too, this experience of dealing with nonlinear dynamics is contrasted with the organisation's assumption of linearity and the expectation of the organisation that staff act in line with prescribed linear processes.

The lived experience of these organisational members is inherently linked to nonlinearity. Conversely, this organisation structures itself as a linear system. The disparity between the formal organisational and the *real world* experience of organisational members is highlighted as a critical feature of the learning and knowledge landscape.

2.6 You can't just tie it in a neat little package and say, 'this is what you will do. For every single person that you come across'.

Customer individuality is an important factor in of the nonlinear dynamics of the customer service employee experience. There is little evidence of repeatable, clear and linear connections between cause and effect in employees' application of organisational rules to individual customer problems. Participants spoke of the discretion they use in solving problems based on this lack of causal relationship in order to address the diversity of problems that emerge in customer interaction.

2.4 …you have to make a lot of discretionary decisions based on, it's almost the right thing…
2.6 What you know to be happening…
2.1 As opposed to what might happen tomorrow!

The organisation's assumption of linearity leads to a collision between the formal (linear) and lived (nonlinear) which impacts sharply on the sharing of knowledge developed through adaptive learning at work.

The disproportionate effect that one variable may have on another as a result of nonlinear dynamics means that participants are dealing continually with novel problems and, as most frequently described, novel problems in interaction with individual customers.

2.8 They're all different, and as [2.7] said, every single customer is going to be different from the one you had two hours ago, even though they present with the same look and feel and everything...
2.4 ...and they all tick the same boxes and [deleted], but they're not the same.

The difficulty in drawing boundaries around what is inside and what is outside the system is introduced in these examples of nonlinear dynamics. In these stories, customers are both part of the aggregate dynamic and part of the environment, the connectedness of all elements in interaction producing nonlinear outcomes.

8.1.1   NONLINEARITY - REAL WORLD

Participants equate the *real world* with their lived experience in a nonlinear dynamic.

2.4 ...there is no way to prepare yourself for the whole, because you get told a lot of things, and you see things on telly but these things are real. And they're real people.

Participants spoke of their perception that the *real world* is something specifically contextual, something to which they require some adjustment. They stress that there is a level of expertise in dealing with the environment that is critical to members' survival within it.

2.4 But you can't put people who are just so new to the organisation, just so new to society, a lot of them! But, they don't, you've just opened up a shell and there they are, you know, and we're about to put them in the real world with our staff and our customers, and they aren't going to cope.

Aside from the impact of human interaction on nonlinear dynamics, participants also spoke about the limitations of technical systems as a result of nonlinearity. When talking about the implications for learning, participants articulated the gap between intent and reality.

Information systems featured in discussion about the *real world* and the limitations of linear assumptions in assisting organisational members in dealing with it.

3.2 …you know, a product's built for a purpose, but the reality of how it actually works in practice can be quite different to the original intent. And that came up later on as well, with other things. So, in terms of like a learning perspective, we need to keep, these things have to be considered up front.

1.1 And that's a real, that's a real issue with lack of… I mean, one of the real issues with any sort of process that we seem to develop in this organisation, is that in the theory it's supposed to be tested in the real world, and yet there's just be 2 or 3 examples where, 'Hey, it's supposed to do this!' and it's supposed to you know, revolutionise the world, and yet…

Nonlinearity features in the narratives of these participants as they attempt to deal with their inability to prepare for the events that they encounter in any day. Their *real world* is illustrated as messy, influenced by interaction with a changing and unpredictable environment within which they struggle to continually learn.

8.1.1.1   *Nonlinearity - Real world - Flexibility*

Dealing with the unexpected problems participants face daily and the persistent novelty that emerges from the nonlinear dynamics of their engagement in their world requires flexibility. They spoke of individual and collective flexibility and problem-solving freedom as critical to surviving within their rugged 'fitness landscape' (Kauffman 1995: 246).

Narratives describe the skills required to support flexibility within the environment. They also highlight the *deviant* behaviour that results from applying rules flexibly (or not applying organisational rules at all in order to maintain flexibility).

In several examples, participants talked about flexibility in the perceived success of learning and organisational knowledge development. In the following example, a participant from head office describes an innovative group and its development within a fairly broad set of goals which provided them with high levels of flexibility. In what he describes as a 'happy' story about learning and knowledge development, this participant discusses scope.

2.5 …so we avoided [deleted] and all that administrative stuff, but technically [we had not met the requirements]. So you just, you know, some of it's relationships within the town with other professionals, or just having some understanding of the system and the rest of it, and they were happy to accommodate. We do that, I would say that sort of thing would happen to us pretty regularly…

3.6 Now, that has changed the whole, the whole way we are operating…. I guess we were led well at the time by a person who gave us the flexibility to feel comfortable in taking those chances.

The perceived unpredictability of their environment prompted participants to discuss their need for flexibility and the constraints that formal process and procedures placed on their ability to *meet the need* of the local environment.

8.1.1.2   *Nonlinearity - Real world - Discretion*

An environment within which prediction of outcome is impossible and novelty is ubiquitous demands discretionary decision-making for these participants. The freedom to use discretion in solving problems is described as vital to participant fitness within the workplace and the effectiveness of the organisation. Use of discretion is illustrated as contributing to the learning of individuals and local aggregates, the knowledge outcomes held close within the aggregate.

Participants spoke about the organisation's insistence of strict application of rules by customer service representatives. This was contrasted with the perceived need for those working at the customer interface to be able to implement legislation in a considered way.

2.6 And since the policy is very vague at times, the legislation, I'm sorry, is very vague and open to interpretation and then we're told we're not allowed to interpret it. ....And when I was at [another government department] we were allowed to interpret, we had a lot of discretion and [this organisation] has taken that away from us, and that has been hard for me to cope with. It quite annoyed me. And still does.... And, I mean, you guys must do that on the counter every day, make discretionary decisions and do workarounds and things for people, especially when there are an unusual set of circumstances that nobody's put in the book.

The lack of flexibility in applying legislation is a strong source of frustration for participants in dealing with their environment and customers. The flexibility inherent in the legislation is described as a flexibility they are not permitted to utilise. Interpretations of legislation are made elsewhere in the organisation and provided to these organisational members, desperate for flexibility, in a structured, non-negotiable set of rules of application.

2.6 The trouble, I think, is that the legislation is so open to interpretation that you cannot then come up with a list of things to do with this...

Organisational members contravene these rules of application in order to meet customer need, and the fear of discovery of this perceived deviant behaviour is highlighted in a number of narratives. Participants describe their concern about ramifications of their problem solving outcomes, and this has important implications for the sharing of learning that emerges in interaction with customers. Closely linked is the impact that the restraint on organisational members has on the organisation's ability to respond to changing customer need.

2.1 ...but I think there are still genuine fears that haven't been allayed about making those discretionary decisions and, yeah, the ramifications that [2.4] was talking about and often that can be enough to stop a [person] making the right decision for a customer, ...but making the right decision for that customer based on their [particular circumstances].

Limitations on organisational knowledge that could emerge from these problem solving activities is described in this example from a customer service employee in response to comments about discretionary decision making and deviance.

2.4 Yeah, this is the truth, but there is a degree of that and a lot of organisational knowledge comes from that, but there's also that cloak over it, because we're all scared of the blanket being lifted not on the fact that we've made a decision, and that we're prepared to stand by the decision, but on, from, or by people who probably wouldn't understand. And that's the reason.

This same participant talks about discretion as important in environments in which uncertainty is a feature, referring not just to the interpretation of legislation, but also about a set of internal rules which participants describe as *the right thing*.

2.4 Yeah, yeah, particularly in management roles, too, where you get, you have to make a lot of discretionary decisions based on, it's almost the right thing...

The conditions within which organisational members exercise discretion is a recurring theme in discussion of the relationship between of *the organisation's* requirements and the requirements of *the real world*. Discretion is not only used in the application of rules in the solution of problems, but also in the extent to which organisational members adhere to organisational imperatives.

In the sense-making workshop the mixed group of participants from both central administration and customer service areas struggled with the narratives about discretion. They discussed its impact on learning and knowledge sharing in the organisation and this excerpt illustrates one participant's grappling with meaning around *right* and *wrong* and the role of discretion.

3.2 So, even if it's not, there's a lot of stuff in here about discretionary decisions, you know, that's, grey areas are always bad, um, but if you don't have grey areas it's black and white which is also bad, because you're either right or you're wrong then, you're not, kind of, you know, right or wrong...

1.1 So the question is, which is worse?

3.2 But, you know, the concept I wrote down was then around, you know, that discretionary decision making can lead to soft options, you know, like, having been there and done that if it's discretionary and it can go one way or the other well the easiest way is to say yes, they go away happy and you never see them again.

This concern perhaps reflects the organisation's rationale for setting clear rules for the solution of problems that are anticipated, a rationale reflecting a perception of linear relationships between cause and effect. This rationale, however, is unable to provide for the unanticipated problems with which organisational members deal.

8.1.1.3 *Nonlinearity - Real world - Crisis*

Participants' interactions with each other and their environment sometimes occur within a state of crisis, organisational members describing the emergence of crisis as related to the nonlinearity of the *real world*. Situations of crisis were recounted by participants in three main ways – either in this first sense, as an indicator of the complexity of the world, secondly, as a source of innovation and change, and thirdly as an opportunity for learning and knowledge sharing.

Again, in the sense-making workshop, participants identified crisis as a feature of the members' experience within the organisational context. There was some discussion as to whether crisis was a feature of the customer service environment or whether it existed throughout organisational levels and geographical areas.

2.8 Well, being in the [operational office] you're pretty much in a crisis mode all the time, in the ACT anyway.

1.1 Well, I'm sure that's common right across the organisation…

The workshop of head office participants offered an example that appears to support this perception. Telling a story of a head office directive for change, the participant says that after feedback,

1.4 …it went berserk, they were running around like chooks with their heads cut off [details of client difficulty as a result of described issue] and the amount of stuff that had to be pulled in to try and work on it to try and help these [customers] was so resource intensive, and it had been done like it's being done now it'd be much better, more humane way of handling it now. But it wouldn't have happened. It had to go through that for what we've got now…

In an important clarification within the group, though, the level of crisis is perceived to be more pressing in situations of individual interaction than it is in organisational ones. This indicates, again, organisational members' prioritisation of the local and immediate.

3.2 That environmental...

1.1 ...to get things to work right, because everybody's different. You know, we've talked about there's difficult customers, you don't see the same situation twice, although it's sort of the same boxes being ticked on the form and all those sorts of things, it's this whole thing about dealing with people in a crisis situation that is..

3.2 ...and their individuality...

1.1 ...and their individual crises as opposed to the organisational crises that overlay that.

This excerpt brings together the components of crisis for these participants as represented by their interaction with the environment, individuality and novelty.

In an example of crisis described in the second sense, one participant talked about pressure and crisis. This participant went on to link this difficult experience with positive impact on her learning.

3.3 'Oh, my God! I've got to do all this by myself!' and [my supervisor] was away and her father was dying and she was going to be away for a while, it wasn't just she was away for two weeks, and there was a lot of pressure about, you know, for me, thinking, well, if we don't have this project, well it's kind of like, it's not my only project, but it's one of three, and what does that mean for me?

Another participant described a time of high activity, production and innovation with a team that developed knowledge that changed process throughout the organisation. For this participant crisis is a positive phenomenon.

3.2 And one of the interesting dynamics we had was that a lot of us were, our lives were almost like a, not a crisis as a bad way, but we were operating off very high stress levels and so it was almost like our work was our outlet, and we just did some absolutely amazing things.

That crisis provides important opportunities for local learning and local sharing of knowledge is illustrated clearly in the narratives of several participants. In these cases, though, participants also describe the lack of wider distribution of knowledge developed as a result of the organisation's assumption and expectation of control.

2.1 I, oh, I felt bad! I was almost yelling at my staff, saying 'Ring the police now!' and at the top of my voice. So not only was I coming back, going, oh, I should have handled that better, but [also] 'Oh, 1, you're such a bitch!' You know, what were you yelling at your staff for? And that, that experience, it becomes, instead of experiences and sharing that knowledge, it becomes, a myth, an urban legend as opposed to getting it out on the table, and let's hash it out, and let's talk about this command situation. So, …

2.6 There is some corporate information that's also not being shared how to manage, how to team…

In the sense-making workshop this theme was developed further.

1.1 You know, I mean people nowadays talk about emotional resilience as a key issue for, for customer service [workers] I've never seen that written in a selection criteria. Because that's, you know, at the end of the day that's what you guys are about, isn't it? Dealing with those difficult, that crisis situation every hour of every day

Crisis is a feature of the nonlinear world in which participants operate. In situations of crisis participants place focus on the individual and the crisis provides an important impetus for innovation, learning and knowledge sharing.

8.1.2   NONLINEARITY - PERFECT WORLD

The *real world* is juxtaposed against the organisation's structuring around *perfect world*. The resulting *disconnect* is discussed in some depth within the concept *flows,* while assumptions of order and linearity inherent in the organisation's structures, policies and processes are outlined here.

1.1   '…I was working [on a project to implement a new quality assurance system] and at [central administration] it was, 'this will be fantastic, it will do everything, increase our accuracy', you know, and when I went out to the [offices where staff work with clients face to face] not really believing that line, but having a fair amount of confidence that we'd done a pretty good job, bloody hell, it was like getting a smack in the face, it was so different. People absolutely hated the product. They'd found lots of ways to work around it that we hadn't even thought of…

1.3   'Where there's a will there's a way…

1.1   'Yeah, it was so poorly received, even though we'd done really good research and we'd tried to do marketing of it and tried to get [end users] involved in the development of it, it went really badly, and what we found because I actually went into the office and sat with a [client service worker] and what I found out about that sort of stuff,… just to see the volume, the amount of stuff that had to get processed in the day and then to sit down with [the supervisor] and say, shit how are you going to get through all that stuff in one day.. and then to go to [another office] and find that they had a different agenda again and then to come back to [central administration] and think, well hang on, this is all really weird… and there wasn't any connection.'

In discussions with head office participants the difference between *real world* and *perfect world* is clearly articulated. *Perfect world* is constructed amongst participants as an artificial world, developed around consistency and control and portrayed as a structural constraint on member adaptation through work.

8.1.2.1   Nonlinearity – Perfect world - Consistency

For these participants the organisation's assumption of certainty and order is evident in demands for consistency. Consistency in the application of rules about services to customers, consistency in interaction with customers and others within the organisation, and strict process are continually described in narratives.

Participants, however, point out that they do not necessarily adhere to the organisational requirement for consistency.

1.1 You take the time to speak to individual [operational members] and stuff like that about the various impressions that they have of how their particular site had implemented this, what was supposed to be a consistent concept, operating principal, and it so, absolutely, without question, was not. And this is about that idea of 'we know what works for us', that kind of stuff, and then the consistency issue is just blown right out of the water.

There is no doubt from the narratives that consistency is an important concept for head office, but one that individuals and aggregates *work around* in practice.

1.1 Now [we're] going out there and saying we're going to give this consistent message, timing blahdy blahdy blah and all the offices are just saying, 'Yep, that's great, all's good' and they're doing what they want to do anyway. And operations management does not work unless it's consistent, so we are cutting ourselves off at the knees straight away.

The extent to which the organisation demands consistency in application of rules and process is caricatured by a customer service member describing the level of direction provided by her supervisor in interacting with customers.

2.7 But, a prime example of that is a manager told a [person working with customers] she said, 'If somebody comes in and says to you, 'how are you today?' you are to answer, 'I'm fine thankyou''.
1.1 Regardless
2.7 Regardless
3.2 So, that's a bit like going to Maccas and you know, 'would you like fries with that?'

A customer service officer's struggle with inconsistency spoke of the dissonance between the expected behaviour she was to display in maintaining consistency, and the behaviour required of her and her team in meeting the need of her environment.

2.4 And we're still getting inconsistencies in, in the application of that. Not in terms of, you will always have the inconsistencies because of the very nature, but I felt really uncomfortable about that, well, you need to take some action, you need to make a decision, you need to do something about that.

Similarly, a head office participant told of the inconsistency that emerges at the customer service end of the organisation as a result of the lack of expert knowledge, the need for operational members to *spread themselves too thin*, and linked this to customer dissatisfaction.

On the other hand, the term *expert* for some employees carried meanings that were negative, reinforcing ideas about the redundancy of stable information and set answers to clear questions.

(Researcher) So, what was the expert thing about that?
2.7 Your perception of what an expert is
1.1 Yeah, I think 3.4 summed it up beautifully that in the old days an expert knew everything because they'd done that particular function or task or whatever, and they knew it inside out. The world doesn't work like that now, and now we are encouraging people or teaching them (and as I say, we don't support it as well as we should) that you don't need to remember it, you need to know where to go and find it.
3.2 …but we have sort of brought that concept of the old expert in through the old, you know it's a [defined expert role]

It is apparent that some participants' constructions of *expert* are antithetic to performance in a nonlinear world. This means that some participants are critical of the role of expert, seeing it as failing to support organisational members.

Some participants identify strategies for engaging experts in the complexity of the real world in order to gather their knowledge within the contemporary context.

1.2 But I think, in working with [the new product relating to knowledge management] and working with [the area of expertise in relation to project management] who are the bods that are supposed to know that stuff, it's just experts like that, in this organisation, always let you down.

1.4 And so one of the things that [this colleague] adopted, and I've started doing too, is taking out [experts] into [our work environment] really early, and giving them an idea of the environment and you've got them on side. They're going back to their team and they're saying, 'well that won't work [in the work environment]. We know, we've been there and experienced it. So, for us, they're really important exercises for us to get them in there.

It is the *nature* of the knowledge that experts are perceived to hold that is the issue for these participants. Participants spoke of the complexity of issues with which they deal, describing the experts as dealing with explicit knowledge, the *easy stuff*, while they deal with the tacit and more elusive.

In this example, consistency is supported by the transfer of explicit knowledge, but inconsistency is implied in the tacit.

2.1 I mean, I handed over to 2.4, I handed over the technicalities, I handed over the staff stuff, I handed over the letters from previous customers, and all the sort of easy stuff that's easy to explain, and easy to handle, but I couldn't say, 'Look, this is how you deal with X, Y, Z' because we're very different people, but at no point did anyone ever say to either of us, 'This is what [this location] is. This is what you may have to deal with and you need to find a way, as a manager, or a senior officer, how you are going to deal with that?'

The complexity of the environment is perceived to demand inconsistency and discretionary choices for employees working at all levels of the organisation, but particularly of the operational level. For some the challenge is overwhelming, not just because the decisions are difficult ones for which they are unsupported, but also because they believe the challenge to be linked to tremendous risk.

In this excerpt the emotion tied to the difficulty of the situation and the fear of reprisal is clear.

2.6 I can remember twice when I've thought to myself, 'If I do this and I lose my job am I willing to do this?' and on those two occasions I was. I made that decision. I don't know whether I can do this and no one could tell me whether I could it, so I did it, documented it, went, 'Head cut off? Head gets cut off'!

Inconsistency, on the other hand, is seen as a response to the nonlinear nature of the context. Narratives describe inconsistency emerging not only from the novelty of problems which members attempt to solve, but also from the interpretation of rules set for problem solving by the organisation. Similarly, narratives reveal members' difficulty with applying rules consistently when even within the organisation, nonlinear dynamics impact on the organisation's internal processes.

2.6 Some people would just go, 'Nup. That's what the rules say, that's what the rules say.'
2.4 And that's where you get a level of inconsistency in the decision-making, because there's that culture of blame underlying this.

1.4 They're getting information from [higher in the hierarchy] saying, 'you have to do this by this deadline', however, once that's happened it could change, you know, so they're trying to get this information out that may or may not change and that's been one of the problems.

Not only are organisational members dealing with novel circumstances at the edge of the organisation while attempting to maintain consistency, but also with the organisation which itself does not remain consistent.

8.1.2.2 *Nonlinearity – Perfect world - Control*

Consistency and control are linked in many narratives which identify the same frustrations about lack of autonomy in spite of a perceived need for it. For many participants, control exerted on them through the organisation's hierarchy is seen to limit their attempts to achieve fitness within the nonlinear landscape.

The influence of hierarchical control is illustrated in each of the narrative workshops and developed within the sense-making workshop through discussion about the tension between consistency and autonomy.

2.7 It's a control thing

3.2 This place isn't too different to some of the stuff we talked about earlier around the [service delivery areas]. You know, all the people that were using it were sending this email saying, 'Oh, this is great! It's a shame it's taken so long to have this' and then people up higher were going, 'Well, no, we haven't signed off yet'. I guess it's establishing boundaries as well.

3.4 That hierarchical thing

3.2 Yeah, hierarchical boundaries, I guess. Accountability…

And yet, conforming with control is affirmed as an important survival behaviour, not within the immediate environment, but within the organisation itself.

3.4 …and you know how you're in the chosen few? You do as you're told

3.2 and also, that you're good at promoting yourself

3.4 mmm. And you do as you're told.

The concept *nonlinearity* provides a language for discussing an important feature of these participants' experience. Through *nonlinearity* the connectedness of experience is highlighted, the difficulty with consistency in a ubiquitously inconsistent world and the need for innovation and flexibility to effectively meet the need of the context are also prominent. The clash between the organisation's requirement for consistency and the participants' need for flexibility has important implications for the sharing of learning from the edges of the organisation and the development and flow of the resultant knowledge for the organisation's advantage.

8.2 FLOWS

'But that's not limited to you, to you individually. What you learn flows into us…' (Participant 1.1)

Flows, in Holland's (1995: 23) work, refers to movement over a network through nodes (agents) and connectors. Examples of flows in organisations include flows of information, physical resources, or sentiment. In complex adaptive systems these flows change in response to the success or failure of agents, their role as nodes and possible connections shifting with the adapting system.

The distance between the perceived experience and understanding of operational members of the organisation and their policy developing counterparts in head office is highlighted above. While each group sees themselves operating within complex environments, those dealing with customers on a daily basis are adamant that the organisation's requirement of them in maintaining consistency and control is untenable.

Through *flows* the impact of power relationships on organisational members' ability to flex to their environment, to learn in interaction with it, their customers and colleagues is highlighted. Narratives provide insight into the ways in which these members learn through exploration when given permission to fail and the impact of fear of the repercussions of exploration when permission is not given. Participants also describe the rhetoric around freedom to explore and contrast it with examples of criticism and blame for negative outcomes and lack of recognition for positive ones.

Participants' perceive a lack of shared understanding across aggregate groups and levels limits the effectiveness of planned learning interventions, serendipitous learning opportunities, knowledge passage into the organisation and knowledge sharing beyond the aggregate boundary.

Through *flows* the impact of the perceived tension between policy and practice in this organisation is developed and organisational members' understandings of the gaps in organisational knowledge sharing is shown to result. *Flows* is presented here through the two main categories that emerged through narratives, *direction* and *disconnection*.

8.2.1 FLOWS - DIRECTION

Power sits at the top of the organisation for these participants. Particular attention is given to the control of head office over the regional and customer service areas of the organisation. Participants in customer service positions describe themselves being positioned as subservient to head office rather than supported by it, and participants from head office themselves recognise their own behaviour in reinforcing this view, *It's just astonishing to me of how we sit up here in our ivory tower, going, 'you will' and they go 'Sure! Sure!' (Participant 1.2).*

Direction for these participants relates to *permission, exploration, risk, blame* and *rhetoric.* Narratives and discussion illustrate the ways in which these properties impact on participants' opportunity to learn through their work and their willingness to share knowledge outside of the local aggregate.

8.2.1.1   *Flows - Direction - Permission*

Permission to respond to local conditions is an important theme in discussion of learning opportunities. Participants in each group and at all levels talked about permission in their stories of informal learning and development within the organisation.

For those in customer service, the stories tend to be about the relationship between a customer service employee and their local supervisor or manager.

2.4 ...and then as soon as he knew he had that permission to do that, that's fine, off he goes, fine, no issues... They want to learn, if they've got permission to make mistakes.

214

Similarly, in stories of attempts to share knowledge, permission is highlighted as an important factor. Endorsement of knowledge sharing activities by those in power within the organisation is described, and the limitations of requiring permission to share lamented, both at the operational level of the organisation and within head office. In this excerpt a manager from head office recalls her experience of attempting to share some knowledge she believed to be important to other members of the organisation.

3.2 And that happened to me last week with something that I was trying to put up to help people as a resource and within two hours of having that put on the website the heavies came straight down and said, 'You'd better remove it because I haven't approved it.'

Head office participants recognise their role in granting permission and its influence on the willingness of individuals and aggregates to share their learnings beyond the aggregate. Occasionally the opportunity arises for these aggregates to share their knowledge more broadly, and it seems that one thing preventing the sharing is permission.

1.5 …we know that from the conference where they stand up and tell everyone what they've done, and you just stand there and think, 'This is great!' and we're still in here trying to pump it out, and they're out there doing it. So I think that they do. And I think that a lot of the time they sit and wait for us to say it's OK.

Leadership is a recurrent theme in discussion of permission, participants describing important learning opportunities as ones in which the leader does not direct or restrict but gives wide permission for autonomy and exploration.

3.6 I guess we were led well at the time by a person who gave us the flexibility to feel comfortable in taking those chances.

3.2 So, can I just ask a question, 3.6? The leadership was the important thing? That you had the clean slate and you had the support of the leadership to enable that to happen in the way that the group had decided was appropriate?
3.6 Yeah. Yeah, well, I guess the knowledge that the leadership wasn't going to quash whatever we came up with, they were prepared to listen to it and we'd always had a sound hearing.

In this example, as in many others, positional power is not a feature of the dynamic of aggregates, those filling the organisational position of power actually absenting themselves from their roles of direction and control within the aggregate.

3.6 Well, it was support more than direction, probably. Didn't leave us alone, but yeah, took on the role of, really, support staff whatever you need, we'll find for you, if you need to find out, well, you can take this, if you need to find out about funding.

One participant, reflecting on the narratives and subsequent discussion about permission and its importance in learning and the transfer of knowledge within the organisation, summarised some important themes for this group in understandings of leadership in the shared narratives.

3.2 I think, you know, … that it probably hadn't occurred to me before putting this in perspective how important leadership is in the success of learning, that learning can be a really positive thing, but it can also be a non-event if you don't have those things in place, the openness and the ability, people, that space they need to create their own solutions, rather than to be given solutions.

Leadership which endorses knowledge sharing and permits local responses to local conditions was described as imperative to these organisational members. Leaders who support rather than direct are said to encourage learning and knowledge sharing in the organisation.

8.2.1.2   Flows – Direction - Exploration

'*The space to create their own solutions*', to explore, was consistently linked by participants to learning, knowledge creation and the movement of that knowledge through the organisation.

In her example of a well-connected team that made an important contribution to organisational knowledge this participant describes the opportunity for exploration available to the team.

3.2 …it was just that open opportunity for people to just have a good look at something in a different way…

For one participant an opportunity to work with another organisation on an international project for a period of time was seen as a great chance to bring new knowledge to the organisation as well as develop her own learning. Having been offered the opportunity the participant asked her managers for their agreement to be seconded to the organisation for a short time. Her managers rejected her approach and she described feeling let down and unsupported in her attempt to develop and bring in external knowledge from new experience.

1.2 I have a chance to explore how something like this can be conveyed in a new public sector environment and all that kind of stuff, and I don't think you've really considered it seriously.

The development of new knowledge within the boundaries of the organisation is alsoseen to be limited by lack of opportunity to explore new solutions.

1.2 There is some difficult issues, and stuff like that, but you should be allowed the room, not only to explore and stuff like that, but to occasionally make mistakes.

The perceived lack of value placed on individuals' exploration in pursuit of personal and organisational development inherent in these excerpts has important implications for the flow of knowledge into the organisation.

8.2.1.3   Flows – Direction - Risk

For many organisational members, operating within a nonlinear environment involves *risk* - risk of repercussions as well as risk of failure and failure to survive. Yet many told stories about members' willingness to take risks and their need to continually employ risk-taking behaviour.

In this example from the head office IT group, a participant describes the frustration resulting from her perception of the organisation's limitations on risk taking.

3.2 But we don't tell people how to do it safely, you know, like, not as a general rule, because we've, when we were working on the [quality assurance tool] there was a bunch of ideas that they had that they wanted to do that were risky. And some of them against current legislation, [detail deleted] so we pushed to have, we pushed the [team] to tell us how they could safely go about doing that to make sure that there were no repercussions...

8.2.1.4   Flows – Direction - Blame

Intimately linked to *permission*, *exploration* and *risk* is *blame*, organisational members telling stories about their fear of blame and its repercussions. Blame is illustrated as limiting their opportunities to learn and share their knowledge more broadly throughout the organisation. This theme was represented in each of the workshops and seen as an important concept in learning and knowledge sharing.

From a flows perspective, blame is seen as a limiter – creating gaps between connectors.

2.4 But nobody told us. And the fear factor there is terrible. Like, what were they… like [2.5] and I would laugh if we saw it, 'You silly Wally, we'll fix it up' you know, that's all right, but that fear that, 'Oh, no, I've screwed up. I'll have to bury it'.

Participants described blaming as part of the organisation's culture.

3.1 There's also the stuff around the blame culture there as well, there are people within our team who have had, actually, lots of ideas in the last week or so who've never had the opportunity to contribute those, haven't been taken seriously, have been told to keep on that little old treadmill.

Culture prompted some interesting exchanges on blame in the organisation.

1.1 I was just going to say it's all about the culture, because there's no point being frank and fearless if every time you put your head, anybody puts their head over the precipice it gets shot off.
3.4 Mmm, fearless in shark territory? I don't think so…

The placing of blame is seen as something so inherent to the behaviour of the organisation's people that it has become self-perpetuating and internally reinforcing. In order for learning to progress, participants agree that the perceived culture of blaming must be removed.

3.2 Mistakes aren't always punished, people often punish themselves, not always other people
1.1 Doesn't have to be external, you know, we're not in the, we don't have a culture where you feel able almost to try something new, because if it goes wrong, you're going to get it in the neck
3.2 Yeah, so it's easier not to bother

In place of blame, participants state, a culture of tolerance is critical. Several participants describe a learning environment as one in which permission to make mistakes is the norm.

2.4 We need to create, we need to take the blame out of the organisation, we need to create that 'You've got permission'. [The CEO] tried that, very early on, when she said, 'I don't mind if you make a, there's no such thing as an incorrect decision, just a learning experience' or something...

2.4 So, how do we get, the question for me, and it's been an ongoing one for a long time is how do we give people permission to make mistakes?

Part of the problem of blame, however, is the lack of trust outside of the aggregate. Within the local aggregate, individuals trust their colleagues to support them, not attributing blame in the event of error. Outside of the aggregate, however, it is perceived that blame is pervasive, and examples illustrate the ways in which blame can be moved between aggregate groups, something 2.1 calls *blame shift*.

2.8 ...or they go to their manager and say, 'can I do this?', 'Yeah' and then they put your name on it.

1.1 So, it's about trust again, isn't it? So what do you become labelled as? Trouble maker or innovator?

3.2 It depends on what the leadership's like, I guess

3.4 ...on the outcome.

Interestingly, this broadly described *culture of blame* was one that for some organisational members didn't seem to be linked, in reality, to repercussions for individuals. In a number of examples, participants described the widespread perception of ramifications, but the lack of ramification in reality.

This conversation between customer service managers, in rationalising the use of discretion in dealing with novel problems attempts to clarify this apparent contradiction.

2.4 The thing is, we put ourselves in that position because people are unable to make decisions. Why don't people make decisions? Because of the ramifications. What ramifications?

2.6 That's what I just said, who has actually lost their job in the past five years because of something like that?

In another example, however, the fear, however poorly founded from managers' perspectives, is tangible. In this exchange, there is a clarification about the source of ramification.

2.4 So we end up with a situation where people are frightened as [2.6] is just saying, there's a bit of fear there about what might be the ramifications. Which I can tell you, there won't be any, but, the point is that…

2.1 There won't be any from this level, and that's the fear. I mean, the people sitting around this table run a [customer service office] and get the customers out and sorted and happy, well, as happy as they can be, but I think there are still genuine fears that haven't been allayed about making those discretionary decisions.

The perception of blame as a consequence of knowledge development is an important limiter to knowledge sharing outside of the local aggregate.

8.2.1.5   Flows – Direction - Rhetoric

The distance between espoused theories and theories in use (Argyris and Schon 1996: 13) is apparent in participants' stories about permission and recognition for risk-taking. In myriad examples, participants describe the verbal encouragement for learning through work and of innovative approaches to work and their actual discouragement in practice.

Participants describe this distance as a barrier.	*1.5 …and there's a barrier. 'This is fantastic, this is wonderful, we think your ideas are all great'….* *1.1 …however, go away* *1.5 Yeah, we only go this far.*
The distance between rhetoric and reality is described as quashing any enthusiasm for novelty and innovation in problem solving and attempting to move emergent knowledge through the organisation.	*3.2 Like token support, like, 'Yeah, yeah, yeah, yeah, we support you, and as soon as you try and supply something then it's like, 'hang on, no. Get back in your box'.*
Participants link the rhetoric about exploration and risk-taking to the organisation's persistent requirement for consistency, recalling halcyon days when consistency was not the most important organisational priority.	*1.1 Do you remember when [this organisation] first started there was a phrase going around that it was better to seek forgiveness than permission [General comment, 'yeah']* *3.2 But we all know that that doesn't actually happen in practice* *3.4 That time has passed. That was the period of the thousand flowers blooming and we're now in a period of consistency!*
However it's not just rhetoric at higher levels in the hierarchy that is seen to be disruptive to flows of information and knowledge through the organisation, head office employees speak of the rhetoric from those working in operational roles in the organisation.	*1.2 …and all the offices are just saying, 'Yep, that's great, all's good' and they're doing what they want to do anyway.*

In the sense-making workshop participants attempted to work through issues of what was required of them organisationally and what was required of them individually and at local collective level, and described themselves as experts in rhetoric.

One participant drew on her interest in organisational learning theory in an attempt to summarise the issue.

3.1 …we have all of these issues about trying to do things differently and trying to capture innovation and we're supposed to be customer focused, we're supposed to be cost effective and really there's such a discrepancy, and we're supposed to practice shared behaviours, and there's such a discrepancy between all of that and what actually happens in practice, I think that we are experts at the rhetoric and the

1.1 So we have this rhetoric/reality gap?
3.1 Yes, the espoused theory versus practice, basically.

The property *rhetoric* of the category *direction* captures the gap between the organisation's official endorsement of learning through work and innovation and the actual discouragement of such activity. It points to the frustration organisational members feel with the formal organisation's lack of connection with localised activity and outcomes.

8.2.2   FLOWS - DISCONNECTION

The theme of *disconnection* emerged early in the first workshop as an *in vivo* term and dominated discussion in the sense-making workshop. The category is one visited by each of the three workshop groups and one which is linked closely to the other central themes around *localisation* and *local group identity*, *structure* and *consistency*, and the emotive group – *fear, repercussion*, and *frustration*.

Participant discussed disconnection in their narratives about *structure, measurement*, and *what we do with information*. These properties relate to the formal organisation, systematic evaluation of member behaviour and   patterns of behaviour around knowledge sharing.

The disconnect in the organisation is highlighted by this head office participant as a disruption in connections between aggregates.

1.2 And the connectivity that we have in the organisation is another interesting issue because of our magnitude. Is that while we, um, while we are good in [this business area] at sharing our experiences and stuff like that, you, at points, I find, and I don't know if anybody feels similar, you kind of feel like its falling on deaf ears.

At one stage the idea of cross level teams was discussed, participants pointing out that such teams didn't work though theoretically they were a great idea. The discussion highlighted the *tagging* of individuals within local environments sharing pressing problems and the difficulty faced in attempting to force connections across hierarchical levels.

2.1 We did try and start something in the area called 'a vertical slice' concept, sort of agenda, that had [people servicing customers] representing each [group] right through to the [manager of the area]. And it's interesting, out of all the meeting formats that we have, that is the one that has never got off the ground, bar the first two hook-ups.
(Researcher) Can you tell, do you know why? Have you…
2.1 I think there's a lot of work required to maintain that,
(Researcher) From what perspective?
2.1 Finding people who have the time to attend the hook-ups, because you are talking about staff who are actually on reception, um, and to be honest, I think, ooh, out on a limb, and off the record, I think some people think they're getting the right information from their sources now, and they don't need to go any further for it… And they're not necessarily getting the right information, but I think this vertical slice didn't go ahead because of the time, energy, um, finding everyone available in one day, um, and I think the other thing probably, and this is a personal opinion, I don't think they knew what to start on.
2.4 Well, I think that's the truth!

Not knowing what to start on, in this example, illustrates that knowledge is only important when it's needed, that manufacturing aggregate is not possible, but that aggregation occurs around a problem leading to the sharing and development of knowledge.

The organisation is designed to meet the needs of two main client groups, the policy developers with whom the organisation works in developing implementation strategy for policy and the customers to whom they deliver the services outlined in the policy.

Structure, for this organisation then, has a duality which participants describe as creating tension between ends of the organisation.

2.4 We run a risk, we're in that sort of middle ground between being a bureaucracy and having a customer focused organisation, so we end up, quite often, trying to play both ends off against the middle. And we're the middle. And so we often find ourselves.

The formal structure of the organisation is seen to interrupt the flow of knowledge through it. Participants describe the separation between levels within the hierarchy, and especially between head office and customer service areas of the organisation as relating to a lack of shared understanding of the others' issues. Importantly, it appears that the tendency of organisational members toward aggregation is confounded by this formal structure.

2.4 The learning and the information flows in that were targeted at - not at an interdependency basis - but rather more independently at the operational arm of the business, and that, that created, gee I could see it, I could see it, well, I've spoken to people about it, but the issue is, it's very, very difficult in this organisation to set up multidisciplinary teams for those reasons. There's totally separate structures. The interdependency we have at the [customer service] level is not mirrored, it is only at the ground that it's mirrored. It's not mirrored further up the organisation, it then very quickly silos, with business. The actual fact that we have business lines and business managers and clusters and this and that, generates a degree of that, breaking down those barriers, creating that learning environment, because there's a lot we can get pick up off each other, um, isn't going to come from the sort of structure we've got now, the sort of involvement we've got now.

For those working in customer service, the structure at head office is seen as irrelevant to their performance, frustrating to members' attempts to meet the pressing need of their complex environment.

2.4 I mean anyone who's worked in National recognises that siloing effect that you get. The one I love is, 'we own this segment of the business'. Well, no you don't we all do. And it really gripes me, I can't stand it, because they've got such a narrow focus. Such a stovepipe focus. That's all they do, so that's what they expect us to focus on all the time. You know, 'here's my barrow' but you've got four or five hundred different barrows.

Participants describe their attempts to overcome the structural barriers to their knowledge sharing, but display frustration with their attempts.

1.1 We always go in with the best intentions, we always build a great relationship with the [experts from the other business area] we do all that sort of stuff, we set the deadlines, we do the timetable we're always going to do it perfectly, and then they let us down. And it's not the person, necessarily, that we're dealing with, it's somebody that we have no influence over.

In some examples, participants stress the way in which the naturalistic formation of aggregate groups and their work together was appropriate and beneficial while outside interference diminished group performance.

1.1 ...It's the, it's exactly what [1.2] just described, it's the people just up the line who, or the client [organisation], or whoever they are external to the relationship that bugger it up.

In this 'happy' narrative a manager at head office describes how the structural interrupt was identified and targeted.

3.6 Over the last three or four years we've got a new leader every time, and I guess that's been the key to our survival, every time we get a new leader, we try and bring them over here and educate them in what we do and how we work, and that's sort of been one of the keys to our success and survival, is being able to ensure that there's a shared understanding.

Participants described the tension that exists between the requirements of the organisations client groups (policy departments) and the organisation's customers (recipients of policy initiatives). The formal structures that exist to support the client requirements for consistency encroach on the flexibility organisational members state they require to meet the individual and unpredictable needs of their client group.

8.2.2.2 Flows – Disconnection - Measurement

Possibly the clearest indicator of the organisation's focus on consistency is through the measures it utilises to oversee member behaviour and outcomes. Measurement of performance through key performance indicators and the comprehensive and complicated set of systems and processes that support them was a common theme in narrative and discussion that related to the disconnect between what the organisation requires and what individual members and their local aggregates require to operate within their environment.

Participants talked about their ability to problem solve within the local field, but their frustration with the measurement systems that punished this behaviour.

2.6 And, but you've also the underlying problem with that too, is, if you're um, if you're being, if your [quality assurance] stuff has been checked, you can't do that [create a novel solution to a local issue] that is no, in a lot of cases. The stuff that you would normally make a decision..., 'Oh, look, all right, I'll just put that through, and then I'll ring the customer and get that information, or I'll double check that or I'll send them a letter after I've paid them'. It's a no no, it's a no go, because of someone's interpretation of what they think they should be [quality checking] you on.

That people are only recognised for what can be measured is a pervasive theme. In this case agents' abilities within their context is not rewarded and the participant highlight the relationship between measurement and recognition.

2.1 But, there's no KPIs on that! And that's the thing. There are people who are signing the business contract, there's no KPI on how good our people are.

The focus for formal learning, too, is on what is measurable, participants describing the training they receive as focused on those attributes of performance identified by *the organisation* as important in maintaining consistency in operation.

3.1 About, when you're talking about the training of people in customer service centres we train them in how to basically meet the KPIs, all the technical stuff, and we make an awful lot of assumptions...

While the formal organisation values measurement against formal organisational goals as a feedback mechanism, participants described their important feedback as emanating from their immediate interaction with customers, coworkers and clients in an immediate and changing context. The disconnection between formal reward and localised reward resulted in lack of motivation for organisational members to highlighting the nature of their localised successes.

8.2.2.3   Flows – Disconnection - What we do with information

In stories that touch on flows of information and knowledge through the organisation, participants describe the varied inhibiters to information flow. For many participants information moves through the organisation in an idiosyncratic way as a result of too much data, too little time for taking in new information (and this is related to the urgency of their localised work environment), *glory seeking*, inaccuracy and lack of links to performance improvement.

Problems with information flow are not considered to be linked to lack of information, participants identifying the sources of information that are available for access, rather that their *real world* pressures limit their ability to actively access.

2.1 we have a system where if anything happens we have the national [information updates on system] so, I mean I tend to not go into them
2.2 You haven't got time...

The redundancy of information is illustrated by an administrator from head office concerned that the link between data, information and performance improvement is not made within the organisation.

3.3 ...data is like the cornerstone of you know, identifying learning opportunities and what you need to look at for performance improvement, because what we do with it, and at the moment we're collecting a whole range of data that we then just don't do anything with.

3.4 continues the discussion, highlighting the organisation's fascination with measuring and collecting data, but not applying the data to solving the problems that members face daily.

3.4 We get truck loads of data, and then we never do anything about it. We measure how bad the problem is and then we don't do anything to fix it.

In a more lengthy example, this participant tells of the inefficiency the disconnect between the operational areas of the organisation and support areas of the organisation causes in real terms.

3.4 One really good example of that is when we did some [feedback activities] for IT to look at the network's perception, um, someone complained about a workaround that meant that they had to key all [transactions of one kind] in twice. I mean, imagine how much work that is, in their office, that they'd been doing for 2 years and they thought it was about time there was a fix. And the IT people there said, the fix has been in for two years. You haven't heard about it. So, you know, and they're not the only ones. So you think of how many people are out there doing that. And that's one that is sort of an officially sanctioned [deleted] fix for a workaround. How many more are being created or going out there that we don't know that there's a better way to do it.

This point is highlighted continually, and is what 1.4 describes as '*Back to the 'we don't know what we don't know'* issue for the organisation.

There are problems, too, with the distance between priorities for those in head office and those in implementation areas of the organisation.

3.4 describes how at different times different aggregates attempt to communicate with other groups, but that the terrain that each operates within is different, and so the priorities for interaction differ.	*3.4 This is what I was talking about in terms of how some offices try and, try and escalate fixes and information that they've got and [central office] doesn't respond, because I've been on the end of trying to source a response, and there'll be some good reason, but it's, you know, just considered to be too much trouble to write the one or two pages that are needed to explain…*
Regardless of this disconnect participants at all levels identify with the goals of the organisation, at least intellectually.	*2.4 You know, and what they're forgetting about is that at the end of the day we're here for our customers.*

Yet aggregate groups are isolated from each other as a result of the differing contexts within which they attempt to survive and improve. It seems that this isolation means that aggregates are unconcerned, in their everyday behaviour, about the survival and improvement of other aggregates.

The *disconnection* apparent in these narratives, and discussed through stories about *structure*, *measurement* and *information sharing*, is critical to understandings of the interaction between the learning of individuals and collectives and the knowledge of the organisation.

8.3   CONCLUSION

The concepts *nonlinearity* and *flows* capture issues in narratives about opportunities for, and barriers to, learning and knowledge in this study. Participants' stories about their inability to predict the outcomes of their daily work as well as solutions to problems they may face are presented in terms of *nonlinearity*. This *nonlinearity* is contrasted with the organisation's construction of a *perfect world* which directly impacts on *flows* of knowledge through the organisation. Through these stories the nature of learning is highlighted as localised, adaptive and problem-focused. Knowledge is described as situated in the local context, emerging from the experiences of individuals and collectives through locally mediated shifts in understandings and protected from organisational censure.

In the following chapter narratives that relate to the impacts of *diversity, internal models* and *building blocks* on the learning and knowledge of participants in this study are presented.

9   FINDINGS – DIVERSITY AND INTERNAL MODELS, INCORPORATING BUILDING BLOCKS

Following on from the exploration of the concepts *aggregation*, *tagging*, *nonlinearity* and *flows*, this chapter focuses on features of the complex environment that both add to, and draw on, novelty and the emergence of knowledge in this organisational context. The concepts *diversity*, *internal models* and *building blocks* are used to make sense of participant narratives.

The three concepts presented here are less prominent in the findings than the four presented earlier. *Diversity* is shown to provide both a concept and a category with only one property identified, *internal models* incorporates discussion of *building blocks* as the concept is not well represented in the data. Discussion about this difference is available in the following chapters.

9.1   DIVERSITY

1.1   '... *yes, there is a synergy*

3.2   '...*that's around that diversity*'

Diversity arises from ongoing adaptation, and each adaptation gives rise to the opportunity for further change through new interactions and new niches in the system. A single agent will not have the aggregate properties or capabilities of a complex adaptive system, but the aggregation of diverse agents provides a distributed base. As a result of diversity and the filling of niches within the system, complex adaptive systems are '...characterised by perpetual novelty' (Waldrop 1994: 147).

Through narratives, participants describe the role of diversity in the survival of aggregates within the organisation as well as on the emergence of novelty. In particular, the ability of members to adjust within aggregate, assume roles or take on new characteristics to improve the aggregate's fitness is highlighted.

3.5 Yeah, most of our group who were there, well, not most, maybe half of our group had come from an IT background, systems support groups, and system testing areas and those sorts of things, and then there was two or three of us who came from a learning background. So, yeah, it had a strong IT focus and that's where, I guess, that's where we, all our original directions had gone, that's where we were going to be heading until we sat down and had this discussion and sort of challenged, well, why wouldn't we do these other things.

Importantly, too, participants told of innovation occurring through interaction of diverse agents, the diversity of the group seen as critical to the emergence of new and substantially different knowledge outcomes. This vignette from narrative workshop 3 captures the relationship between the diversity of the aggregate, its dynamic and the novel outcomes that emerge as a result of their interaction. 3.4 starts by describing a work team which was brought together to review a learning strategy within the organisation,

3.4 '…and it I guess it was also an unusual situation because the people who made up that team were all relatively new, but from a huge diverse range of backgrounds, so we had someone from another government department, for example, who'd been there when I got there, and I was the last one to get there, … I was there, not even from [this organization] but my previous experience had been in [an organization in commerce] the team leader at the time, the team leader there had been there the longest… and had a new business manager, and her background was HR, it wasn't actually learning, it was more the industrial relations type stuff. So, through a series of circumstances, you know, we had what appeared to be a huge amount of work to do, and lots, I guess, lots of different people and a lot of very different dynamics….and so we were able to really revolutionise, is a big word, but in [that part of the organization] it's pretty much what happened… a classic is the development now of what we call [a particular quality assurance process] which supposedly sits outside of learning, but is, in actual fact, is the same process that we use for our learning is now used for a business process of that, and just like our recruitment was also then going to start linking into what some of our expectations were, based on the outcomes that we'd identified from the learning. So there was just, you know, what started off, and what used to be a very isolated team on its own, the influence of the work that it had done had actually created this enormous sort of span outside of it. And within [the service areas] as well as within [the administrative core].

This example clearly illustrates the close relationship between diversity, innovation, learning and knowledge development within the aggregate and provides a rare example of the impact of the learning aggregate on the organisation's knowledge.

9.1.1   DIVERSITY - NOVELTY

The sense-making workshop group spent some time drilling down into the stories around diversity, comparing the contribution of diversity to innovation, with *blockers* and the relationship of those blockers to stagnation.

236

This excerpt from their discussion highlights the group's perception of diversity as important to novelty and to learning. The discussion begins from the group's discussion of a part of the metanarrative that relates to blocks to innovation and leads to discussion about the story provided in the vignette above.

3.2 ...which is interesting because I was just going to say that in the next story in (3.4) it's quite the opposite, where you didn't have the blockers and the, you know, the politics and stuff in the first story, second story talks about diversity and energy

3.1 yeah, I think it was...

3.4 that was actually more than one story

3.2 So when we have diversity and we don't have those barriers, it creates a ball of energy which leads to some really great things. So, I guess, that's the opposite of ...

1.1 revolutionise is a word in that story that I think is really powerful

3.2 ...everything else we've talked about

3.4 and also they had complementary skills,

1.1 yes, there is a synergy

3.2 that's around that diversity

The impact of freedom on innovation was discussed earlier in *Nonlinearity*, and here we also see the impact of diversity. After discussion of a learning experience that led to shifts in the organisation's knowledge this participant reinforces the former point and introduces the second.

(Researcher) What was it about that particular group, do you think, that made it so innovative?

3.6 OK, I guess we were, two things, we were given a clean slate we weren't bound by all the things that other people have talked about already in the constraints of the organisation, because, you know, I guess no one had a preconceived idea of where the thing should go or what it should do exactly. So, that was, I guess, an environmental benefit we had, the other thing was, we were all new to the sort of work it was going to do, none of us had any great preconceived ideas, we all had strong backgrounds in a particular area, some in IT development, programming, those sorts of things, some in IT support, some in learning, and various areas. We all had our own ideas of, 'Oh, we could do this, and we could do this,' I guess the diversity of background of the group, even though it was a, had a strong IT focus, they came from different backgrounds in IT and different directions…

Sometimes it is the novelty of a newcomer to the group that leads to novel outcomes. The added diversity created by the introduction of a naïve agent into the group is discussed on several occasions. In this example a participant recalls a time when she was working under some duress on what she considered a difficult project. A new member joined her and didn't understand the restrictions she perceived as limiting the success of the project.

3.3 And so, he came, this guy came up and I do remember the conversation, because I remember him saying, like with this really quizzical sort of, 'It's not rocket science,...' and that sort of change in thought... which led to new approaches to the project.

This newcomer's action in prompting reconsideration of the internal models restricting innovation is something a second participant in the narrative workshop responded to quite explicitly.

3.2 That's why I think it's interesting, comments about the [telephone service] environment when she went into is that people didn't, people came in from different backgrounds and in, as she said, a high stress situation, and people asked the same, 'but why?'.

Diversity is both a function and a product of the complexity of the organisation. Not only does the diversity of the population contribute to the continuity and coherence of the aggregate, but diversity contributes to adaptation that opens up possibility for further diversity.

9.2   INTERNAL MODELS (INCORPORATING BUILDING BLOCKS)

1.2 But you haven't had any negative feedback...

1.4 Yeah, which is good, because you always know when you haven't...

1.1 Yeah, you'll find out about it when you get it wrong.

Built to form filtering rules that agents apply in decision-making, *internal models* are a mechanism of complex adaptive systems and are used as an anticipatory device; these *internal models* comprise a set of inputs which includes: all possible action/decisions that agents are capable of taking, combined with all possible pairings of current and future states, and the concept of desired outcome or *fitness function* (Rhodes and MacKechnie 2003: 59). *Internal models* provide the complex adaptive system with an active ability to continually make predictions about its environment and act on that prediction. Indeed, Holland (1995: 31 - 34) assures us that every complex adaptive system builds models to anticipate the world . In the narratives provided by participants, strong internal models are evident in two main categories, *the normal confines* (defined as a tacit organisational internal model) and *the right thing* (tacit personal/collective internal model).

For Holland (1995: 34) *building blocks* are continuously revised and rearranged as complex adaptive systems gain experience. At one level, *building blocks* are the component parts of which internal models are built. Internal models may be deconstructed and their building blocks recombined to apply to new situations. At another level internal models become the building blocks of behaviour (Waldrop 1994: 169), and so on, so that each level of organisation becomes the building block of the next, ready to be tested, refined, and rearranged. This nesting hierarchy feature of complex adaptive systems is not identified in narratives, although the influence of internal models on learning and knowledge in the organisation was discussed quite broadly.

In the following example the participant describes a time that was ripe for learning with and through the work and the production of new knowledge that may have contributed to the organisation's knowledge but for the schema of a person in a position of power.

3.1 There was no room for anything else. So, he couldn't understand, didn't matter what we did, he couldn't understand what was being proposed, and he didn't see the value of it, and that makes life quite difficult...

Participants spoke, too, about their own internal models, in this case as a puzzle, and the ones that exist within their aggregate.

2.3 … and it was a real, like, Bam! That thing that I've been looking for, … Like I hadn't asked the right questions, or we'd been looking way too narrow, so yeah, that was a real, OK, now I can see that's the missing piece of the jigsaw puzzle.

Opportunities for collective learning are perceived to be related to the absence of restrictive internal models within aggregate members and the aggregate itself.

3.2 And because the blockers weren't there, there was no, 'Well, because we've always done it this way… because they weren't wedded to the past, and they weren't restrained by anyone else, it was just that free environment they were learning in.

Internal models are shown to exist within collectives and the organisation as well as within individuals. Participants spoke about their own internal models and the ones that exist within their aggregate.

9.2.1 INTERNAL MODELS - THE NORMAL CONFINES (TACIT ORGANISATIONAL)

Stories in this study do not separate the internal model from the whole - shifts in internal models are described as *reconceptualising, a new way of thinking*, and *letting go* and are spoken of within broader experiences of the individual and collective in maximising their fit with their work environment.

Organisational structures and processes may be seen as the organisation's internal models (structured as they are to assist the organisation to respond to its environment and assist in anticipation of future events). In this case, tacit organisational structures are illustrated as restricting *brain space*, as contrary to learning.

3.2 …one of the problems that 3.4 and I often talk about is how many ideas we actually have and how great things could be …but, because we're so busy, you know, trying to keep up with all the processes and you know, sign the right forms and you know have the right reports in on time and all that processy type stuff, we never have that brain space we keep talking about to actually do the innovative stuff, even though we probably are well positioned where we sit to actually be able to do that. So we never get to it, so it's one of those things that's almost a luxury, that it, you know, I'd really like to do that but I can't because this finance report's due or whatever.

Internal models assist the organisation to replicate outcomes, and in this organisation, the replication maintains priority over new learning and knowledge development.

3.2 …we don't actually focus on innovation and that's picked up in a number of these other stories, too, that we tend to do more of the same rather than to look at innovative or different ways of doing things to achieve the outcome.

The tacit imperatives of the organisation also reduce members' range of sensory experience by adding weight to organisational members' load.

Internal models are displayed in participants' discussion about unwritten rules in the organisation, the *ropes*, or perhaps the culture. Lakomski (2001: 73) develops the notion of culture as existing through the shared schema of connected members, in the collective mind of the organisation.

The internal models illustrated in narratives of these organisational members are tacit rules about the organisation which instruct organisational members indirectly.

As illustrated with reference to *flows*, the culture of the organisation is sometimes described as an inhibitor, characteristics of the culture ranging from blame to stealing others' ideas.

1.5   Well, there's not a particular person up there who says, 'You can't do this, ...', so isn't it more... I think it's more of a culture.

1.4   It's a culture, I think it is too.

3.4 We just don't invest in solutions

3.2 We don't ever see any surprises

1.1 It almost comes back to that, what I said before, about, we've made a mistake and...

3.2 and blame someone else

3.4 We can't fix it so we won't worry. Ignore it and it might go away.

1.1 that sounds like putting your head in the sand

3.4 ...or, or, the blame culture thing - find someone to pin it on... Or you might suggest an idea, or whatever, and put it in someone's mind and then they run with it, and get the recognition, which then, you think, I'm not going to bother any more.

In this example the participant describes culture within culture – the aggregate's culture (as explicitly stated) within the organisational culture, *the normal confines*.

3.6 That's sort of been one of the keys to our success and survival, is being able to ensure that there's a shared understanding, or a, of our culture, if you want to call it that, or on our philosophy on how we work and what we do and what we provide, um, because that without that we're sunk, basically. Because, we don't operate within the normal confines of the organisation.

Participants refer to the building of corporate memory through retention of organisational internal models.

1.2 We have an extensive corporate memory and we don't forget.

For these participants, the memory of the organisation is maintained through recruitment practices as well as by what Argyris and Schon (1996: 20) would refer to as 'single-loop' learning. Organisational members claim that the organisation protects itself from change by obstructing opportunities for innovative practice and schematic redefinition.

3.4 Or, they bring someone in from outside and people select people like themselves. So you just get more of the same culture.

1.1 So we just repeat the same . Well, can I then say that it's a cry for help that doesn't get heard, that, 'no, I'm not going to put my hand up and to be team leader, no I'm not going to put my hand up to be team leader, no I'm not going to put my hand up to be team leader' when you look at that, it's 'Shit, this being a team leader's rubbish and nobody should oughta do it' um, maybe there's a fundamental problem with the system, but we don't address that issue, we go, 'Oh, we need a team leader, you'll do.'

Tacit organisational models are illustrated in these narratives as restricting innovation and limiting the sharing of locally developed knowledge.

A result of the fixedness of organisational internal models from these participants' perspectives is that rather than the routine or process supporting organisational members to meet the need of their environment, often the impetus shifts to the organisational member to support the routine and make the system work.

In this way, the internal model of the organisation is seen to drive outcome, regardless of its fit with the environment.

3.4 It's people at the shop front who've got to link it and make it work and we don't count the cost to our people.

While the underlying internal models for organisational strategy remain unchallenged repetition is more common than innovation. Stories provide numerous descriptions of programs, practices and products that, though apparently ineffectual, are perpetuated within the organisation.

3.5 …and the program had been run in the [organisation] for, you know, under a thousand different names and whatever over about three or four years, and had never really been very successful.

Focusing on the organisation's internal models highlights important issues for knowledge development in this organisation. If internal models are not in contact with feedback, then opportunities for change are restricted. Lack of aggregate feedback resulting from disconnection between aggregates and aggregate levels mean that as an organisation participants comment that they, *Just recycle everything. We don't invent anything.* Invention, of course, is what participants talk about needing to do every day to deal with the novelty of their environment.

The tension that is articulated here is a function of the members' seemingly inherent need to maximise their own performance in their work context against the apparent constraints of the organisation's internal models. That the internal models do not shift as a result of feedback from the environment is a continuing issue of frustration for these organisational members.

Participants also describe the organisation's internal models as restricting critical perspectives on organisational strategy. Structures and systems developed over time and in response to past organisational need remain within the organisation and are entrenched in the organisation's ways of doing.

The notion that process should be challenged is problematic in this environment.

1.1 We seem to have said, 'Shit, we've committed resources, money, time, whatever into this and we've got to make it work, regardless', when, you know, it seems plain that, hang on, we've made a fundamental error here, and it's never going to fly. Let's cut our losses and accept that we, we got...

Letting go refers to the shifting of tacit as well as explicit personal and organisational internal models. The redefinition of internal models on both scales is described in participant stories about the development of organisational products and processes, and identified as problematic for both the organisation and its members.

3.2 ...because that was the right idea to do at the time, because that was going to be the be all and end all

1.1 Ok, but now that idea's proven to be not the right idea, why don't we just shelve [it]?

Indeed, letting go, or redefining internal models is illustrated as an emotionally disrupting process, frustrating and often lonely.

1.3 I'm also just at the point where you have to see that there are some things you can and can't do... and I really do feel just like I'm on my own at the moment.

For one participant, attempting to let go of her own framework was agonising.

> *1.2 ...and, um, you can only bang your head against a brick wall so many times before you're beaten and bloody and you just go, well, that's... I'm not prepared to die in a ditch over this one. And, and, but... when I first started here I would have and, but... when I first started here I would have. I would have, I would have been prepared to have somebody say to me, and say, and come to me and say, 'You need to let that one go, because you're just driving it to the wall, and it's not going to happen...'*

The organisation's internal models put pressure on organisational members to let go of their own internal models – both tacit and explicit. This redefinition is describes as uncomfortable and disruptive as opposed to participants descriptions of their adaptation in response to environmental feedback which was describes as necessary and organic.

9.2.2   INTERNAL MODELS - THE RIGHT THING (TACIT PERSONAL)

Many participants, particularly those working directly with customers, rely on their internal schema to predict *the right thing* in outcome. For people working with customers, this means using their own fairly simple rules to make decisions about the actions they take in meeting the need of customers.

Participants spoke about *the right thing* as if it were clear – if not to the organisation, at least to them, and often they acted on this internal schema in the absence of what they considered appropriate organisational rules.

> *2.4 We get ourselves bound up quite often in what we don't know, and not what we're allowed to do. There's a little bit about, if we don't know something, what are we allowed to do? Under the circumstances, what's the right thing to do? And quite often, what I say to people is, if it makes sense, it makes sense, if its logical, no one's going to beat you over the head for making a logical decision.*

Indeed, in many cases participants give priority to their internal sense of *the right thing* over the legislation that governs their interaction with customers. In this case the participant talks about maintaining focus on the customer.

2.1 ...making the right decision for a customer, whether or not it is in the legislation is irrelevant, but making the right decision for that customer based on their [particular circumstances].

The sense of acting according to a personal framework of what is right is not restricted to those working with customers. In head office participants spoke of attempting to solve problems for their internal customers, and of *the right thing* being about helping others, finding new ways and doing their jobs well.

3.2 ...whilst we try and do the right thing and doing our jobs and helping people and trying to find new ways to provide new resources for people, there's always that peer factor of, 'Well, what if I get it wrong? What if someone doesn't approve of what I'm trying to do? Or well, if I try something new, well who is going to be upset that I'm not doing it the way it's always been done.'

9.2.2.1   Internal models – The right thing - Good faith

Related to personal internal rule sets about *the right thing* is the theme *good faith*, the action related to following one's sense of the right thing. Acting on good faith is an interesting thread in narratives and stories describing situations where or innovating according to internal rules about *the right thing* leads to positive outcomes.

In this vignette, a participant describes working in a customer service area of the organisation where his sense of the right thing leads to innovations that are recognised and endorsed by the organisation.

2.4   There's a lot to be said here about learning about good faith. If you take action in good faith then you should be, that should be acknowledged. And I've had experiences of that myself. Very quick example, we did a bodgie in South Australia [detail deleted] and oh! Policy found out about it, and Nationals, and I got hauled in front of the [senior] manager in South Australia, me and [another manager], and he said, 'well, how much trouble do you think we're in?' and I said, 'Oh, not a lot, because I think I've got away around this.' And he said, 'Oh good. I'll do all the talking.' I said, 'All right'. He got about three words in and the [senior manager] said, 'Hang on, I want to hear what [2.4] has to say about this. And I said, 'Well, this was the best outcome for the customer'. Now, legal or not, I don't think we did anything harmful and there was no intent there to do anything wrong, so I think that we've acted in good faith and that's enough for me. And she said to Nationals, 'Well, I think that you should be acknowledging that this is quite an innovative solution. Incorrect though it was…' or something along those lines. She said it was an innovative way of approaching it, and in actual fact, the new legislation is going to cover these things anyway. So, we were just thinking ahead and trying to… and we tested a small groups of trustworthy customers that we figured there's not much risk, and what's the harm? If anything had gone wrong we could have just [solved it quite simply] anyway. So I figured, 'All right, I'm riding pretty close to the wind here, but I'll give it a bash'. Now, I never got in trouble for it, but I certainly got questioned and I was worried, I must admit there was a bit of sleep lost the night before about what the hell am I going to say…

This story highlights the opportunity, not only for learning through interaction with the environment, but also the opportunity for sharing the knowledge that arises from innovation. In this case, a problem encountered at the fringes of the organisation has important implications for legislation, as illustrated by the development of new legislation underway at the time. The lost opportunity for other knowledge developed at the edge of the organisation to inform policy is suggested by this vignette. The reluctance of organisational members to share their *bodgies* has implications for the relevance and speed of change of legislation to meet the need of the groups it aims to serve.

9.2.2.2   Internal models – The right thing - What I know

Highlighted in participant stories are apparent truths which guide the behaviour of individuals and the collectives with whom they interact. *What I know* refers to these fairly static sets of rules that are assumed to be stable over time and shift only in response to some stimulus or irritant. Participants provide some insight into the structure of their internal models, their stories illustrating these models as static, fixed, and changing abruptly in response to novelty, challenge or confrontation.

While Holland (1995: 33) describes the redefinition of internal models as critical to lookahead in changing environments, admitting that current models do not meet the need of the environment is described as unacceptable within this organisation.

2.2 ...this organisation is not good at allowing staff to say something like 'I don't know how to do that'.

For these participants, the inability to admit their lack of knowledge means that the organisation is unable to predict gaps in the knowledge it holds. As a result participants feel that the organisation is unable to respond to its own unanticipated needs or those of its clients.

1.2 ...we know what we know, we know what we don't know and then we don't know what we don't know and it's the don't know what we don't know bit, and the integration and coordination of all that stuff is, we are so phenomenally bad at!

Participant stories offer examples of the structure of internal models, their disruption and reconfiguration within context. Internal models are shown to be held at individual, collective and organisational levels, although the relationship between the levels is not clear. Individual mental models are not shown to be building blocks of organisational internal models, rather that individual and collective truths and personal rules affect local behaviour. The contribution of these individual and local models to the organisation's schema as participants described it is not clear.

9.3   CONCLUSIONS ON FINDINGS

The properties and mechanisms of complex adaptive systems emerged from narratives of learning and knowledge development in this organisational context. Participant discussion about the nature of localised groups learning and sharing knowledge through their engagement in work found new language in *aggregation* and *tagging*, the problems with 'organisational knowledge' and of developing knowledge more broadly in the organisation was addressed in discussion of *nonlinearity* and *flows*; and the features that contribute to creativity and new knowledge are discussed alongside those that limit creativity through *diversity* and *internal models*.

Although presented separately, the six concepts can be seen in the preceding chapters to be interrelated, each impacting on the other, each contributing to understandings of the other, and consideration of each leading to contemplation on the others. The use of the complex adaptive system heuristic guides attention to aspects of organisation, learning and knowledge that allow for new insights into their emergence and connection. Holland's (1995) complex adaptive systems model, while resonant with the findings and useful in making sense of the data, is not perfectly aligned to the lived experience of the participants in this study. Discussion about the ways in which this experience relates to complexity and the use of the heuristic are discussed in some detail in the following chapters.

10 DISCUSSION AND IMPLICATIONS

Inherent to the research question *What is the relationship between workplace learning experience and organisational knowledge?* are two major queries; first, *What are the workplace learning experiences of participants?* and second, *What is the relationship between these experiences and organisational knowledge?* In this chapter the first query is addressed under the heading 'Workplace learning experience', the second and the integration of the two parts in the research question, under the heading 'Toward a holistic model'.

The transcendent themes which emerge from participant narratives in this study suggest a complex adaptive systems framework. This framework, in turn, is coherent with the three major threads around which organisational learning and knowledge management converge. These central themes: Individual and collective learning and knowledge; knowledge portrayed as complex, situated and active; and disruption of mental models, adaptation and generative learning, are gathered together under complexity. Its language and conceptual base are put to use in their discussion and analysis.

In attempting to present a connected discussion, this chapter progresses through each of the major themes identified in the review of the literature, drawing on the critical application of complexity metaphors to workplace learning experience and comparing findings with knowledge management, organisational learning and workplace learning theory.

The chapter then goes on to relate these experiences to their perceived impact on organisational knowledge. Complexity provides a language for the discussion of learning and knowledge within one frame and an opportunity to develop an integrated model of learning and knowledge in organisations.

It is important to note that this study derives its findings from the participant descriptions of their experience through narrative and that this narrative is constructed within organisational and cultural discourses which frame and to some extent form them.

10.1 WORKPLACE LEARNING EXPERIENCE

Holland's model provides ' ...a new, active, grammar... to facilitate the analysis of those complex relations which exist within the passive constructs of management and organization' (Collins 2000: 12), a useful yet too simplistic a frame for a complete discussion of findings in this study. Holland's grammar is insufficient as, while it illuminates some aspects of learning and knowledge in this organisation, it obscures others from view.

The findings of this research suggest a deep structure (Haggis 2005) aligned with complexity, but it is important that this deep structure neither blinds the researcher to the diversity of the organisation's individuals nor reduces the rich interconnectedness of their experience to neat categories. While the categories of complex adaptive systems theory provide novel insights into aspects of organisational experience, they do not sit cleanly and separately – they are interwoven. This chapter discusses this problematic and attempts to provide a perspective in which the complexity of experience is explored in a more holistic way.

10.1.1 EXPERIENCE AND THEORY

The workplace learning experiences of this study's participants highlight issues around the social nature of learning, its emergence through individual and collective engagement with a changing and challenging environment, and the iterative development of knowledge through myriad interactions with diverse others. Participants' narratives, too, underline the processes through which they learn to cope with the challenges of the work environment through their identification of, and selective interaction with, entities that could support their success. Their stories tell of the ways in which this selective interaction contributes to the success of the collective rather than the success of the organisation because of interruptions in the flow of knowledge between groups. The mechanisms for sharing across boundaries are described as limited by individual as well as organisational structures and schema, participants pointing to the need for structures to be broken down and recombined in response to contextual change.

These experiences are richly suggestive not only of the properties and mechanisms of complex adaptive systems (Holland 1995) but also of major themes across the literatures. Resonance is clear in the relationship between the theme of individual and collective learning and knowledge and the concepts that emerged from the findings around aggregation and tagging. Similarly, consideration of knowledge as complex, situated and active aligns with the findings, particularly those categorized under nonlinearity and flows. The third major theme, disruption of mental models, adaptation and generative learning (or emergent learning) is mirrored in the findings categorized in internal models, diversity and building blocks.

When approached in interaction rather than in separate categories these themes link with, and provide an opportunity for, integration of theoretical perspectives described in contemporary workplace learning, organisational learning and knowledge management literatures (for example, Fenwick 2001; Winch and Ingram 2002; Vera and Crossan 2003; Fenwick and Tennant 2004; Field 2004).

10.1.2   INDIVIDUAL AND COLLECTIVE LEARNING AND KNOWLEDGE

Attention to the relationship between the individual and the collective is central to the tenets of complexity. From a complexity perspective, the individual is irreducible from the collective; the individual and the collective are each a single learning entity. The focus in complexity is on the patterns that emerge from the collectivity of interaction of individual agents – that is, in complexity the individual and the collective are not discrete, rather, the individual and the collective are at once formed and forming, being and becoming. The unit of analysis for learning is unclear when individual and collective are indiscrete and learning emerges from, and contributes to, the dynamic interaction of the two.

Collective behaviour emerges from the interaction of agents – the learning of the collective not reducible to the learning of any individual agent nor a collection of individually learning agents, rather to the collectivity of the learning that occurs in interactivity. Backstrom's (2004: 466) definition of collective learning as '...rather enduring changes in a collective as a result of interaction between the collective and its context', captures a notion of collective learning concomitant with complexity although the findings of this study suggest that its separation of collective and context is inappropriate.

Figure 5 Individual and Collective

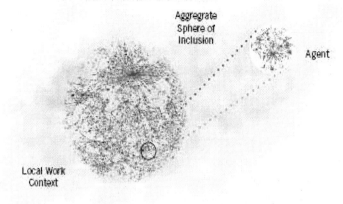

The model above (see figure 5) illustrates the individual and collective as co-emerging in their interconnection in context, each formed by and forming the collective within the work context. It highlights the nature of aggregation as the clustering of interaction and stresses the ways in which the interaction is imbued with contextuality. Individual, aggregate and context are irreducible from their web of interaction, learning and knowledge intricately caught up in the patterns of relationships in which they at once draw on and contribute to each other.

10.1.2.1 Individuals learn with and from those in their local aggregate.

Complex adaptive systems are, above all else, learning systems. The learning that occurs in such systems does so in response to adaptation to contextual change and in struggles to improve fitness within the local landscape. Stacey (2003a) states that patterns of meaning develop through iterated interaction occurring in the *local* interaction between people; the localisation is important as it allows the agents to be sufficiently connected to one another.

In this study the experiences of the participants clearly illustrate the localised nature of learning in interaction with their local colleagues and their shared environment. In complex systems agents act only in response to information within '…their immediate environment, from the few agents connected to them in a feedback loop' (Anderson 1999: 222) and as a result, continually evolving niches are formed from local adaptation. For Cohen, Burkhart et al (1995: 1) it is the ways through which '…individuals and local interests assert themselves at the expense of more global and organisational concerns ('the diversity of 'fitness' forces')' that is important in understanding tension between emergent organisation and behaviour and formal organisation.

This understanding promotes a focus on learning in a specific environment, within a specific time and with specific others. This situated learning view is developed through social learning theories in which learning is recognised to be '…grounded in interaction, activity and practice in everyday organisational life and work' (Visser 2005: 211).

It is this local interaction where each agent receives inputs from only a few others within the local environment which leads to the somewhat isolated local neighbourhoods (Anderson 1999: 220) described by participants as their learning and knowledge sharing *spheres of inclusion*. The feedback loops reinforce (or extinguish) approaches and behaviours depending on their suitability to the local environment, leading to adaptation at the local level.

This phenomenon poses a crucial issue for the organisation as a whole and links with the theme *disconnect* visited below. At the same time it highlights issues around validation of knowledge. What is clear in this study as in others (for example, Brookfield 1985), however, is regardless of how the resultant knowledge may be adopted and used, agents learn through interaction within local settings. As Visser (2005: 211) states, 'learning and knowing are viewed in terms of behavioural interaction at the level of context and relationship'.

The participants in this study describe their involvement in communities of practice that develop in their common locale, interests and work problems. Lave and

Wenger's work on communities of practice (Lave and Wenger 1991; Wenger, McDermott et al. 2002; Snyder, Wenger et al. 2004; Wenger 2004)has brought this notion of learning embedded in practice and interaction to the fore, maintaining that learning is embedded not in the head of the individual but in their active engagement in the situation and the community of practice.

The findings of this study are supported by Lave and Wenger's assertion that learning occurs through access to and engagement with competent others in a practising community. Like their study of apprenticeship (Lave and Wenger 1991) this current study puts the emphasis on the development of new knowledge as a result of this engagement. The creation of knowledge is prominent in narratives although the distribution of knowledge within aggregate is also highlighted.

This research highlights the localised, connected networks of members within which the individual learns, but through which both the individual and collective emerges and acts. In this study knowledge grows from experimentation and problem-solving within which the divide between individual and collective is blurred. It is the distinction between the individual learner and the community in Lave and Wenger's work which differentiates it, if not in substance, at least in nuance, from the findings of this current study. Lave and Wenger's (2000: 171) use of the term community as '...participation in an activity system about which participants share understandings concerning what they are doing and what that means in their lives and for their communities' does not quite capture the experience of those in this study. In Lave and Wenger's work focus is placed on participation in a collective whereas this research reveals the construction of collective, simultaneously creating and being created by engagement with others in context as central to experiences of learning and knowledge. Lave and Wenger's use implies a collection of learning individuals while this study places emphasis on their complex interconnection.

10.1.2.2 Individuals tag others for interaction on the basis of locality and shared experience

In this study aggregates are not hierarchically determined or limited, membership is multi-level and aggregates exist at all levels. Boundary formation around aggregates is not related to organisational level or role, rather to situation and experience. Interaction is purposeful and selective, creating conditions in which specialisation and cooperation are fostered. Participants told of their preferred interaction with those in their local environment who have shared understandings of *the right thing*, a similar level of commitment to the work and philosophy of the organisation and capacity to share useful information to support the participant's success in the environment.

The selection of others with shared understandings, however, is not unproblematic, there is not a direct relationship between the selection of others with similar values and approaches and learning – again, the individual and aggregate is at once formed and forming. The aggregate develops amongst itself, through its interaction, a shared meaning around *the right thing* and commitment to work and this in turn impacts on each individual's tagging of others in the aggregate. Concerns about self-perpetuating action and limits to learning are valid in environments where diversity is constrained and feedback continues to support restricted practice and selection. From a complexity perspective, adaptation requires sufficient diversity (Holland 1995: 27) and this may take the form of differing schematic sets or the introduction of novelty to the context. In the narratives offered in this study, the context provided ceaselessly novel conditions which contributed to the continual adaptation of aggregates and their generation of new knowledge.

Localisation is a prominent theme in discussions about selective interaction and this prominence is reflected in a range of studies on information sharing and knowledge development in organisations. For example, in a study of knowledge sharing using information and communication technologies Ackerman, Pipek et al. (2003) find that technologies are secondary to the networks created through facilitation of physical contact between experts. Similarly Cross, Parker et al. (2001) find that personal connections are by far the preferred source of knowledge for immunologists in their study, and as cited above, Lave and Wenger's (1991) work on communities of practice similarly finds that individuals in common work contexts are bound by their work roles and informal relationships.

These studies highlight issues of connection between members and their perceived trustworthiness as knowledge sources, but also provide insight into the role of others' willingness to become involved in problem solving and the generation of new knowledge. These factors are reflected in the findings of this study, however, for these participants the factors blended within one of locality.

This study highlights the ways in which localisation provides for this personal connection. Localisation facilitates the individual's knowledge about the trustworthiness of knowledge sources and the capacity for problem solving in the agent's context. Localisation also enables accessibility and increases the connectivity between agents which is critical to learning. Anderson and McMillan (2003: 35) stress that individuals are attracted to others within their vicinity when they require help on a task. The increased connectivity that localisation provides contributes to the interactivity of agents in the context which in turn facilitates learning and adaptation.

The increased interconnectivity that arises from tagging for locality reflects what Anderson (1999: 225) describes as 'A fundamental aspect of complex adaptive systems' pointing to their characteristic allowance of '...local behavior to generate global characteristics that then alter the way agents interact'. In this study Anderson's assertion only partially holds. While the global behaviours described by participants as emerging from their local interaction do appear to alter their local behaviour, they do not, except in some notable examples, appear to contribute to changing behaviours throughout the organisation.

The boundaries formed by tagging for locality and experience were described by participants in their analysis of narratives as *sphere of inclusion*. This boundary is marked and the language used to discriminate between those within and those outside of the aggregate boundary is clear. Participants articulated how the boundaries are drawn focusing particularly on locality but also recognizing skills, work experience (in the *real world*), and immediate context problem solving capacity.

There is a tension inherent in this *sphere of inclusion* which was articulated in the analysis phases of the research. The *sphere of inclusion* is predominantly localised (as discussed above) and yet, for many members, concern for the organisation, its goals and vision is simultaneously a tag for selective interaction. That is, for some members, selection of others with whom to interact locally is dependent on their own and others' concern for, and commitment to, the organisation's mission. Participants reduce this dissonance through their shared understanding of *the right thing*, basing local action on their local construction of appropriate organisational behaviour.

10.1.2.3 *Learning and knowledge are seen as both individual and collective*

References to their learning as individual members and in collectivity are interchangeable for participants in this study. Participants do not delineate between personal shifts in understanding or changes in behaviour and those of the collective when they discuss their learning. The connectivity of the individual within the collective is illustrated by the stories of learning which show a seamlessness – the collective learning through, from and with each other in their iterative interaction in the work environment.

The comment, *What you learn flows into us* is a delightful illustration of participants' recognition of 'the learner' as both individual and aggregate – 'you' as a learning entity, 'us' as a learning entity. Davis and Sumara's (2001: 92) work in school organisations supports this finding. In a long term study the authors noted a shift in a community group's development within which, 'This emergent habit of talking about themselves as much in terms of 'us' as 'me' highlights the human capacity to float somewhere between individual and collective identification'. The current study, challenges this statement, highlighting instead the human capacity to exist not just between the two, but simultaneously as both.

The findings of this study sit comfortably with Stacey's (2003a) reflections on learning as an activity of interdependent people. For Stacey, the mind is not an internal world which holds representations of the real world within a bounded space (the head), it is, rather, a web of interactions within which the iterative development of patterns of meaning emerge (Stacey 2003b: 356). This perspective resonates in some regard with the work of Lakomski (2001), her focus, though, on the lack of boundary between 'private knowledge' and 'public culture'. While the current study and the work of Stacey illustrate a relationship between the individual and collective in *learning* and *knowing*, Lakomski highlights the relationship between the individual and collective in *culture* and its influence on learning. Her work is discussed with reference to internal models below.

Collectivity in learning is illustrated as central to experiences of learning and knowledge in this study, and this is supported in many ways by Weick's (2001) insights into the collective mind. For Weick (2001: 267), the collective mind is located in the process of interrelating and provides a 'transindividual' quality in learning. In Weick's account, however, the shifting schema of individuals is not represented in the comprehension of the collective mind, and the collective precedes the individual mind. This perspective aligns with the thoughts of Vygotsky (1962).

This study suggests, rather, that the collectivity is not *between* individuals or that the collectivity *precedes* the individual, rather that the two exist in the present through the interactivity of people who are closely connected. The findings of this study are better represented by Spender's (1996: 71) statement,

> '...learning at the collective level is the outcome of the interplay between the conscious and automatic types of knowledge, and between the individual and collective types of knowledge as they interact through the social processes of the collective'.

Michel Foucault (1984) in his deliberation on external space states that

> '... we do not live in a kind of void, inside of which we could place individuals and things. We do not live inside a void that could be colored with diverse shades of light, we live inside a set of relations that delineates sites which are irreducible to one another and absolutely not superimposable on one another'.

This reflection has strong resonance with the findings of this study and to the precepts of complexity. For these participants, 'sites' of learning are in the web of interactions that make up their experience and they are at once individual and collective.

10.1.2.4 The aggregate self-organises to increase payoff

That learning emerges from struggles to maintain effectiveness in ever-changing environments is a central theme in this study. Individuals and self-organised groups respond to local conditions and restructure their thinking and behaviour in response to feedback from their work and their workplace.

In a complex adapting context each individual acts on local information to increase payoff (or fitness function) and, because each agent's attempts to increase payoff impacts on the attempts of each other agent in the environment, complex behaviour emerges. Anderson and McMillan (2003: 34) describe this group level, adaptive behaviour as emergent from an '...appropriate set of feedback, interindividual interactions, and proximate mechanisms'. In what Kurtz and Snowden (2003: 467) describe as 'human patterns of complexity', properties emerging from interaction include groupthink, rumour, internal conflict, and ambiguity.

The properties that emerge from the groups' self-organisation in this study also include innovations in technique and process including workarounds, individual and group protection, support and maintenance strategies and behaviours, commitment, cohesiveness and group consciousness, each of which contributes to the pursuit of fitness. The self-organising groups exemplified in this study come together in response to a pressing issue or workplace problem and take action collectively to resolve it.

The coherent, collective action that occurs within aggregates self-organises without direction in the experience of these participants. This finding is in accord with Anderson and McMillan's (2003: 34) assertion that '...a simple individual-level rule generates an adaptive group-level functional unit – the team – without any hint of explicit coordination, direction, or command and control'. Indeed, attempts at direction are seen as limiting to group behaviour.

Direction and control are consistently linked with frustration while group autonomy, permission to explore and freedom to make mistakes all link with the emergence of adaptive and in many cases high-performing groups. Similarly, outcomes emerge from group interaction rather than from any formalized plans or goals. Several stories told of the emergence at the edge of *bubbling chaos* of extremely high powered aggregates who make important, even *revolutionary* impacts on the group (and in some cases on the organisation). In these narratives there appears a pattern of complex behaviour that Kauffman (1995) describes in reference to selective advantage of complex adapting systems. These narratives highlight self-organising groups working in crisis where small changes have great impacts, in Anderson's (1999: 224) words, when '…small changes in behaviour lead to wildly different fitness levels (as occurs in chaotic environments) systems can reach extraordinary fitness peaks but cannot remain on them'. Morel and Ramanujam (1999: 283) underline the role of connectivity in their reflections on this phenomenon of self-organisation, stating that '…when the connectivity is allowed to increase, these systems can display self-organizing behavior before becoming chaotic'.

This characteristic of complexity is evident in participants' discussion of the group consuming vast amounts energy in learning and innovating in its environment, then being unable to maintain itself, *self-destructing* as the fitness environment shifted. Anderson describes this kind of phenomenon as the type which allows systems to leap ahead to higher fitness levels rather than the slower route of 'evolutionary refinement' (Anderson 1999: 224).

The notion of fitness function for these participants is difficult to define. Rhodes and MacKechnie (2003: 67) suggest that defining the content of fitness function is '…secondary to specifying the agents' processes of defining fitness and then acting based on that definition'. In examples of action based on a collective understanding of *cutting it* in the customer service context, fitness means doing *the right thing* for the customer. In many examples this leads to behaviour that is at odds with the formal rules of the organisation. *The right thing* was developed by participants from their understanding of the underlying principles of the formal rules coupled with their experience of the work and of life.

Participants in this study use these self-developed definitions to substantiate practice that is in defiance of formalized organisational rules and processes, drawing on the collective to protect the deviant on the basis of a shared understanding of *the right thing*. Fenwick and Tennant (2004: 63) cite the work of Gold et al. (2000) in their analysis of the development of collective constructions of 'good' and 'right', emphasizing the role of language in determining what the community defines as truth and reality. While participants do not explicitly refer to language as a contributing feature in the development of collective understandings in this study, the theory offers insight into the relationship between the collective definition of *the right thing* and *real world* and the collective's self-protection.

In the peaky fitness landscape of this study site, fitness function is about working to maximise positive outcomes in interactions with both internal and external customers. In these interactions agents act to attract positive feedback and minimize negative feedback. This can be seen in examples of participants innovating to solve immediate problems to satisfy customers with whom they interact and hiding this behaviour from *'the organisation'* from which feedback may be negative.

10.1.2.5 *Aggregates self-organise to support, stretch and protect the aggregate*

An emergent property of the communicative interaction of individuals in aggregate is the aggregate's support, motivation and protection of individuals and the aggregate itself. A very strong theme in collected narratives, this finding is supported by recent learning theory (Fenwick and Tennant 2004; Field 2004). This feature of learning aggregates is at once an opportunity for important learning that can contribute to the organisation's adaptation within its environment as well as a site for development of deviant, destructive and oppressive schema and practices.

The positive aspects of this self-organisation are presented in narratives in this study, participants discussing the ways in which innovation emerges from participants' support of each other and aggregate behaviour that protects individuals and the aggregate itself from organisational censure. Participants also described the ways in which members within aggregates support each other with their knowledge or assistance in problem solving, how they encourage one another to make decisions and try new innovations, and how individual members learn new skills and assume new roles to meet the need of the aggregate.

However, a number of stories highlight innovative solutions to pressing issues that remain localised as a result of protection. Participants recognise this activity as one which obscures deviant behaviour from scrutiny outside of the aggregate. Field (2004:

212) describes the phenomenon as well known in the psychoanalytical literature, citing '…ample evidence that groups with common interests have an unconscious tendency to preserve and protect themselves'. The strength of this unofficial underlying ideology (or shadow theme (Stacey 2003b)) emerges from the connectedness of the aggregate and has important implications for learning and knowledge sharing in the organisation.

Fenwick acknowledges the emergent properties of highly connected aggregates (2001: 7; Fenwick and Tennant 2004: 67) highlighting the difficulties that may accompany them, stating that '…problematic knowledge may become authoritative through continuous reinforcement in social learning processes and resistant to change' (2001: 7). This links to identified issues around the construction of *the right thing*, and in this study, the organisation's concern would be with the emergence of patterns of behaviour that Blackman and Henderson (2005: 158) call the development of a community of poor or inappropriate practice .

Learning is reinforced at the local level without any other check than that which supports or extinguishes adaptation at the local level – feedback taking the form of responses in the local environment. While success at the local level leads to the aggregate's adaptation to the immediate environment, there is no apparent parallel feedback mechanisms to support learning at higher levels of organisation. This means that learning and adaptation support aggregate outcomes, but there is no clear link to organisational outcomes.

This problem is recognised in critical literature (Billett 2001; Bella, King et al. 2003). The concern in such work is that learning reinforced within the local environment and passed to newcomers to the environment may indeed be problematic knowledge that is continuously reinforced and resistant to change. Bella, King, et al.'s concern is with emergence of systematic distortion of information, where individual behaviours that lead to distortion do not stand out as abnormal. If such distortions were self-harming they would not persist, but these distortions can be seen as beneficial, and so sustain and promote behaviours within aggregate. Self-correction, as a result, is not observed.

In this current study the vast weight of discussion is around the effectiveness of localised learning in facilitating the adaptation of local aggregates to meet the need of their context. Hill (2004: 227) talks about this 'grassroots' knowledge as 'fugitive', '...generated by common folks who understood that meaning was complex, conflicted, and ambiguous' and characterized by its situatedness and production in specific social, temporal and cultural context. The validity of this knowledge for group performance and survival is underlined in Hill's work as it is by the participants of the current study.

For Blackman and Henderson the concern resides with the *system's* inability to validate appropriate knowledge under such conditions. In their words (2005: 163), 'There will be a much greater focus on constructed development and the importance of sharing, but no checks and balances to ensure that relationships do not take over all aspects of the KMS [knowledge management system]'. In this study, however, validation is provided by the local relationships, any validation external to the relationship irrelevant if it does not contribute to the local fitness of the collective.

Authors such as Fenwick (2001: 7) offer additional criticism of the nature of self-organising groups, suggesting that their tendency to '... conserve, protect, and recycle their knowledge' limits the aggregate's ability to challenge and extend their knowledge. These participants did talk about conserving and protecting their knowledge, but their focus is on its invention rather than its recycling in most cases. There are examples of local knowledge being recycled (regardless of its correctness from an organisational perspective) uncritically, but more frequent are examples of critical appraisal of situations and the information and knowledge available to the aggregate for problem solution.

Occasionally, though, participants' comments hinted at their recognition of the negative outcomes of their protective behaviours. Members lamented the difficulty in opening up the aggregate to disclose deviant behaviour.

The concern of theorists and of this study's participants alike again points to the epistemological issue about the very nature of knowledge and its validity. Who defines deviant? Who decrees validity? In communities of practice, 'peers in the execution of real work' (Cavaleri 2004: 166) determine what is true and valid, evaluating as a community what is reliable and works well over time.

Using complexity to help make sense of this issue, both recycling and invention may be seen as emerging from interaction – positive feedback loops which reward effectiveness in the local context derive from interactions with other organisational members as well as from success in meeting the need of others within the environment. The uptake of new knowledge or the recycling of old depends on the ability of each to meet the need of the individual agent in producing appropriate outcomes within the context.

In Holland's (1995) complexity the role of positive feedback is '*the* fundamental issue' (Waldrop 1994: 180) in the learning that results from the agents interaction with others and the environment. Given this fundamental then behaviour which is not reinforced through feedback from context it will be extinguished. The learnt behaviour must be seen as beneficial to performance within the fitness landscape to persist. In this study, the feedback from the immediate context leads to the creation of new knowledge where a problem is novel in the experience of the aggregate. On the other hand, where others within the localised environment have experience of the problem their knowledge is (largely) uncritically recycled. In cases where more than one individual in the area has knowledge to support a solution the aggregate offers a range of options to the individual who then works with the problem, the context, the aggregate and their own schema to act.

10.1.3   KNOWLEDGE IS COMPLEX, SITUATED AND ACTIVE

The nature of knowledge as an emergent property of the iterative interaction of agents in context is highlighted in learning and knowledge management literatures which are influenced by or draw on complexity theories. In this study, the role of the individual and collective learner in the development of knowledge through engagement with work is highlighted. The situated nature of the knowledge emerging from this engagement and its local production in localised activity of organisational members' nonlinear dynamics is similarly important. The tension that this emergence creates in the formal organisation which is focused on client (that is, policy developer) requirements for consistency leads to frustration for members, lack of sharing outside of the aggregate, and protection of the aggregate.

Figure 6 Knowledge is Complex, Situated and Active

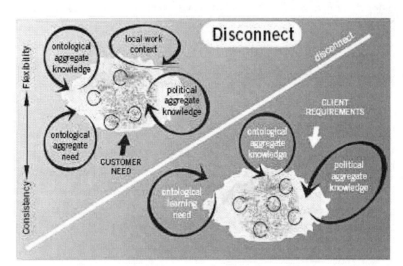

These features of knowledge as outlined in the experience of this study's participants are illustrated in the model above (see Figure 6). The tensions inherent in this experience at the intersection between policy and delivery (Halligan 2004: 149) leading to learning from ontological and political interest (Field 2004) and creating a disconnect between emergent and organisationally sanctioned knowledge.

10.1.3.1 Learning emerges from engagement with work

Learning in this study directs focus to the information, tasks, rules and structures that define participants' work role as well as the colleagues, clients and customers with whom they engage in social and organisationally driven communication.

In this study narratives show learning to occur *through* the work that participants do, learning embedded in the work, a result of iterative interaction with the aggregate, the organisation and the context (Fenwick 2001). This finding accords with the work of Marsick and Watkins (1999) which shows that the learning during informal practice when members have the opportunity to listen, question, practice, check, and reflect on their work far outweighs the contribution of formalized learning programs. This concept of learning *through* work shifts focus from traditional perspectives of workplace learning on learning *at* work, in which the location of the learning is prominent and the nature of learning seen as separable from context; learning *to* work, in which individualised, skills based training remains in the fore of a utilitarian understanding; and learning *for* work, in which the technical-economic interests of the employer dominate.

In contrast to these traditional approaches to workplace learning, the findings of this study highlight the interconnectedness of learner and context and prioritise the creation of knowledge through engagement and action. The findings reflect what Fenwick (2001; 2004; Fenwick and Tennant 2004) refers to as embodied co-emergence, the situated, inventive, self-modifying interconnective learning that occurs through interaction and which intricately entwines learner and context.

10.1.3.2 Learning emerges from nonlinear dynamics

Nonlinearity features in every understanding of complexity (as illustrated in the literature review) and is essential in differentiating complexity perspectives from Cartesian ones. Understanding the interconnectedness of agents and contexts, their interdependence, and the influence of nonlinear interactions is critical in better understanding the learning that occurs as a result. It is critical, too, in understanding the impact this learning has on the organisation.

In this study the learning aggregate and the environment can be said to be coevolving, the interaction between the two creating shifts in each. As discussed in the findings, there is some difficulty here defining the boundary between the aggregate and the environment as the two are mutually constructing and changing, '...context is not a separate background for any particular system such as an individual actor' (Fenwick 2003: 148). The findings illustrate the complex relationship between participants and context that results in their learning. Each actor can be seen as coevolving with the structures that emerge from the learning of other actors, the influence of others in the environment creating opportunities for learning and adaptation (Allen and Strathern 2003: 31).

The phenomenon of the co-emergence of learner and context through their interaction is not new. Dewey, in 1933 (in Elkjaer 2004: 420), wrote of the mutual formation of the individual and the environment through the interaction of individuals with each other their context. Recently in learning literatures (for example, Elkjaer 2004; Fenwick 2004; Visser 2005) greater emphasis is placed on the ways in which cognition, identity and context emerge together through learning.

In this study, participants spoke meaningfully about the complexity of their work and working life and the result this has on their learning. A strong theme in the narratives, these organisational members described their attempts to maintain effectiveness in an environment in which *every day is different*. The eternally novel experiences that result from the dynamics of their work and environment means that members are often unable to accurately predict outcomes or apply set solutions to complex problems.

10.1.3.3 *Formal structures interfere with flows between levels of aggregation*

As discussed above, some aggregate constructions of appropriate behaviour are recognised within the aggregate as deviant and this recognition interrupts flows between organisational entities, particularly between local aggregate and other aggregates within the organisation. It is at this point that the findings of this study diverge markedly from complex adaptive systems theory as defined by Holland (1995).

A central finding in this study is that aggregation does not build hierarchy. Participants spoke at length about aggregate learning and their localised sharing of knowledge, but the emergence of a knowledge hierarchy which self-organises through higher levels of aggregation is not apparent. This finding challenges the direct application of complex adaptive systems theory to human organisations.

That aggregates 'nest' is important property of complex adaptive systems. In the words of Davis and Sumara (2001: 91),

> *'Complex systems might be described as nested. Individuals come together into flexible clusters, clusters come together into larger clusters, and so on. At each level, more global purposes emerge that affect the overall project and individual activities alike'.*

The nature of aggregation in complexity leads to the development of hierarchies, the organic organisation of individuals and aggregates who self-organise, each aggregate a building block in the next level of aggregation, a phenomenon described in the organisational learning literatures as 'ladders of aggregation' (Argyris and Schon 1996: 26).

Cilliers (2005 in his introduction to Simon's (1962) paper) points out that complex systems are not *simply* hierarchical systems, not neatly nested, but 'cross-cutting'. He states, however, that in complexity, the less important cross-cutting interactions are limited enough to allow approximations of hierarchy to become apparent.

In this study, however, the nested nature of aggregation is not demonstrated, even approximately. Adaptation occurs at the local aggregate level but is limited in its contribution to organisational adaptation. Anderson (1999: 228) describes adaptation as '... the passage of an organization through an endless series of organizational microstates that emerge from local interactions among agents trying to improve their local payoffs'. However, the aggregation occurring at the local level in this study is not mirrored at higher levels, participants describing the self-protection of the individual and the aggregate as limiting the formation of higher levels of aggregation.

Narratives abound in this study, too, about the *disconnect* between the local aggregate and the formal hierarchy of the organisation. Lave and Wenger's (1991) work adds credence to this finding, suggesting that the contradictory forces that place the organisation's core at odds with the members' working, learning and innovating drive learning communities to hide the insights gained through their work from the broader organisation (Brown and Duguid 2000: 158).

For the participants in this current study, the use of pronouns reflects an important disconnect within the learning context. Participants used the pronoun *us* in relation to the local aggregate and *them* as *the organisation*. Regardless of the position of the participant in the organisation, *the organisation* was discussed as though it had its own identity set aside from that of the individual or the aggregate.

The described interrupts to the flow of knowledge through the organisation are a result of the preferred behaviour of individuals working in aggregate. Their assumptions about the deviance of noncanonical knowledge (Brown and Duguid 2000: 147), that is, knowledge not supplied as 'official' knowledge or endorsed by the organisation, limits the aggregate's ability to cluster at higher levels of aggregation.

Feedback loops again emerge as important to the learning aggregate's context – positive feedback from the immediate context reinforcing innovation and problem solving which increases local fitness is set against negative feedback loops from the formal organisation for the same behaviour. The formal organisation, with its focus on organisational purpose, task and its role in the larger community supports a technical-economic interest which leads to formal processes targeted to productivity and consistency based on a formalised understanding of the organisational context. What this interest does not account for is the individual, localised, changeable, contextually influenced interactions of the individuals carrying out the tasks.

Recent work (Field 2004) sheds light on the nature of the learning occurring in these local aggregates as a result of these differing feedback loops. On one hand, the aggregate shows learning from what Field (2004: 212) calls 'ontological interest', shared interest group learning which supports self-protection, security and reduction of anxiety. This learning is prompted by the threat of changing environments and expectations and scaffolds adaptation and continuity of the local aggregate. The ontological interest can be seen in the learning that emerges from aggregate struggles to keep innovations and deviance close, create boundaries around membership and build social supports to assist members to make sense of *frantic palaver* and absorb failure.

Field (2004: 208) also discusses 'political interest', referring to Habermas in his contention that '…considerable knowledge and learning result from efforts to avoid becoming hemmed in by such things as bureaucracy, institutions and the financial market'. It is this political interest learning that can be seen to emerge from the aggregate's response to organisational feedback in the technical-economic (Field 2004: 201) interest. The learning that emerges from the political interest of these local aggregates is evident in their innovations and workarounds. Their hoarding of locally developed knowledge, their breaking of rules, and their operating as if they were autonomous groups illustrates these participants' attempts to reduce the tension between organisational imperatives and immediate local ones.

Learning and adaptation, then, occur at the local aggregate level in response to feedback from the work environment in support of both the ontological and political interests of the aggregate. In the first instance, learning occurs in response to interaction with a changing work context in which individuals work collectively to ensure their survival, improving their fitness in carrying out the work of the aggregate and protecting themselves from the assaults of ambiguity and uncertainty. They do so through interaction with the organisation in which individuals strive to protect themselves from censure, gain recognition for themselves and their aggregate. In the second instance, learning occurs through political interest in which the aggregate strives for autonomy and power over their work, attempting to gain advantage over organisational constraints in order to effectively meet the demands of their work life.

This finding illustrates the complexity of the relationship between the formal organisation and the emergent organisation. Learning is shown to occur continually, emerging from the context and interactions with it, however, it can also be seen to be limited to the immediate context. The formal organisation creates an environment within which organic emergence of organisation cannot take place. In this case, the formal constraints act as a block to flow across the emergent organisation.

The findings of this study are supported by Beesley's (2004) assertion that 'Organizations themselves do not learn *per se*' and that '...organizations contain static (rules, norms and procedures) and dynamic (social relationships), elements that mutually influence the degree to which knowledge is acquired and utilized in organizational settings...', however her statement that '...learning occurs *within* those who constitute their membership' (emphasis added) is at odds with these findings. In this case, static and dynamic elements mediate learning, but learning is not confined to individual members, rather learning emerges from and takes place in individual engagement and interaction in collective and in context.

The emergent themes in this study of *diversity* and *internal models* are coherent with important debates in theories of workplace and organisational learning, and those of knowledge management. In Holland's (1995) work, internal models are central to notions of learning, '*All* complex, adaptive systems – economies, minds, organisms, build models that allow them to anticipate the world' (Waldrop 1994: 177).

In this research, however, learning cannot be seen to be unproblematically attributable to expanding cognitive models. Learning is illustrated, rather, as emerging from myriad influences and linked to the whole, interactive learner (whether this be individual or collective) within a context and time.

Figure 7 Disruption of Mental Models, Adaptation and Generative Learning

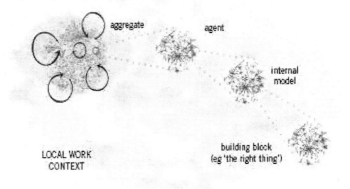

The model above (see Figure 7) illustrates the relationship between aggregate, agent, internal model and building block through interconnection and context. It prompts consideration of internal models as connections, composed in the individual and collective, patterns of networks emerging from immersion and engagement in the work context. The model highlights the role of feedback as influencing connections and interactions and impacting on the emergence of aggregate properties.

10.1.4.1 Learning includes but is not defined by recombining building blocks in individual mental models

Waldrop (1994: 179), from his complexity perspective, finds cognition to be simple, learning purely centred on cognitive shifts through recombination of mental models,

> *This was Darwin's great insight, that an agent can improve its internal models without any paranormal guidance whatsoever. It simply has to try the models out, see how well their predictions work in the real world, and – if it survives the experience- adjust the models to do better next time…In biology, of course, the agents are individual organisms, the feedback is provided by natural selection, and the steady improvement of the models is called evolution. But in cognition, the process is essentially the same: the agents are individual minds, the feedback comes from teachers and direct experience and the improvement is called learning'.*

Simple and fundamental as it may appear to Waldrop, however, shifting mental models alone cannot account for the idiosyncratic nature of learning through work described in this study, the limitations imposed by structural, social, emotional and political influences and the intricate entwinement of individual and collective. This is not to say that the individual, with its behaviour guided by a cognitive structure that evolves over time, does not exist. It is, however, the connectedness of agents where the behaviour of one impacting on the behaviour of others leads to nonlinearity and the emergence of patterns across the collective. It is this interdependency that leads to aggregate evolution and change.

With a notable exception where a participant spoke of a manager's need to *shift his mental model*, participants did not speak of mental models as though they are stable, exist aside from context or within an individual alone – the concept is a lot messier. The narratives of these participants describe shifting internal models in terms of the shifts in meaning that emerge from exploration, interaction, novelty, surprise and even naivety. Waldrop's (1994) cited representation of the role of mental models in learning aligns with a cognitivist perspective in education, where learning is seen to be the individual's acquisition of ever more accurate maps of the way of the world. The findings of this study contrast sharply with such narrow constructions of learning and knowledge, and yet mental models do emerge as a clear theme.

The notion of internal models presented in narrative sits closely with Maturana and Varela's construction of mental processing as one of 'bringing forth a world' (1992: 11), actively engaging in continual mental reconstruction resulting from interaction with context. These narratives similarly highlight the context of the shift but unlike Maturana and Varela's construction they also present the mental processing as something not entirely personal and individual. For these participants learning is both about individual mental processing as well as about social and relational being. Participants describe learning as *a holistic thing* and recognise shifting internal models to be a part of the complexity of learning.

Using complexity as a lens, participants can be seen to be using their own sets of rules to make decisions and to improve their effectiveness in their role and aggregate and from this learning emerges. Anderson and McMillan (2003: 34) would concur with this interpretation, finding that '...individuals make their own simple decisions using information garnered from the local environment, or through signals and interactions among individuals'.

The right thing provides a clear example of the relatively simple rules from which complex behaviour emerges (Holland 1995: 7). Participants working in customer service using this rule for action (which would vary between participants as a result of their diverse experience) and through their interaction produce a range of complex behaviours at the aggregate level as described above. Particularly obvious in this example is collective protective behaviour.

Similarly, the improvisation apparent in the actions of organisational members illustrates shifting mental models. The continuous process of reconstructing processes and designs, altering, revising, creating solutions and discovering new opportunities for improvement are obvious in these narratives and accord with Weick's (2001) discussion of sense-making in organisations.

Mezirow (1990) uses 'frame of reference' or 'habits of mind' in much the same way that Holland uses 'internal models'. Mezirow describes reflection on experience in relation to these frames of reference leading to expansion and transformation of meaning and in creation of new knowledge that complement existing frames of reference. In each case, learning occurs through the recombination of the building blocks of mental models or habits of mind in response to interaction within a given context.

Adjustment of mental models occurs as a result of *reflection* on learning to identify and correct distortions in content, process or premise, through discourse and through action in Mezirow's (1990) theory of adult learning. In this study, however, participants did not refer at any stage to reflection in their narratives of learning experience and this is perhaps due to their interactive practice. In a 2004 study of CEOs, Sherlock and Nathan (2004) found that CEOs related their reflective practice to a lack of peers in the organisation with whom to engage. In this study, all participants spoke of their communicative practice, their access to peers and others. Even so, the lack of explicit reference is surprising given the weight of literature on reflective practice (for example, Argyris and Schon 1978; Kolb 1983; Mezirow 1990; Fook 2004).

This absence links to a gap in findings in relation to Holland's (1995) *building blocks* mechanism. In this study, participants discussed shifts in understanding occurring *in* the action or interaction, rather than through *reflection on* the experience. In this way, the findings of this study provide a different perspective on adult learning than that which has some support in the literatures and leaves a gap in understanding the internal, individual processes of adjustment to mental models described by Holland (1995).

The messiness of the relationship between shifting mental models and learning in aggregate prompts questions about assumptions of organisational learning. Akgun, Lynn et al. (2003: 842), for example, discuss learning at both individual and organisational levels as changes in states of knowledge – in particular, '...as changes in knowledge structures or schemas' and Schein (1999: 168) asserts that organisational learning requires 'cognitive redefinition'. Lakomski (2001: 69) develops discussion of the role of internal models in organisational learning through her 'neural net account' of organisational cognition and learning. The findings of this study as described above, however, suggest that shifting individual and aggregate mental models do not necessarily (and in fact do rarely) contribute to the development of organisationally held schematic sets.

Schein and Lakomski's work leads to a notion in which organisational culture can be seen as the organisation's mental model, a view that roots organisational culture in cognitivist perspectives. Literature abounds, however, on the problematic nature of organisational culture – its emergence through negotiation between the organisation and its members, its embeddedness and resistance to change, its fragmented nature such that organisations are said to have multiple cultures as well as subcultures (Burnes 1992). It seems that organisational schematic sets share similar attributes to those at individual and collective levels.

Developments in cognitive science add another dimension to the conceptualization of mental models and their role in learning. Gonczi (2004: 19) describes patterns as being stored not in the mind, but of the mind interacting with the environment to produce appropriate patterns, that is, patterns sit within the environment and our brains act intelligently to make sense of the patterns. Others, (Lakomski 2001) use connectionist or cognitive network theories to explain shifts in understanding, stating that the patterns of activation in neural nets are stored for reference and reconstructed in response to new information. These new perspectives provide some clues to the nature of the individual and context in interaction and hint at the emergence of collective learning, its social nature or contextual influences on its emergence.

10.1.4.2 Aggregate diversity and importing naivety support learning

Diversity is mentioned quite infrequently relative to other important themes in this study. However, when participants did tell of experiences in which diversity or naivety feature, these narratives tell of great learning, innovation or generative change within the work unit (and occasionally in the organisation more widely).

The role of novelty in reconstructing schema in stressed in the work of Anderson (1999: 225),

'... complex adaptive systems can evolve when new agents or new schemata are introduced. They may be drawn from a pool of candidates outside the systems, or they can be generated by recombining elements of existing agents or schemata' and that '... recombination [is] a fundamental requisite for adaptation on rugged fitness landscapes'.

Diversity as also a critical feature in the transformation of systems, Stacey explaining that in order for systems to move spontaneously from one attractor to another there must be sufficient heterogeneity in the agents and the system as well as in their interactions(2003b: 375). In his words,

'Transformation is possible only when the entities, their interactions with each other and their interaction with entities in the system's environment are sufficiently heterogenous, that is sufficiently diverse'.

This view is supported by Holland (1995: 29), who points to the nature of adaptation as at once drawing on, and contributing to, the diversity of the system.

In several narratives that related instances of diversity leading to important learning for the individual or aggregate participants spoke of tension and energy resulting from the diversity. For Stacey (2003b: 376) it is the miscommunication and misunderstanding in the interactions of diverse groups that leads to their transformation, the work of each in trying to understand the other leading to substantially new knowledge.

This understanding of diversity points to an important role for naivety in learning and innovation. In this study naivety emerges alongside diversity as a factor in shifts in the understanding of participants which leads to radical change in practice. Using Stacey's theory, these naïve agents in the new environment lack the language of the environment that allows them to interact using a shared vocabulary. As a result of the imperfect cross-over from one environment to the other, misunderstanding results and leads to new understanding for both the naïve newcomer and expert in the environment.

It is not merely the diversity within the aggregate that contributes to adaptation, however, and this study illustrates the impact of diverse interactions with other contextual actors. The diversity of the work environment within which these aggregates struggle to perform features prominently in narratives. Stories illustrate clearly how diverse and changing environments lead to the adaptation of the aggregate – an important finding from learning and organisational knowledge point of view and one which stimulates discussion about the relationship between work and learning.

10.1.4.3 Learning and innovation are closely linked

When participants spoke about their learning they often used the terms learning and innovation in close association. Importantly, when participants offered examples of times when their learning contributed to broader organisational knowledge they described instances of innovation. The focus on generation of new knowledge as an outcome of learning through work offers a critical link between learning and knowledge that adds strength to the potential synergy between learning and knowledge approaches in organisations.

Chakravarthy, McEvily et al (2003) describe all knowledge accumulation as learning. This study, however, suggests that 'accumulation' is too narrow a defining feature of learning and that the innovation that is a product of participants' engagement with work directs focus to the creativity involved in learning. It is held that innovation is risky, '...unpredictable...', often long term, labor intensive, idiosyncratic and often require substantial human capital investments' (Holstrom 1989 in Foss and Mahnke 2003: 86), however, in this study, innovation is portrayed as an everyday feature of survival within a changing context.

10.1.4.4 Learning is also about generating knowledge

The linking of learning and innovation in this study contributes a different perspective to understandings of organisational learning to that presented in the literature review. In Elkjaer's (2004) discussion of metaphors for organisational learning *acquisition*, *participation* and *the third way* (in which learning situated in organisational dynamics is highlighted) are presented are primary perspectives. This study, however, suggests that it is *generation* which is prominent in discussion of organisational learning. Perspectives on acquisition, participation, and *generation* situated with organisational dynamics presents a more complete view of learning in this organisation.

The traditional understanding of learning as acquisition in both adult learning and organisational learning discourses puts focus on the '...individual, and particularly that person's conscious, rational activities of perceiving, interpreting, categorizing and storing knowledge' (Fenwick and Tennant 2004: 57), what Ford and Ogilvie (in Huzzard 2004) describe as a systems-structural view. While criticized in both streams of literature for this 'mentalist' focus and its lack of attention to social, cultural and political influences on learning, acquisition of knowledge does emerge as a theme in the findings of this study. This is not to say that such cognitive constructions are sufficient in explaining the findings of the study, merely that acquisition does emerge as a feature of the learning of these participants.

It is the conception of knowledge as stable and additive in this acquisitionist perspective (discussed in Elkjaer 2004; Fenwick and Tennant 2004) where the point of divergence from this study lies. Indeed, organisational members did speak of their individual learning within aggregate and the resultant changes in their own schema which contributes to the usable knowledge of the collective. Acquisition of knowledge theories, however, suggest that knowledge is a definite, substantial and stable thing. A core finding in this study, however, is that knowledge is rather something that grows from the interactivity of the group in its environment, constructed within the aggregate through interactivity of entities and context and retained, shared, utilized and *discarded* in response to feedback from the context. In this way learning as acquisition can be seen as a *part* of a dynamic and complex system of learning and knowledge rather than a defining feature.

Theories of learning as participation more closely reflect the experiences of the participants in this study but, again, fail to completely explain the findings. Aligned with the findings, participation theories focus on the learning that occurs in everyday life and work through participation in communities of practice, theories which move the focus from learning as intellectual shifts in the minds of individuals to learning as rooted in the situation in which the individual participates (Fenwick 2001). Such theories put the focus on meaning creation through action (Spender 1996) and in these theories learning is seen as contextual and relational, inventive and embedded in action. The difference lies, however, in participation's emphasis on the individual and collective as separate entities and the delineation of learner and context. The recognition of the adjustment of individual and collective schema in this study is also an important diversion from mainstream discussion of participation.

In Elkjaer's (2004) *third way* of understanding organisational learning, acquisition is recognised as a feature of organisational learning and participation is reiterated as part of the experience of iterative transaction and mutual adjustment of the individual and the environment. Her interest, as stated above, is on the situated experiences of participants emerging in context which is at once evolving in response to as well as contributing to changes in the environment. This study, however, also places emphasis on the generation of new knowledge as a result of iterative interaction of dynamic aggregates in practice grounded in uncertainty (Spender 2006: 15). Outcomes from this nonlinear interaction increase the fitness of the aggregate and are reinforced within the aggregate.

In this way learning centres around the generation of knowledge within the collective which is active and dynamic, formed in doing and forming the context, emerging from interaction, misunderstanding and an environment of flux.

10.1.5   CONCLUSIONS ON WORKPLACE LEARNING EXPERIENCE

The discussion about experiences of workplace learning above draws out the ways in which the experience of participants in this study corresponds to theories of learning, knowledge management and complexity. In short, the learning experiences of the participants in this study are self-organising, individual as well as collective, they draw on diversity, and emerge through the nonlinearity and interactivity of practice.

The experience of these organisational members offers some fresh perspectives to theory available in contemporary literatures, particularly on the relationship between the individual and collective, the situated nature of the emergent knowledge, the disconnect between formal and emergent organisation, the role of mental models in learning, and the focus on innovation in learning.

The following discusses the interaction of these learning experiences with the knowledge of the organisation, finding problems with theoretical constructions of 'organisational learning' as well as with the management of knowledge.

10.2   TOWARD A HOLISTIC MODEL

The first part of this chapter discusses the findings of this research in their relationship to the complex adaptive systems metaphor and to major themes in the learning and knowledge management literatures. While the preceding discussion is occupied with investigating the learning that occurs in the experience of these participants, the chapter now goes on to highlight the problematic nature of the contribution of that learning to organisational knowledge.

Developing the discussion about learning through work, the following posits a shift toward learning as a more complex and iterative relationship between organisational members, their work and their interactions in context. This shift draws attention away from an emphasis on teleological, instrumental perspectives and directed approaches to learning. It acknowledges issues around assumptions of predictive causality, communicative interaction, ladders of aggregation and, ultimately, the problematic conceptualization of 'organisation' and its relationship to learning.

Progress in this section is through discussion of the relationship between learning and organisational knowledge, to the use of the complexity metaphor in making sense of these findings. It continues on to the ways in which the heuristic use of complexity metaphors may have obfuscated other important issues in the experience of participants.

10.2.1   LEARNING EXPERIENCE AND ORGANISATIONAL KNOWLEDGE

Narratives collected here suggest that while this organisation reflects features of complex adapting phenomena it cannot be described as a complex adaptive system. In Morel and Ramanujam's words (1999: 284) '...the organisational structure is an emergent property resulting from the interactions of many adaptive agents' – in complex adaptive systems organisation emerges from the interactions of adaptive agents and context. In this study, however, organisation is seen to emerge from the interactions of adaptive agents engaged in the work of the organisation in local aggregates, and yet, *the organisation* does not.

A key finding in this research is that the formal organisation constricts the emergence of organisation. This finding contributes not only to the understanding of this organisation, but also to assumptions inherent in the application of complex adaptive systems theory to organisations. The aims, processes, rules and 'ropes' of the formal organisation effectively disrupt the nesting of hierarchies and flows across connectors in the emergent organisation.

In this organisation, learning is an integral part of workplace experience, but the technological-economic focus of the organisation creates tension in which consistency and member autonomy compete. This tension manifests itself in extremely limited opportunities for organisational knowledge to grow from the learning of organisational members.

Related to this outcome is the problematic nature of knowledge management. Knowledge is valued by organisational members for its emergence and situation within the immediate problem-solving context. Its validation by aggregate members for its usefulness and verisimilitude within the local and temporal context is particularly important. Knowledge thus defined is difficult to manage, even at the local level. The notion that it might be captured for organisational consumption in support of consistency is problematic given the findings of this study.

Problems of organisational learning and of knowledge management are identified in the narratives of the participants, the interweaving reasons given for the problem illustrated below following Bella, King et al. (2003). The model (see Figure 8) is designed to illustrate the connectedness of the issues described, reflecting the interconnection between major themes in the research and underlining the relationships between experiences of learning and knowledge in this organisational context.

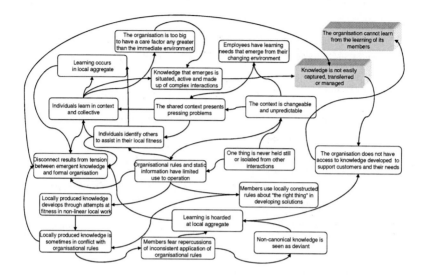

Figure 8 Connecting experiences of learning and knowledge in the organisation

(following Bella 1987 in Bella, King et al. (2003)). Start anywhere in the diagram and read forward or backward along arrows, saying 'therefore' when moving forward and 'because' when moving backward. Moving forward and backward along the loops of the entire sketch provides a sense of the whole.

10.2.1.1 The learning individual, the learning collective and the organisation

A critical finding in this study was that the construction of meaning around the term *the organisation* was problematic. The term was used by members in each of the narrative groups to represent the structures and rules that direct their behaviour rather than to describe any network of human beings. The relationship between individual members, their collectivity and *the organisation* is discussed below at some length as it is a crucial to the research question.

The clear delineation between the organic learning aggregate and the purposive construction which was continually referred to as *the organisation* or *head office* is defined in this study as a *disconnect*. The lack of segregation between the individual and the learning

285

collective at the local level is not reflected at the next level of aggregation, between collective and *the organisation*. In this study *the organisation* includes any level beyond the self-organising local aggregate level. Critten (2003: 17) describes the link between individual and organisational learning as elusive, and this elusiveness is reflected in this study as it is in the literature.

Gioia and Sims' (1986: 7) state that:

> *'Given the nature of organisations as socially constructed entities, and the nature of individuals as socially immersed and influenced, the lines defining what is an individual phenomenon and what is an organisational phenomenon are very blurred indeed.'*

In contrast to Gioia and Sims this study shows delineation of *the organisation* from the individual and collective to be quite clear. The findings of this study, however, show the lines defining what is individual and what is local collective to be blurred, indeed there is much blurring between what is individual, collective or contextual.

Field (2004: 201) speaks of 'shared-interest-group learning' in clarification of organisational learning, and it is a term which may well be used to describe the learning articulated in narratives in this study. The shared-interest-group is a far more useful unit of analysis for the learning that occurs in this organisation than is the organisational level, stories consistently relating the experiences of members and their predominantly localised interactions with known others in solving immediate and pressing problems. Scarbrough, Bresnen et al. (2004: 492) also identify this phenomenon in their study of project work. Their preamble '...suggesting a sharp contrast between the abundant generation of learning *within* projects and the more limited prospects for the diffusion of such learning *across* the wider organisational context (Ayas and Zeniuk, 2001)' (emphases in original).

Spender's (1996: 64) assertion that '...organisations and individuals are clearly not functionally equivalent...Organisations are artefacts, constructed for a purpose. Individuals are not' leads to some consideration of the formal and the informal, emergent properties of organisation. While Spender's focus is on the relationship between the individual and the organisational, and his contention is that organisations can indeed learn, know and memorise through a collective mind, his distinction here is an important one. The structure of formal organisation is purposive, the emergence of collective is self-organising and undirected. The contrast between the two in this study leads to rifts in the knowledge base of the organisation.

In other work, Stacey (2003a: 326), looking to overcome the dualism evident between individual and organisational in learning and organisational literatures, suggests that a paradox exists within which '…individual and group/organisation are aspects of the same process of interaction between people'. This study supports the view of individual and group in such a light, however, where Stacey describes the group and organisation as existing in the same process, the participants in this study clearly distinguish between the individual/collective and the organisation. The findings of this study suggest that rather than the individual and group/organisation being aspects of the same process between individuals, the individual and group are aspects of the same process of interaction between people while the organisation is a structural constraint on the development of processes of interaction between these groups.

The findings clearly illustrate the dynamic of the aggregate and the emergent properties that result from its interactions. Yet, they just as clearly highlight the boundaries around the aggregate and the blocks to flow created by the aggregate's self-protection and inability to cluster at the next level of aggregation to build learning hierarchies. The delineation of organisational entities points to the limitations of knowledge development and sharing that emerge from agents' interaction with context.

The delineation reveals limits to this organisation's ability to know all that its members know; that is, the membership of this organisation can know more than the organisation can access. To extend Snowden's (2006) take on Polanyi's (1967) words, not only can we know more than we can say and say more than we can write down, we can also know more collectively than we do organisationally.

Participants in this study cite organisational structures and processes as the root of the *disconnect* between collective and organisation. Their narratives describe the magnitude of difficulty engendered by the organisation's requirement for consistency driven by policy and the organisational members' requirement for flexibility driven by their engagement in the organisational context.

The relationship between the learning individual, the learning collective and the organisation is shown in this study to be difficult. Firstly, the notion of organisation is problematic, representing a purposive structure disconnected from the activity of the local aggregate. Secondly, the seeming boundarilessness between the individual, collective and context is juxtaposed against the clear delineation between aggregate and organisation, and thirdly, this disconnect between the two is shown to cleave the knowledge flows of the organisation.

10.2.1.2 Consistency, autonomy, and knowledge

In many of the collected narratives, the organisation's expectations are illustrated as at odds with participants' drive to maintain fitness in their work environment. This theme is developed in analysis to reflect a tension between the *policy end* of the organisation and its *operational end*, a tension inherent in the role of organisations of this type (Halligan 2004: 152). Organisational members attempting to implement policy, or to support those who do, spoke of their need for flexibility in meeting the needs of their work. Flexibility is a contemporaneous theme in organisational and workplace learning literatures as well as knowledge management discourse (for example, Fenwick 2001; Koopmans 2005). Underpinning the discussion is a deeper issue which again resonates with arguments about the nature of knowledge.

Organisational rules, processes and rituals which reify consistency are bound up with a notion of knowledge as fixed, verifiable and rooted in truth. Within this notion there is a presumption that knowledge remains stable and is discrete from context. The assumption is also made that there is a clear and direct relationship between cause and effect which leads to the application of specific, stable knowledge in every instance in which a certain phenomenon is displayed. This assumption allows for consistent solution to standard problems apparent in the work.

For the participants of this study, however, knowledge is not about some authoritative description of reality and truth so much as it is constructed in the doing, constructed in the collective, dependent on context and continually changing. Participants are unable to predict the conditions that present in their work day and find that official knowledge provided on the assumption of linear processes is unable to assist them in improving their fitness in these contexts. Assumptions of consistency and predictive causality are inappropriate where nonlinearity features. In these cases, autonomy is said to be critical to participants' ability to perform.

A lack of shared understanding about what constitutes effective performance in this organisation leads to the dislocation of local aggregate from the formal organisation and indeed from other levels of aggregation that could emerge from the clustering of local aggregates. Through complexity, it should not be surprising that this phenomenon was described in each of the narrative groups regardless of the member's role in the organisation. For each group issues of autonomy, permission, tolerance of error and experimentation were cited as crucial to their capacity to learn and perform effectively, and for each organisational rules and processes were seen to constrain their effectiveness. These concerns are common regardless of whether the group is delivering services to customers or developing strategies for the implementation of policy. In all groups the conditions of complexity hold – the interactions between members and context are nonlinear and lead to novel, unpredictable outcomes for which they require flexibility.

10.2.1.3 *The technological-economic interest and learning through work*

This study shows learning occurring continuously in small clusters throughout the organisation to be poorly recognised, unsupported, largely unvalued, even discouraged. The work itself provides a significant and fruitful learning space and does indeed produce great knowledge outcomes for individuals and collectives. This learning space, however, is underutilized in this organisation – work treated as separate from both the worker and learning, formal and directed learning and knowledge systems and processes imposed upon organisational members with the goal of providing consistency in performance.

Of course, the organisation is focused on delivering training and information to members which supports its technological and economic (and in the case of this public sector organisation) (big P) Political aims. Managers' imperatives dominate and this leads to functional perspectives of learning and knowledge (Koopmans 2005). The technical-economic interest of the organisation drives the workplace learning and knowledge management systems. In this organisation that drive leads to formal in-situ or training room training and on-line knowledge management tools.

The technical-economic interest of the organisation, however, can be served by the learning that takes place through engagement with work. Participants provided numerous accounts of the serendipitous learning that has the technical-economic/Political interest of the organisation at its core. Abundant examples were offered of individuals expending generous amounts energy through their work to solve problems and find innovative approaches to improve effectiveness and in so doing develop valuable knowledge.

What is also apparent, however, is that is not just the technical-economic/Political interest of the organisation that is served by learning through work. As Field (2004) suggests, shared-interest group learning occurs at ontological and (small p) political levels as well. The learning that emerges through local aggregate interaction is rich and multi-dimensional, but is not directed or goal-oriented, and this poses problems for organisations built on traditions of management and control. It also poses problems for organisations concerned with maintaining direction toward aims and this is, after all, the reason that organisations exist.

It cannot be assumed that all learning that occurs through work will support the aims of the organisation, in fact, it can be assumed that much will not. In the examples offered by participants in this study many hinted at risks for the organisation although these examples were proffered with claims of working *in good faith* (and difficulties with construction of *the right thing* and *in good faith* have been discussed earlier). Much of the learning that occurs does so in response to the immediate environment, feedback from the local environment reinforcing or extinguishing new knowledge without exposure more broadly in the organisation.

10.2.1.4 Organisational knowledge and learning through work

In this study learning is shown to emerge through the work of each of the three narrative groups, regardless of the type of work they undertake. This finding challenges Koopmans (2005) statement that the importance of the relationship between learning and work increases as a result of the growing intensity of knowledge work and pressure to innovate. The persistent change of the work environment and the nonlinearity of interactions within it means that regardless of varying knowledge loads or intensity, learning through work remains the dominant theme in discussions about learning that contributes to the knowledge of the organisation. The perceived sophistication of the role from a knowledge perspective does not impact on the ways participants spoke of their learning. This study suggests that the relationship between learning and work increases not so much as a result of centrality of knowledge in our society so much as a result of its changedness and its complexity.

It is perhaps for this reason that participants seldom mentioned official knowledge management systems in their narratives, even when discussing circumstances in which they sought information to solve immediate problems. While many narratives provide insight into individuals seeking out knowledgeable others for interaction, no example of mechanical transfer from the knowledge management system to the individual or collective is described. It is the relationship that is highlighted, again, the interactivity of the context prominent in discussions of accessing knowledge.

This organisation is awarded for its knowledge management systems and yet these systems were discussed in narratives only in reference to their limitations. Instead of knowledge management systems, these participants rely on members in their immediate vicinity for assistance, fielding the solutions offered and utilising whichever solutions fit most neatly with their need and expectations. This is an expected finding and one which accords with a weight of knowledge management research (Cross and Israelit 2000; Dixon 2000; Cross, Parker et al. 2001).

Again, this raises important concerns for the organisation in relation to its need for consistency in pursuing its aims. Organisational members access knowledge from sources which may not be the best source of official organisational information. For organisational members, though, the value of the knowledge is based on its identification and validation in context.

10.2.1.5 Organisational learning? Knowledge management?

While this study illustrates much about learning in this organisation, it provides little support for the notion of organisational learning. This study, like that of Matthews (2005) and the theorising of Field (2004) finds that although organisational members invest much in developing new knowledge, only in limited circumstances is this knowledge available to the larger organisation.

The contention that the organisation is not the appropriate level for focus in considering organisational learning is supported by the findings of this study. It contributes to the debate in the literature around the relationship between the individual and the organisational – putting focus at the local collective level rather than the organisational. It is the learning of the local aggregate which is highlighted, the organisation as a learning entity problematised.

Organisational learning is touted as important to organisational effectiveness and yet the experience of these participants suggests that it is individual and collective learning that occurs and is critical to the success of organisational members dealing with the pressures of their environment. Participants described in detail their frustration with connecting with *the organisation* and of their preference for local interaction. Because aggregates do not nest into organic hierarchies, learning remains pocketed, tightly linked to immediate context and localised problems. Valuable knowledge about the needs of internal and external customers and the limitations of the organisation is developed and hoarded within aggregates, not building through emergent organisation. Nyhan, Cressey et al. (2004) suggest that expectations of perfect organisational learning are unrealistic give the complex interaction between tangible and intangible dimensions of an organisation, its learning goals and those of its individual members, and this study supports their claim.

While the organisation exists to structure the interaction of the individuals within it and the interactions between its members and the environment, the individuals and collectives themselves self-organise to maximise their effectiveness in practice. Although organisational members learn in order to solve problems on the organisation's behalf, in this case there is little evidence of this learning impacting on the schema of the organisation. Occasionally, some learning that occurs through the interactivity of local agents may be drawn up into the organisation's memory (for example, a workaround that is passed through to *Head Office*) but the altered memory of the organisation is rarely shown to result in behavioural change at the organisational level.

This research suggests that learning occurs in an ad hoc way and that adaptation occurring at the edges of the organisation better facilitates the performance of individual members and small collectives. In this incremental way, the organisation's components may demonstrate localised shifts in understanding and behaviour, yet the internal models the organisation uses to anticipate and respond to its environment *as a whole* remain unchanged. The emergent hierarchy, so critical to adaptation is absent in this case organisation and, as Waldrop (1994: 169) states, '...a hierarchical, building-block structure utterly transforms a system's ability to learn, evolve, and adapt'.

Akgun, Lynn et al.'s (2003: 842) social cognitivist perspective on learning presents learning as changes in knowledge structures or schemas. If this definition of learning is used in the definition for organisational learning, then the organisation in this study is shown not to learn even though learning occurs within and through it. Carroll, Rudolph et al.'s (2003) definition of learning as a change in situation-action linkages similarly excludes the experience of this organisation from examples of organisations that learn.

The finding that exogenous shocks are absorbed at the periphery of the organisation leaving the organisational structures unchanged, challenges Stymne's complexity-inspired definition. In this definition '...organisational learning is a function of the interaction of exogenous shocks and the existing organisational structures that are partly functions of previous shocks (Stymne 1970)' (Frank and Fahrback 1999: 270).

Chakravarthy, McEvily et al. (2003), however, describe learning as the process of acquiring comprehension, or 'knowledge accumulation'. In their terms, '...knowledge is accumulated when units within the firm or the organisation as a whole gains new understanding' (2003: 307). Within this definition, then, the learning of local aggregates is indeed seen to provide the organisation with learning. But this research questions acquisitionist constructions of learning and challenges whether the organisation can be described as learning given that its underlying schema and ongoing behaviour remain unchanged as a result of the experience of its members.

Similarly, this study highlights knowledge and its development as intimately entwined with learning, and does not support suggestion of its nature as something 'manageable'. The findings of this study align with Alvesson and Karreman's claim that '…knowledge is an ambiguous, unspecific and dynamic phenomenon, intrinsically related to meaning, understanding and process, and therefore difficult to manage' (2001: 995). Participants' representations of knowledge underline its emergence through interaction, its validity in application and local support, its contestability, situatedness and construction. Such representations are at odds with conceptions of control and management and as such support contemporary perspectives of knowledge in organisations (Stacey 2001; Snowden 2002; Wenger, McDermott et al. 2002; Stacey 2003b; 2003a).

The detachment of individual from collective, of mind from body, of knowledge from context are inherent in mechanical systems of knowledge management and to some extent in more human perspectives in the knowledge management literatures (for example, Nonaka 1991). This detachment is not apparent in these findings and such representations of knowledge management are not supported by this study.

The findings of this study problematise the notion of organisational learning, questioning the assumption that that the organisation can be seen as a whole, learning entity. Rather, this study illustrates learning entities (individuals and aggregates) that may contribute to adaptation at the organisation's periphery. The study also questions the notion of knowledge management, the findings highlighting the self-organisation inherent in knowledge activities in organisation.

The section above illustrates the interdependence of learning and knowledge, and raises problems with the relationship between aggregate learning and organisational knowledge. Issues that emerge from the tension between organisational requirements for consistency and operational requirements for flexibility in this study are also presented, particularly with reference to flows of information and knowledge through the organisation. Given the complexity of the work and the knowledge that emerges through it, the limitations of knowledge management approaches are also discussed and the contentions made that the organisation could not be said to learn and that its knowledge could not be described as manageable.

Complexity provides a lens through which learning and knowledge are seen as forming and being formed by one another in the iterative interactivity of organisational members within their work context. Recognising the interdependency of the two leads to suggestions for practice that bring together the 'learning' and 'knowledge' specialist areas in organisations. Engaging organisational members in learning that contributes to organisational knowledge through their immersion in work highlights opportunities for more holistic considerations of members and their needs, developmentally, socially, technically and motivationally. Simultaneously, it highlights opportunities for *the organisation* to benefit from the experience of its members' interaction in the real world, providing insights and learning that can contribute to its competitiveness in its fast-changing environment.

10.3 IMPLICATIONS FOR PRACTICE

The findings of this study do suggest that opportunity exists for the blending of learning and knowledge approaches in organisations. Once data and the information management systems that are so often bundled up with knowledge systems are differentiated from the systems of learning and knowledge reflected in this study, then approaches which look to develop knowledge inherently place emphasis on workplace learning. Knowledge and learning are entwined and inseparable, each contributing to and being formed in the other.

Within this integrationist perspective and through complexity, implications for practice relate to the three major themes visited above. The focus on the learner as at once individual and collective highlights strategies that promote interactivity and emergence; the recognition of knowledge as complex, situated and active points to expansive environments (Fuller and Unwin 2004), strategies that support autonomy, tolerate risk and provide opportunities for collectives to work on shared problems; and better understanding of the role of internal models and diversity leads to consideration of optimal diversity and encouraging practice and opinion that disrupts stagnant internal models at individual, collective and organisational levels.

This research is not unique in its *wish* to '...find 'a' reality of effectiveness and legitimation that can be transferred onto other social situations' (Luhman 2005: 20), indeed, some responsibility for doing so is assumed (Strauss and Corbin 1998a: 177). However, no claims to its *ability* to do so are made here. So, while no suggestion is made that the findings of this study are generalisable to broader contexts, this study does prompt a consideration of organisation in terms of complexity.

The broad implications for practice from a complexivist perspective hover around the futility of tightly structured and fixed organisational structures, plans and goals. Complexity highlights the emergence of surprise outcomes resulting from the interaction of individuals, the self-organising capacity of groups and the concerning limitations inherent in attempts to direct groups. It provides a perspective within which the system can be seen as less rational (Frank and Fahrback 1999: 269) than traditional views on organisation suggest. It focuses attention on the influence of exogenous impacts on individuals and their interaction within the organisation, and the impact of the context or landscape within which individuals attempt to improve their fitness (Anderson 1999).

10.3.1 INDIVIDUAL/COLLECTIVE LEARNING AND KNOWLEDGE

This research adds weight to the current conceptual shift in the literature to a social perspective on learning in organisations (Visser 2005). It questions the predominantly formal and individualistic perspectives of workplace learning approaches in the Australian context and strengthens discussion on the definition of 'the learner' (see, for example, Davis and Sumara 2001). This research also refocuses knowledge processes on human and social aspects of organisation, accommodating knowledge as emergent and active.

10.3.1.1 Accommodating emergence

Recognising organisational members' learning *through* work places emphasis on the nature of the work and the opportunities for learning that practice affords the member. As Conlon (2003: 291) states,

> *'With a large percentage of employee knowledge emerging from informal learning, it would appear organisations should seek ways to allow and plan for it while staying on the sidelines to let it work. It is likely that much of the learning that goes on at work is unnoticed by researchers and even employers, who unwittingly depend on their employees learning informally and who could not function without the significant contributions employees make in work organisation and technology'.*

Accommodating emergence may mean redesigning work so that it maximises opportunity for learning, providing opportunities for experimentation and error in the solution of real workplace problems. Focusing on work as a conduit for learning supports Nyhan, Cressey et al.'s research which suggests that 'One of the keys to promoting learning organisations is to organize work in such a way that it promotes human development' (2004: 67).

10.3.1.2 Making organisation's need for member learning a member problem

Learning is shown in this study to emerge from individual and collective effort to maintain fitness within a specific and changing context. The demands of the context prompt innovation and adaptation without direction or control and lead to important knowledge developments. This finding suggests that where organisational and personal imperatives conflict, the organisation's attempts at *teaching* organisational members will fail.

In the work of Dovey and White (2005), aligning the personal interest of organisational members with project goals is an important component of developing strong bonds between organisational members. Given that learning is shown to emerge from the interactivity of these members, allowing groups to coalesce around problems that impact on their daily life and work appears critical to the development of knowledge in the organisation.

This study illustrates difficulties with forcing the development of work groups that are not focused on immediate and pressing problems. Support of learning communities that do form organically in the workplace would be an appropriate strategy for maximizing opportunities for learning, knowledge development and sharing.

10.3.1.3 Letting local aggregates drive

This notion of aggregates coalescing around work issues leads to an important learning about the relevance of centralised knowledge management and training programs. This study highlights the role of aggregates in making sense of, and innovating to adjust to, their localised environments. These localised groups are in an appropriate position to determine their *real learning needs* as well as the usefulness of their knowledge outcomes.

While the dilemma this creates for traditional management is discussed earlier, the opportunities localised learning provides the organisation cannot be ignored. If local aggregates have the opportunity to identify and access additional learning opportunities they require for performance in their work context, then the local aggregate has the opportunity to maximise its own performance.

10.3.1.4 Tolerating exploration and failure within boundaries

Providing autonomy at the local level, however, may increase discomfort. While the participants in this study state their need for exploration and control over their decision-making, they also speak of fear of reprisal if they fail. This concern is one reflected in the literatures, authors from Schein to Stacey highlight anxiety in learning. Schein (1999: 168) strongly maintains that generative learning '…is an inherently anxiety-provoking process that will be resisted' and Stacey (2003a: 330) states that learning in this frame '…will inevitably give rise to anxiety… In a social order that greatly prizes competence, understood as knowing, it is deeply shaming not to know.'

It may be very difficult for learners to experiment, even when fear of reprisal from management for failing in attempts to improve performance has been removed. Stacey and Schein's work suggests that encouragement of attempts to innovate must be coupled with support to reduce anxiety and discomfort.

10.3.1.5 Using narrative

This study draws upon collective constructions of reality through group narrative. The process is important in grasping participant versions of reality, and is recognised as important in knowledge development and sharing. Bruner (1991) asserts that narrative is critical to organising human experience, its interpretation leading to important shifts in understanding. The breaching of canonical knowledge, described by participants as critical to improving performance, is central to narrative. Narrative accounts provide organisational members with the tools for validating 'deviant' behaviour.

From a workplace learning point of view, narrative provides the learning and knowledge facilitator with a role as interpreter. In Fenwick's (2003: 151) words, 'Within organisations, story-making is one way that educators listen and interpret a system's relationships and activities, and mirror it back to itself.'

10.3.2 KNOWLEDGE IS COMPLEX, SITUATED AND ACTIVE

Constructions of knowledge in this study underline its nature as emergent, valued in its relevance and application within a specific time and locale, its social construction and verification through local feedback. As Spencer (2002: 300) reminds us, 'Workers have always "learned at work" '. This study highlights knowledge as emergent in interaction and situated in work.

10.3.2.1 Supporting interactivity

Providing space and time for interactivity at the local level supports development of situated knowledge at the place and in the time it is required. Ellstrom (2001: 431), for example, discusses integration of work and learning requiring working conditions which include access to adequate learning resources such as time and space. Englehardt and Simmons (2002: 43) use the complex adaptive systems metaphor set to explore ideas about the emergence of learning and the provision of space outside of formal organisation to accommodate emergence.

The notion that time and space apart from the constraints of formal organisation are beneficial to learning is reinforced by the findings of this study. Examples of self-organising teams operating outside of formal organisational direction, or loosely bounded by organisational direction, provide illustrations of important learning in the study organisation.

This research, like others cited earlier, illustrates organisational members' preference for dealing with accessible and trusted others in learning and sharing knowledge. The implication for practice, of course, is to provide opportunities for such interaction and to let go of information systems as the basis for knowledge sharing approaches.

10.3.2.2 Providing information on underlying philosophy

This is not to say that access to information is not important. These organisational members describe a need to interpret the information within their local context and in application to local problems. Issues emerging from the disconnection of policy and operational imperatives in this organisation were shown to be related to members' rejection of canonical scripts in preference for their own construction of *the right thing*. Providing these members with the philosophy underlying such rules, terms and policies may well support members' knowledge development and decision-making in uncertain environments.

Related to this notion of flexibility underpinned by understanding is recognition that the development, hoarding and verification of knowledge at the local level is both an opportunity for, and a threat to, the organisation's success. Locally developed knowledge may lead to negative outcomes for the organisation as the learning may be appropriate for local fitness but inappropriate for organisational effectiveness. Recognising the nonlinearity of the work experience and providing learning problems which provide underpinning concepts and problem-solving and networking skills, for example, may provide learners with the opportunity to still work flexibly while representing the organisational imperative effectively

10.3.2.3 Consider taking learning out of the training room

This and other studies '...challenge prevailing orthodoxy that worthwhile knowledge is canonical and that legitimate education is planned and monitored by professionals' (Fenwick 2003: 142). This study, rather than privileging formal information and training, underlines organisational members' self-validation of locally produced and shared knowledge and their focus on its value in application within the immediate context. The organisation's focus on disseminating dislocated information through formal training, internal communication and knowledge management approaches is ridiculed by participants.

Formal programs are often derided in this study for being unhelpful to the performance needs of organisational members. According to one member, '*what head office thinks our learning needs are, they aren't!*'. Formal learning programs which are based on linear principles, assuming consistent experience with consistent solutions, do not meet the needs of these organisational members in their nonlinear experience.

There is some criticism of formal training in a broad range of literatures. In environmental management, for example, authors are critical of such approaches,

> *'If contextual knowledge is seen as paramount to resolving localized environmental issues, centralized organisations that invest considerable tax dollars into generalizable knowledge-based 'solutions'... should rethink their focus.'* (Keen, Brown et al. 2005).

This research supports the questioning of such foci. The participants of this study display little respect for the organisation's attempts to educate them through formal training initiatives, seeing such approaches as redundant in their ever-changing work contexts.

Rather than being about formalised systems and programs for learning and knowledge sharing, this study supports the insight offered by Fenwick (2001: 8) that, '...workplace learning is becoming understood as relational processes of continuous invention and exploration', placing learning in authentic, community focused contexts a significant challenge for learning in this century (Atkin 2000).

Taking learning out of the training room and repositioning it in practice endorses the legitimacy of emergent knowledge. In doing so, it provides a conduit for openness of such knowledge to other aggregates within the organisation, removing, as it does, local concerns about deviance and protection.

10.3.3   DISRUPTING MENTAL MODELS, ADAPTATION AND GENERATIVE LEARNING

This study reveals fixed mental models in individuals and internal models in collective and organisation as contributing to difficulties with innovation and knowledge development in the organisation. Participant narratives illustrate the opportunities afforded collectives through importing naivety and disrupting the status quo.

10.3.3.1 Moving people around

While the participants in this study stressed the parochialism inherent in the formation and survival of aggregates, some authors in complexity suggest that there is a level of 'optimal parochialism' (Bowles and Gintis 2000) beyond which survival is better served by importing diversity.

Requisite diversity has long been proposed as critical to creative social interaction and innovation (Nonaka and Takeuchi 1995). As Kauffman (1995: 296) succinctly states, 'Diversity begets diversity'. Other authors in organisational theory who draw on complexity add weight to the appropriateness of the strategy of 'mixing it up', Stacey (2003b: 375) asserting that,

> *Transformation is possible only when the entities, their interactions with each other and their interaction with entities in the system's environment are sufficiently heterogeneous, that is sufficiently diverse' so that 'New themes emerge as people struggle to understand each other and as their conversations are cross-fertilised through conversations with people in other communities and disciplines' (Stacey 2003a: 417).*

Workplaces, therefore, which limit diversity in workplace experience or 'inter-subjective encounters' (Dovey and White 2005: 246) constrain opportunities for learning and development of new workplace knowledge.

Exposure to contextual change opens new niches within which diversity can emerge through opportunities for new interactions. In a continuous way diversity provides opportunities that can result in increased diversity to respond to new environmental opportunities. Diversity, then, leads to the development of new knowledge through the interaction and relationships between individuals in diverse collectives.

10.3.3.2 Encouraging challenge to status quo

Uncomfortable as it may well be, challenging *the normal confines*, what might be called 'troubling work', is apparent in this study as critical to knowledge development. Fenwick (2003: 151) uses the verb 'disturb' in her references to strategies for development of new insights in organisation. For her, challenge is designed to '…interrupt the normative, decentre it, and invert the terms of reference' in order for new knowledge to emerge.

Of course this notion of challenge is inherent in the earliest work in organisational learning (Argyris and Schon 1978; Argyris 1995; Argyris and Schon 1996; Argyris 1999) and continues to be important in contemporary theory building (for example, Calhoun and Starbuck 2003). The power constraints imperative in this practice implication are clear and are discussed later in a critical appraisal of the use of the complexity heuristic.

10.3.3.3 Rewarding innovation

Reward features in its absence in narratives in this current study, with participants conveying their disappointment that their innovations are not recognised (and worse, often credited to others). This disappointment is often linked in their narratives to issues of aggregate ownership, hoarding and protection of knowledge. Evans and Kersh's (2004: 63) work illustrates that expansive or stimulating workplace environment provides recognition for, and development of, tacit skills as well as opportunities to engage in learning.

In order to facilitate knowledge development beyond the collective it appears critical to reward innovation where is occurs, thereby removing any sense of deviance in the activity that leads to the new knowledge.

10.3.4   CONCLUSIONS ON IMPLICATIONS FOR PRACTICE

The findings of this study in their alignment with complexity metaphors leads to reflection on traditional notions of formal learning and knowledge management practice. The complex adaptive system metaphor set prompts discussion using a new language which accommodates focus on connection and self-organisation. The metaphor set portrays some features of the experience in relief and it is these features which have informed discussion to this point. Fuller understanding, however, can only emerge in consideration of what exists in the background when some features are brought to the fore.

10.4   WHAT SITS OUTSIDE THE HEURISTIC?

To counter any risk of compartmentalising human experience this next section attempts to identify the themes which sit outside of the model – the aspects of the participants' lived experience that are not fully represented by the categories and definitions of the complex adaptive systems model. This is not to say that broader dimensions are not accessible through complexity, rather that the distinct properties and mechanisms of Holland's (1995) model do not immediately point to their analysis.

10.4.1.1 *Power and politics*

In this study issues of power, economics and politics emerged on the periphery of analysis in relation to emergence and organisational limitations to building hierarchy through aggregation. While the links between organisational learning and power and politics have only recently gained prominence (Easterby-Smith, Crossan et al. 2000; Huzzard 2004), for some theorists (for example, Schein 1999; Huzzard 2004) these themes are central to understandings of learning and organisational dynamics. Issues around coercion, oppression, control, and direction are tied up with notions of moral force. Such notions challenge hegemonic logic in learning and organisation including the superiority of expert, scientific and disciplinary knowledge, and the orthodox positioning of the professional educator as the legitimate vessel for valued knowledge (Fenwick 2003). While not explicitly accessible through categories of complex adaptive systems, this study does highlight such issues, the narratives confronting traditional assumptions about legitimate organisational themes, allowing consideration of shadow themes.

Perspectives such as Holmes' (2004) which challenge assumptions of empowerment through learning and Schein's (1999) related preoccupation with organisational learning as coercion, provide insights into deeper issues on the complexity of power relationships in workplace and organisational learning. In this study participants' views supported a perspective in which learning (rather than training) prompts and promotes workers' opportunities for more autonomous action while simultaneously opportunities for autonomous action lead to learning.

Schein's (1999) concerns about coercion are also important in this study, however, his assertion that employees are coerced to shift their individual schematic sets to meet cultural change is challenged by the findings. Schein suggests that generative change by the individual requires free choice of exit, and that employment limits freedom to exit. While there is no argument with this claim, this study illustrates that individuals also exercise their freedom of exit by merely meeting the needs of *the organisation* rhetorically while persisting in behaviour that maximises their effectiveness in the immediate environment.

The experiences of the participants accords with Contu and Willmott's (2003) conceptualization of power as articulated through social constructions of truth and exercised in localised practices and relationships. *Empowerment*, for the participants in this study, reflects a meaning in which the employee assumes power over the workplace rather than one in which the employer delivers power to the employee (Field 1997: 149). In this way, this study provides insight into the problematic and largely unaddressed relationship (Huzzard 2004: 350) between learning and power in situated learning theories.

10.4.1.2 Emotion

The complex adaptive systems model suggests an arrangement whereby action based on simple rules impacts on others taking action and from which patterns emerge. Indeed, mathematical simulations of complexity do just this. It would be easy then, using the model, to consider the interactions that occur in the workplace to be merely mechanical processes of selection, interaction, and response. However, as Spender (2003: 267) asserts, '…it is no longer empirically acceptable to avoid dealing with emotion in our organizational theorizing'. This study illustrates, and much literature supports, the recognition of the influence of emotion on the interaction and emergent properties of interaction (for example, Weick 2001; Fenwick 2003; Fineman 2003; Marshall and Simpson 2005).

In this study, the nonlinearity of the participants' experience would be expected to lead to high levels of arousal. Weick (2001) develops an argument where the novel events in technology rich environments increase interruption to and pressure in the work environment which in turn increases emotion. In the study site participants spoke of ubiquitous novelty and change, of *frantic palaver* and *bubbling chaos*. Participants spoke emotionally about their experience and their stories reflect emotion as an emergent property of their interaction within the work context, again, emotion emerging from and contributing to the interaction and the resulting patterns of behaviour.

Emotion is a theme which emerges, too, in the feminist literatures (Hayes and Flannery 2000 in Bierema 2001; Reger 2004) in discussion of the choices for interaction and learning women make in the workplace. This literature supports the findings of this study which illustrates the value placed on relationships for learning and knowledge sharing in aggregate. In this study, however, both male and female participants discussed the emotion in connections, the *sphere of inclusion* theme carrying with it important issues about the role of emotion is selecting others for interaction and the development of supporting relationships based on trust.

10.4.1.3 Intelligence

The complex adaptive system model does not provide a frame for discussion of intelligence as a singularly individual characteristic. Using the model, intelligence is held in the agent's ever-changing mental models, in their selection of others with whom to interact and in the iterative interaction itself. In this way, intelligence from a complexity perspective sits at once within the individual and the context, but alone in neither. The 'inherent capacity' aspect of intelligence theory (Fenwick and Tennant 2004: 57) is not recognised in this model, unless it can be reduced to the mental models of the individual. Such a cognitivist construction is at odds with the narratives collected here.

The findings accord with Spender's (1996: 65) conceptualization of intelligence as '...both the ability to experience and the facility to abstract from that experience', a behaviour noted in this study in individual and collective pursuit of effectiveness in the environment.

10.4.1.4 Ethics

A variety of ethical issues in work associated with the activity of organisational members in their learning and knowledge sharing emerge from this study. While the model does not lend itself immediately to discussion of ethics it is an important peripheral theme.

Ethics emerge in narratives of knowledge *ownership* and the equity of formal relationships in the organisation. Several narratives describe experiences where knowledge developed within the local aggregate is appropriated by others at higher levels of the organisation, these others then receiving recognition for it as their own. Similarly, they reflect a hierarchical structure and rules system in which conformist behaviour is seen as good and nonconformist as bad. Stacey (2003b: 395) positions this view of ethics as one in which '...leadership and ethics become matters of explicating the rules of qualities of the harmonious whole and of individuals conforming to it'. In this study, in which no harmonious whole is seen to exist as *the organisation* and in which non-conformity is seen to be critical to acting ethically, ethics takes on a new form.

The ethical considerations participants make are based on an emergent understanding of ethical behaviour as discussed in relation to *the right thing*. This local construction of the ethics of work practice is open to development within the context but closed to other areas of the organisation, thereby allowing for a construction deviant from organisationally or even societally sanctioned ethical standards.

Ethics in this study is not about participants adhering to a clear set of standards based on universally held codes of conduct developed rationally by individuals. It is much more closely aligned with the thinking of Griffin (2001) whose focus on the interaction of agents with one another in the development of ethical approaches is based in context and moment. Such constructions of ethical behaviour make it impossible to shirk responsibility for one's own action. This study, however, also highlights the role of the iterative construction of ethical action as defined by the group, the aggregate providing an opportunity for the individual to claim group responsibility for action.

There are several examples of individuals acting on their local ethical standard and being prepared to lose respectability (and employment) as a result. This is an important consideration when reflecting on self-organisation, learning through work and the development of ethical practice and knowledge in the organisation.

10.5   CONCLUSION

This chapter highlights the relationship between learning and knowledge in this organisation, placing the two in one frame. The contentions made here are that organisations as whole entities do not learn, rather that aggregates within their boundaries learn, and that knowledge as described by the participants of this study is not a commodity that can be managed. Implications for practice that integrates learning and knowledge are offered with reference to the three converging themes which thread through this dissertation. In view of this study's critical use of the complex adaptive systems model, this chapter concludes with a discussion of important themes which are not directly addressed through the complexity metaphor. The final chapter that follows this one is a short conclusion to the study.

11 CONCLUSION

The introduction to this dissertation argued that learning and knowledge are artificially separated in organisations and promised that this research would offer an exploration of the relationship between the two. The integrated view which guided the exploration led to the development of an innovative methodological approach and findings which make a contribution to the body of knowledge in organisational learning, knowledge management, workplace learning and in the application of complexity theories to organisation. In doing so, this dissertation answered calls to research in a number of fields and went some way toward addressing the silence apparent in extant literature on experiences of learning and knowledge at work.

In attending to the question, '*What is the relationship between workplace learning experience and organisational knowledge?*', this monograph developed an argument in which learning and knowledge are conceived as complex and entwined in each other as they are in interaction, situation and practice. In this concluding chapter, the development of that argument is reviewed with reference to its contribution to organisational research and to implications for further research.

11.1 THE THESIS

This research was prompted by organisational theorising in which learning and knowledge are treated with increasing sophistication, leading to the convergence of central themes across discourse areas. The convergence was illustrated as occurring in premises which align with core features of complexity theories and these themes were developed in a discussion across the literatures.

The call for research which explores the relationship between learning and knowledge in organisations in holistic ways was presented alongside a silence in the empirical literature. While much is theorised about the relationship between learning and knowledge in organisations through complexity, no empirical exploration of the relationship is available. In its attempt to '...clos[e] the embarrassing gap between theory and empirical research' (Glaser and Strauss 1967: vii), this research analysed the narrated experience of organisational members, grounding discussion in tangible examples of workplace learning and knowledge. It explored the phenomena within temporal and physical contexts and accommodated the emergence of novel perspectives on their interaction.

The use of a methodology developed in close reference to the informing theory provided a sound research base for the findings. The research combined methodological approaches in order to remain true to the question and to the theory. In this study concepts were induced from diverse data and then comparisons were made with theory and deductions about the relevance of the developing concepts developed with participants.

The findings of the study were many. Firstly, the complexity metaphor set was shown to provide important insights into learning and knowledge in the organisation by highlighting the inexorable interconnectedness of learning, interacting and knowledge, and allowing more holistic perspectives on the nature of learning and knowledge through work. The recognition invites consideration of the ecological nature of organisational life, the role of improvisation, incidental and informal learning, innovation, relationships, networks, the foundations of knowledge, sources of order, dialogue and narrative.

However, the direct application of the complex adaptive systems metaphor to organisational experience was shown in this study to be problematic, the findings offering some clarification of the limitations of current conceptions of complexity and their relevance to work organisations. In its critical discussion of the findings this study also contributed to the developing theory of complexity.

Secondly, this research revealed the unit of analysis for learning to be unclear, the individual and collective entwined, learning emerging from self-organisation through interaction in context.

Thirdly, the relationship between learning, innovation and work was highlighted. Central findings showed that organisational members' struggles with the diversity and changeability of their work put focus on the generation of new knowledge as an outcome of learning, suggesting a significant opportunity for the merging of learning and knowledge strategies in organisations.

Fourthly, organisational experience was presented as tied up with the tension between the organisation's assumption of Taylorist principles, focusing on linearity, measurement and control, and organisational members experiencing uncertainty in their interaction with each other and their practice. This tension plays itself out in behaviours that restrict learning and knowledge sharing to the local context.

Fifthly, vital issues were raised in this study about the construction of 'organisation' as a learning entity, illustrating learning as confined to local level interaction and knowledge to be held in interaction at its periphery. This research explicitly challenged the assumption that organisations can learn.

An important sixth finding was in the construction of meaning around the term 'knowledge'. In this research knowledge was understood to be active and continually changing, valued in its local verisimilitude, constructed in the collective and within context and moment. The validity of canonical knowledge was questioned and formalised training approaches and knowledge management systems were revealed to be antithetic to participants' notions of valuable learning and valid knowledge.

Finally, this dissertation demonstrated that learning and knowledge in the organisation are bound up with each other in fundamental ways which defy their separation. Learning and knowledge were shown to co-emerge in the activity of organisational members in performance of their work, in struggles to maintain effectiveness in a localised and changing context. When notions of learning and knowledge are understood in the ways they are represented by the participants of this study and decoupled from discourse about manageable features of organisational systems such as data and information, then the blending of the strategies that support them is imperative.

Broad implications were suggested in this study's finding of learning as both individual and collective, each formed in and forming the other; the situatedness of knowledge and its value in it local verisimilitude and application; and the self-organising activity of individuals and collectives in pursuit of effectiveness in their immediate environment. The implications of this study for organisational practice revolved around the complexity of the experience of learning and knowledge in this organisation. The study pointed to a range of strategies for workplace learning and knowledge development that are well represented (though contested) at the broadest level in the literatures as, '…establishing and modifying environments within which effective, improvised, self-organised solutions can evolve' (Anderson 1999: 216). Implications hinge on the accommodation of chance events and uncertainty.

11.2 CONTRIBUTION OF THIS STUDY

The study made contributions to the body of knowledge in organisational learning, knowledge management, and workplace learning theory through its theoretical and empirical support for integration across the fields. It contributed fresh perspectives to each of the fields through their integration as well as through the application of complexity metaphors.

The dissertation addressed the aim of the research by positing discussion of learning and knowledge that aspired to a holistic representation of experience in this study organisation. This discussion highlighted the entwinement of learning and knowledge and their inseparability from individual and collective interaction within context.

The study fulfilled its objectives by describing and developing dimensions and characteristics for central themes that emerged in narratives about learning and knowledge in the subject organisation. It illustrated the relationships between these emergent themes with close and critical reference to metaphors derived from complex adaptive systems theory. The study's development and application of a tightly structured methodology aligned with complexivist understandings was an innovation which strengthened the study's theoretical integrity, and the findings informed a range of learning and knowledge facilitation strategies.

The study was of consequence in its empirical validation of the relevance of complexity thinking to human experience in organisations. Its problematisation of the role of internal models in learning made a contribution to the developing theory of complexity. The study provided additional clarification about the role of the local interest group in the development of knowledge and provided further empirical support for this level as an important one for focus in discussion of organisational learning.

The research contributed several models of learning and knowledge experience which illustrated the two as occurring in networks of interaction imbued with, and reinforced by, context and supported practice predicated on the recognition of learning and knowledge as intimately tied up with interaction and with practice.

11.3   MEETING CALLS FOR RESEARCH

This research reponded to strident calls for research across three bodies of literature. These calls addressed the phenomena of collectivity in learning (Mirvis 1996), the relationship between the individual and collective and the learning of the organisation (Karakowsky and McBey 1999), learning flows (Bontis, Crossan et al. 2002), and the application of complexity theory to organisation (van Eijnatten 2004). Calls are also made for cross-disciplinary (McElroy 2000) and non-positivist organisational research (Chaston, Badger et al. 2000), particularly that which generates novel hypotheses through the application of complexity (Rhodes and MacKechnie 2003). This study met these calls solidly, providing analysis and discussion grounded in experience and linked through narrative to holistic representations of the phenomena explored.

11.4   FURTHER RESEARCH

While this research went some way to providing clearer insight into the relationship between learning and organisational knowledge in the experience of organisational members, a number of important issues were exposed in its progress which call for further exploration. These issues centre around the notion of organisation, its boundaries and context, the validity of broader application of complexitivist metaphors to organisation, the role of internal models in learning and knowledge, and the efficacy of practice which integrates learning and knowledge facilitation and draws on complexity. They are presented here as future research questions;

What is an organisation that it may learn? What is the relationship between emergent organisation and formal organisation and how does this relationship impact on organisational alignment with environment?

How is learning and knowledge in the organisation shaped by the interaction of the organisation in its context?

Does the complexity metaphor set emerge in narratives of learning and knowledge in other organisations?

Does the complexity metaphor set emerge in narratives of learning and knowledge across international cultures?

What part do mental models play in the learning of individuals and collectives?

Does the implementation of practice suggested by the complexity metaphor set and the findings of this study improve learning experience for organisational members and improve opportunities for organisational knowledge development?

What are the constraints on the merging of learning and knowledge facilitation functions in organisations and how might these be overcome?

11.5   FINAL COMMENTS

This study emerged from a background of increasing focus on the competitive advantage of learning and knowledge in organisations to provide a glimpse of the ways in which human learning interacts with the knowledge of the organisation. In the study, learning and knowledge were represented within a single frame, providing a clearer and more complete perspective on the ways in which people learn at work and the relationship of that learning to the knowledge the organisation holds. The dissertation illustrated the entanglement of learning and knowledge in context and interactivity through engagement with work and juxtaposed organisational reality with organisational structure and process.

It is indeed surprising, given the theoretical support to the contrary and the findings of this study, that learning and knowledge functions are dealt with separately in organisations. This study showed learning and knowledge to be intimately entwined in the practice of organisational members. Their consideration within a single frame through complexity suggests important opportunities for richer learning experiences and more knowledgeable, responsive organisation.

Ackerman, M. S., V. Pipek, et al. (2003). Sharing Expertise: Beyond Knowledge Management. Cambridge, Mass.; London, MIT Press.

Ackermann, R. J. (1976). The Philosophy of Karl Popper. Amherst, University of Massachusetts Press.

Akgun, A., E, G. S. Lynn, et al. (2003). "Organizational Learning: A Socio-Cognitive Framework." Human Relations 56(7): 839-868.

Alavi, M. and A. Tiwana (2003). Knowledge Management: The Information Technology Dimension. The Blackwell Handbook of Organizational Learning and Knowledge Management. M. Easterby-Smith and M. Lyles. Carlton, Victoria, Blackwell Publishing.

Allen, P. M. and M. Strathern (2003). "Evolution, Emergence, and Learning in Complex Systems." Emergence 5(4): 8-33.

Alvesson, M. and D. Karreman (2001). "Odd Couple: Making Sense of the Curious Concept of Knowledge Management." Journal of Management Studies 38(7): 995-1018.

Anderson, C. and E. McMillan (2003). "Of Ants and Men: Self-Organized Teams in Human and Insect Organisations." Emergence 5(2): 29-41.

Anderson, D., M. Brown, et al. (2004). Vocational Education and Training. Dimensions of Adult Learning: Adult Education and Training in a Global Era. G. Foley. Crows Nest, NSW, Allen and Unwin: 234-250.

Anderson, P. (1999). "Complexity Theory and Organization Science." Organization Science 10(3): 216-232.

Appelbaum, S. and L. Goransson (1997). "Transformational and Adaptive Learning within the Learning Organization: A Framework for Research and Application." The Learning Organization 4(3): 115-128.

Appleyard, M. M. and G. A. Kalsow (1999). "Knowledge Diffusion in the Semiconductor Industry." Journal of Knowledge Management 3(4): 288-295.

Argyris, C. (1995). "Action Science and Organizational Learning." Journal of Managerial Psychology 10(6): 20-26.

Argyris, C. (1999). On Organizational Learning. Malden, Mass., Blackwell Business.

Argyris, C. and D. Schon (1978). Organizational Learning. Reading, MA, Harvard University.

Argyris, C. and D. Schon (1996). Organizational Learning II: Theory, Method and Practice. Sydney, Addison-Wesley.

Atkin, J. (2000). "Styles of Learning." Journal of the Australian College of Education 26(3): 50.

Backstrom, T. (2004). "Collective Learning: A Way over the Ridge to a New Organizational Attractor." The Learning Organisation 11(6): 466-477.

Baets, W., Ed. (2005). Knowledge Management and Management Learning: Extending the Horizons of Knowledge-Based Management. Springer's Integrated Series in Information Systems. New York, Springer.

Baets, W. and G. Van der Linden (2005). Knowledge Management and Mangement Learning: What Computers can still do. Knowledge Management and Management Learning: Extending the Horizons of Knowledge-Based Management. Springer's Integrated Series in Information Systems. New York, Springer: 59-84

Baker, W. E. and J. M. Sinkula (1999). "The Synergistic Effect of Market Orientation and Learning Orientation on Organizational Performance." Journal of Marketing Science 27: 411-427.

Bapuji, H., M. Crossan, et al. (2005). Organizational Learning, Methodological and Measurement Issues. The Passion for Learning and Knowing: 6th International Conference on Organizational Learning and Knowledge, University of Trento - Italy, University of Trento.

Bartlett, D. and S. Payne (1997). Grounded Theory - Its Basis, Rationale and Procedures. Understanding Social Research: Perspectives on Methodology and Practice. R. Usher, G. W. McKenzie and J. Powell. London; Washington, D.C., Falmer Press: vii, 242.

Beesley, L. (2004). "Multi-Level Complexity in the Management of Knowledge Networks." Journal of Knowledge Management 8(3): 71-88.

Bella, D., J. King, et al. (2003). "The Dark Side of Organizations and a Method to Reveal It." Emergence 5(3): 60-82.

Benjamin, A. (1995). "Complexity: Achitecture/Art/Philosophy." Journal of Philosophy and the Visual Arts **6**: 1-96.

Bierema, L. L. (2001). Women, Work, and Learning. Sociocultural Perspectives on Learning through Work. T. Fenwick. San Francisco, Jossey-Bass. **92**: 53-62.

Billett, S. (2001). Co-Participation: Affordance and Engagement at Work. Scoiocultural Perspectives on Learning through Work. T. Fenwick. San Francisco, Jossey-Bass.

Blackman, D. and S. Henderson (2005). "Know Ways in Knowledge Management." The Learning Organization **12**(2): 152-168.

Bontis, N., M. Crossan, et al. (2002). "Managing an Organizational Learning System by Aligning Stocks and Flows." Journal of Management Studies **39**(4): 437-470.

Bowles, S. and H. Gintis (2000). Optimal Parochialism: The Dynamics of Trust and Exclusion in Networks, Department of Economics, University of Massachusetts.

Brookfield, S. (1985). Self-Directed Learning: A Critical Review of Research. Self-Directed Learning: From Theory to Practice. S. Brookfield. San Francisco, Jossey-Bass. **25**: 5 -16.

Brown, J. S. and P. Duguid (2000). Organizational Learning and Communities-of-Practice: Toward a Unified View of Working, Learning, and Innovation. Strategic Learning in a Knowledge Economy: Individual, Collective, and Organizational Learning Process. R. Cross and S. B. Israelit. Boston, Butterworth Heinemann: 143-165.

Bruner, J. (1991). "The Narrative Construction of Reality." Critical Inquiry **18**(Autumn): 1-21.

Bryans, P. R. S. (2000). "Beyond Training: Reconceptualising Learning at Work." Journal of Workplace Learning **12**(6): 228-235.

Burnes, B. (1992). Managing Change. London, Pitman.

Burnes, B., C. Cooper, et al. (2003). "Organisational Learning: The New Management Paradigm?" Management Decision **41**(5): 452-464.

Burns, R. (2002). The Adult Learner at Work: The Challenges of Lifelong Education in the New Millennium. Sydney, Allen & Unwin.

Calhoun, M. A. and W. H. Starbuck (2003). Barriers to Creating Knowledge. The Blackwell Handbook of Organizational Learning and Knowledge Management. M. Easterby-Smith and M. Lyles. Carlton, Vic., Blackwell Publishing: 473-492.

Call, D. (2005). "Knowledge Management - Not Rocket Science." Journal of Knowledge Management 9(2): 19-20.

Callahan, S., A. Rixon, et al. (2006). "Avoiding Change Management Failure Using Narrative." Anecdote White Papers Retrieved 4 May, 2006, from http://www.anecdote.com.au/whitepapers.php?wpid=7.

Capra, F. (1983). The Turning Point: Science, Society and the Rising of Culture. London, Fontana Paperbacks.

Carroll, J. S., J. W. Rudolph, et al. (2003). Learning from Organizational Experience. The Blackwell Handbook of Organizational Learning and Knowledge Management. M. Easterby-Smith and M. Lyles. Carlton, Vic., Blackwell Publishing.

Cavaleri, S. (2004). "Leveraging Organizational Learning for Knowledge and Performance." The Learning Organization 11(2): 159-176.

Chakravarthy, B., S. McEvily, et al. (2003). Knowledge Management and Completitive Advantage. The Blackwell Handbook of Organizational Learning and Knowledge Management. M. Easterby-Smith and M. Lyles. Carlton, Vic., Blackwell Publishing.

Chappell, C., G. Hawke, et al. (2003). High Level Review of Training Packages: Phase 1 Report. Brisbane, Australian National Training Authority.

Charles, C. M. and C. A. Mertler (2002). Introduction to Educational Research. Boston, Allyn and Bacon.

Charmaz, K. (2000). Grounded Theory: Objectivist and Constructivist Methods. Handbook of Qualitative Research. N. K. Denzin and Y. S. Lincoln. London, Sage publications: 509 - 536.

Chaston, I., B. Badger, et al. (2000). "Organizational Learning Style and Competences." European Journal of Marketing 34(5/6): 625-642.

Child, J. and S. Rodrigues (2003). Social Identity and Organizational Learning. The Blackwell Handbook of Organizational Learning and Knowledge Management. M. Easterby-Smith and M. Lyles. Carlton, Victoria, Blackwell Publishing: 535-556.

Choo, C. W. (1998). The Knowing Organization: How Organizations Use Information to Construct Meaning, Create Knowledge, and Make Decisions. New York, Oxford University Press.

Choo, C. W. and N. Bontis (2002). The Strategic Management of Intellectual Capital and Organizational Knowledge. New York, Oxford University Press.

Cilliers, P. (2002). "Why We Cannot Know Complex Things Completely." Emergence 4(1/2): 77-84.

Cilliers, P. (2005). "The Architecture of Complexity: An Introduction by Paul Cilliers, University of Stellenbosch." E:CO 7(3-4): 138.

Clandinin, D. and F. M. Connelly (2000). Narrative Inquiry - Experience and Story in Qualitative Research. San Francisco, Jossey-Bass.

Cohen, M. D. (1999). "Commentary of the Organization Science Special Issue on Complexity." Organization Science 10(3): 373-376.

Cohen, M. D. and R. Axelrod (1984). "Coping with Complexity: The Adaptive Value of Changing Utility." The American Economic Review(March 1984): 30 - 42.

Cohen, M. D., R. Burkhart, et al. (1995). Routines and Other Recurring Action Patterns of Organizations: Contemporary Research Issues. Santa Fe Institute Working Paper. Santa Fe, Santa Fe Institute - International Institute of Applied Systems Analysis: 1-51.

Colarelli, S. M. (1998). "Psychological Interventions in Organizations." American Psychologist 53(9): 1044-1055.

Collins, D. (2000). Management Fads and Buzzwords: Critical-Practical Perspectives. London, Routledge.

Conlon, T. J. (2003). "A Review of Informal Learning Literature, Theory and Implications for Practice in Developing Global Professional Competence." Journal of European Industrial Training 28(2/3/4): 283-295.

Contu, A. and H. Willmott (2003). "Re-Embedding Situatedness: The Importance of Power Relations in Learning Theory." Organization Science 14(3): 283-296.

Critten, P. (2003). "A New Role for HRD for Emergent Organizations: Going with the Flow." Development and Learning in Organizations **17**(6): 15-17.

Cross, R. and S. B. Israelit (2000). Strategic Learning in a Knowledge Economy: Individual, Collective, and Organizational Learning Process. Boston, MA; Oxford, Butterworth Heinemann.

Cross, R., A. Parker, et al. (2001). "Knowing What We Know: Supporting Knowledge Creation an Sharing in Social Networks." Organizational Dynamics **30**(2): 100-120.

Cross, R. and L. Prusak (2002). "The People Who Make Organizations Go - or Stop." Harvard Business Review **80**(6): 104-112.

Crossan, M., H.W. Lane and R.E. White (1999). "An Organizational Learning Framework; from Intuition to Institution." Academy of Management Review **24**(3): 522-538.

Crossan, M. (2003). "Altering Theories of Learning and Action: An Interview with Chris Argyris." Academy of Management Executive **17**(2): 40-47.

Crotty, M. (1998). The Foundations of Social Research: Meaning and Perspective in the Research Process. St Leonards, NSW, Allen & Unwin.

Daudelin, M. W. (2000). Learning from Experience through Reflection. Strategic Learning in a Knowledge Economy: Individua, Collective, and Organizational Learning Process. R. Cross and S. Israelit. Melbourne, Butterworth Heinemann.

Davenport, T. H. and D. W. De Long (1998). "Successful Knowledge Management Projects." Sloan Management Review **39**(2): 43-58.

Davenport, T. H. and L. Prusak (1998). Working Knowledge: How Organizations Manage What They Know. Boston, Mass., Harvard Business School Press.

Davis, B., R. Phelps, et al. (2004). "Complicity: An Introduction and a Welcome." Complicity: An International Journal of Complexity and Education **1**(1): 1-7.

Davis, B. and D. Sumara (2001). Learning Communities: Understanding the Workplace as a Complex System. Sociocultural Perspectives on Learning through Work. T. Fenwick. San Francisco, Jossey-Bass. **92:** 85-95.

Denzin, N. K. and Y. S. Lincoln (1998). The Landscape of Qualitative Research: Theories and Issues. Thousand Oaks, Calif., Sage Publications.

Denzin, N. K. and Y. S. Lincoln (2000a). The Discipline and Practice of Qualititative Research. Handbook of Qualitative Research. N. K. Denzin and Y. S. Lincoln. London, Sage Publications: 1-28.

Denzin, N. K. and Y. S. Lincoln (2000b). The Handbook of Qualitative Research. Thousand Oaks, Calif., Sage Publications.

Dixon, N. M. (2000). Common Knowledge: How Companies Thrive by Sharing What They Know. Boston, Mass., Harvard Business School Press.

Dooley, K. J. and A. H. Van de Ven (1999). "Explaining Complex Organizational Dynamics." Organization Science 10(3): 358-372.

Dovey, K. and R. White (2005). "Learning About Learning in Knowledge-Intense Organizations." The Learning Organisation 12(3): 246-260.

Drew, S. A. W. and P. A. C. Smith (1995). "The Learning Organization: "Change Proofing" and Strategy." The Learning Organisation 2(1): 4-14.

Drucker, P. F. (1988). "The Coming of the New Organization." Harvard Business Review January-February 1988: 45-53.

Earl, M. (2001). "Knowledge Management Strategies: Toward a Taxonomy." Journal of Management Information Systems 18(1): 215-233.

Easterby-Smith, M., E. Antonacopoulou, et al. (2004). "Constructing Contributions to Organizational Learning: Argyris and the Next Generation." Management Learning 35(4): 371-380.

Easterby-Smith, M., M. Crossan, et al. (2000). "Organizational Learning: Debates Past, Present and Future." Journal of Management Studies 37(6): 783-797.

Elkjaer, B. (2004). "Organizational Learning: The 'Third Way'." Management Learning 35(4): 419-434.

Ellstrom, P.-E. (2001). "Integrating Learning and Work: Problems and Prospects." Human Resource Development Quarterly 12(4): 421-435.

Englehardt, C. and P. Simmons (2002). "Creating an Organizational Space for Learning." The Learning Organisation 9(1): 39-47.

Evans, K. and N. Kersh (2004). "Recognition of Tacit Skills and Knowledge - Sustaining Learning Outcomes in Workplace Environments." Journal of Workplace Learning 16(1/2): 63-74.

Farrell, M. (2000). "Developing a Market-Oriented Learning Organisation." Australian Journal of Management 25(2): 201-222.

Fenwick, T. (2001). Tides of Change: New Themes and Questions in Workplace Learning. Sociocultural Perspectives on Learning through Work. T. Fenwick. San Francisco, Jossey-Bass. 92: 3-18.

Fenwick, T. (2003). "Reclaiming and Re-Embodying Experiential Learning through Complexity Science." Studies in the Education of Adults 35(2): 123-141.

Fenwick, T. (2004). "Rethinking Processes of Adult Learning." Retrieved 19 November 2004, from www.ualberta.ca/~tfenwick/ext/pubs/print/adultlearning.htm.

Fenwick, T. and M. Tennant (2004). Understanding Adult Learners. Dimensions of Adult Learning. G. Foley. Sydney, Allen & Unwin: 55-73.

Field, L. (1997). "Impediments to Empowerment and Learning within Organisations." The Learning Organisation 4(4): 149-158.

Field, L. (2000). Organisational Learning: Basic Concepts. Understanding Adult Education and Training. G. Foley. Sydney, Allen and Unwin.

Field, L. (2004). Rethinking 'Organisational ' Learning. Dimensions of Adult Learning: Adult Education and Training in a Global Era. G. Foley. Sydney, Allen and Unwin: 201-218.

Fineman, S. (2003). Emotionalizing Organizational Learning. The Blackwell Handbook of Organizational Learning and Knowledge Management. M. Easterby Smith and M. Lyles. Carlton, Victoria, Blackwell Publishing: 557-574.

Fiol, C. M. and M. Lyles (1985). "Organizational Learning." Academy of Management Review 10(4): 803-813.

Firestone, J. M. and M. W. McElroy. (2002). "Generations of Knowledge Management." Retrieved 25 June, 2006, from http://www.knowledgeboard.com/doclibrary/knowledgeboard/generations_of_km.pdf.

Firestone, J. M. and M. W. McElroy (2003). Key Issues in the New Knowledge Management. Boston, MA, Butterworth-Heinemann.

Firestone, J. M. and M. W. McElroy (2004). "Organizational Learning and Knowledge Management: The Relationship." The Learning Organisation 11(2): 177-184.

Fook, J. (2004). Critical Reflection and Organizational Learning and Change, a Case Study. Social Work, Critical Reflection and the Learning Organization. N. Gould and M. Baldwin. Aldershot, England, Ashgate: 57-74.

Foss, N. J. and V. Mahnke (2003). Knowledge Management: What Can Organizational Economics Contribute? The Blackwell Handbook of Organizational Learning and Knowledge Management. M. Easterby-Smith and M. Lyles. Carlton, Vic, Blackwell Publishing.

Foucault, M. (1984). "Des Espace Autres." Retrieved 13 March, 2006, from http://foucault.info/documents/heteroTopia/foucault.heteroTopia.en.html.

Frank, K. A. and K. Fahrback (1999). "Organizational Culture as a Complex System: Balance and Information in Models of Influence and Selection." Organization Science 10(3): 253-277.

Fuller, A. and L. Unwin (2004). Expansive Learning Environments: Integrating Organizational and Personal Development. Workplace Learning in Context. H. Rainbird, A. Fuller and A. Munro. London, Routledge: 126-144.

Garavan, T., P. Gunnigle, et al. (2000). "Contemporary HRD Research: A Triarchy of Theoretical Perspectives and Their Prescriptions for HRD." Journal of European Industrial Training 24(2/3/4): 65-93.

Garavan, T., M. Morley, et al. (2002). "Human Resource Development and Workplace Learning: Emerging Theoretical Perspectives and Organisational Practices." Journal of European Industrial Training 26(2/3/4): 60-71.

Garvin, D. (1993). "Building a Learning Organisation." Harvard Business Review 71(4): 78-91.

Geisler, E. and B. Ritter (2003). "Differences in Additive Complexity between Biological Evolution and the Progress of Human Knowledge." Emergence 5(2): 42-55.

Ghosh, A. (2004). "Learning in Strategic Alliances: A Vygotskian Perspective." The Learning Organisation 11(4/5): 302-311.

Glaser, B. G. and A. L. Strauss (1967). The Discovery of Grounded Theory: Strategies for Qualitative Research. Chicago, Aldine Pub. Co.

Gloet, M. and M. Berrell (2003). "The Dual Paradigm Nature of Knowledge Management: Implications for Achieving Quality Outcomes in Human Resource Management." Journal of Knowledge Management 7(1): 78-89.

Gonczi, A. (2004). The New Professional and Vocational Education. Dimensions of Adult Learning: Adult Education and Training in a Global Era. G. Foley. Crows Nest, NSW, Allen & Unwin: 19-34.

Gough, N. (1999). Understanding Curriculum Systems. Understanding Democratic Curriculum Leadership. S. Henderson and K. Kesson. New York and London, Teachers College Press: 47-69.

Griego, O., G. Geroy, et al. (2000). "Predictors of Learning Organizations: A Human Resource Development Practitioner's Perspective." The Learning Organisation 7(1): 5-12.

Griffin, C. (2001). From Education Policy to Lifelong Learning Strategies. The Age of Learning. P. Jarvis. London, Kogan Page: 38-55.

Gubrium, J. F. and J. Holstein, A. (2000). Analyzing Interpretive Practice. Handbook of Qualitative Research. N. K. Denzin and Y. S. Lincoln. London, Sage Publications: 487-508.

Haggis, T. (2005). "Knowledge Must Be Contextual": Some Possible Implications of Complexity and Dynamic Systems Theories for Educational Research. Complexity Science and Society Conference 2005, Liverpook, UK.

Halligan, J. (2004). "The Quasi-Autonomous Agency in an Ambiguous Environment: The Centrelink Case." Public Administration and Development 24: 147-156.

Hamel, G. and L. Valikangas (2003). "The Quest for Resilience." Harvard Business Review 81(9): 52-63.

Hansen, M., N. Nohria, et al. (1999). "What's Your Strategy for Managing Knowledge?" Harvard Business Review March-April: 106-111.

Harkema, S. (2003). "A Complex Adaptive Perspective on Learning within Innovation Projects." The Learning Organisation **10**(6): 340-346.

Harkema, S. (2005). Emergent Learning Processes in Innovation Projects. Knowledge Management and Management Learning: Extending the Horizons of Knowledge-Based Management. W. Baets. New York, Springer: 287-316.

Hawking, S. (2000). "Complexity Digest." Retrieved 22 April, 2006, from http://www.comdig.com/stephen-hawking.php.

Hayles, N. K. (1990). Chaos Bound: Orderly Disorder in Contemporary Literature and Science. Ithaca, N.Y., Cornell University Press.

Hayles, N. K. (1991). Chaos and Order: Complex Dynamics in Literature and Science. Chicago, University of Chicago Press.

Hayles, N. K. (1999). How We Became Posthuman: Virtual Bodies in Cybernetics, Literature, and Informatics. Chicago, Ill., University of Chicago Press.

Hedberg, B. (1980). How Organizations Learn and Unlearn. Handbook of Organizational Design. P. C. Nystrom and W. H. Starbuck. Oxford; New York, Oxford University Press: 8-27.

Hedberg, B. L. T., P. C. Nystrom, et al. (1976). "Camping on Seesaws: Prescriptions for a Self-Designing Organization." Administrative Science Quarterly **21**(1): 41.

Hill, R. J. (2004). "Fugitive and Codified Knowledge: Implications for Communities Struggling to Control the Meaning of Local Environmental Hazards." International Journal of Lifelong Education **23**(3): 221-242.

Hitt, D. (1995). "The Learning Organization: Some Reflections on Organizational Renewal." Leadership and Organisation Development Journal **16**(8): 17 - 24.

Hitt, M., R. Hoskisson, et al. (1994). "Human Capital and Strategic Competitiveness in the 1990s." Journal of Management Development **13**(1): 35-46.

Holland, J. H. (1995). Hidden Order - How Adaptation Builds Complexity. Reading, Massachusetts, Perseus Books.

Holmes, L. (2004). "Challenging the Learning Turn in Education and Training." Journal of European Industrial Training 28(8/9): 625-638.

Huber, G. (1991). "Organizational Learning: The Contributing Processes and the Literatures." Organization Science 2(1): 88-115.

Hurley, R. (2002). "Putting People Back into Organizational Learning." The Journal of Business and Industrial Marketing 17(4): 270-281.

Huzzard, T. (2004). "Communities of Domination? Reconceptualising Organisational Learning and Power." The Journal of Workplace Learning 16(6): 350-361.

Ikehara, H. T. (1999). "Implications of Gestalt Theory and Practice for the Learning Organization." The learning organization 6(2): 63-69.

Ives, W., B. Torrey, et al. (1998). "Knowledge Management - an Emerging Discipline with a Long History." Journal of Knowledge Management 1(4): 269-274.

Janesick, J. (2000). The Choreography of Qualitative Research Design. Handbook of Qualitative Research. N. K. Denzin and Y. S. Lincoln. Thousand Oaks, California, Sage Publications: 379-399.

Jun, J. (2005). "The Self in the Social Construction of Organizational Reality: Eastern and Western Views." Public Administration Theory Network 27(1): 86-110.

Karakowsky, L. and K. McBey (1999). "The Lessons of Work: Toward an Understanding of the Implications of the Workplace for Adult Learning and Development." Journal of Workplace Learning 11(6): 192-201.

Kauffman, S. A. (1993). The Origins of Order: Self-Organization and Selection in Evolution. New York, Oxford University Press.

Kauffman, S. A. (1995). At Home in the Universe: The Search for Laws of Self-Organization and Complexity. New York, Oxford University Press.

Keen, M., V. A. Brown, et al. (2005). Social Learning in Environmental Management: Towards a Sustainable Future. London, Earthscan.

Keeves, J. P. (1997). Educational Research Methodology and Measurement: An International Handbook. Cambridge, Pergamon.

Keeves, J. P. (1999). Overview of Issues in Educational Research. Issues in Educational Research. J. P. Keeves and G. Lakomski. Oxford, Pergamon.

Kennedy, M. (2004). Knowledge Management and Workplace Learning - Changing Perspectives, Issues and Understandings. 3rd International Lifelong Learning Conference., Rockhampton, Australia, Central Queensland University Press.

Kennedy, M. (2005). "Exploring Experiences of Learning and Knowing at Work: Findings from a Public Sector Case Study." actKM Online Journal of Knowledge Management 2(1).

Kolb, D. A. (1983). Problem Management: Learning from Experience. The Executive Mind: New Insights on Managerial Thought and Action. S. Srivastva. San Francicsco, Jossey-Bass.

Koopmans, H. (2005). A Symbiosis of Learning and Work-Practice. Knowledge Management and Management Learning: Extending the Horizons of Knowledge-Based Management. W. Baets. New York, Springer: 165-180.

Kuhn, T. (1970). The Structure of Scientific Revolutions. Chicago, The University of Chicago Press.

Kurtz, C. F. and D. J. Snowden (2003). "The New Dynamics of Strategy - Sense-Making in a Complex-Complicated World." IBM Systems Journal 42(3): 462-484.

Lakomski, G. (1998). Leadership, Distributed Cognition and the Learning Organization. Exploring New Horizons in School Leadership. O. Johansson and L. Lindberg. Umea, Centrum fur Skolledartveckling: 98-111.

Lakomski, G. (2001). "Organizational Change, Leadership and Learning: Culture as Cognitive Process." The International Journal of Educational Management 15(2): 68-77.

Lam, Y. L. J. (2001). "Toward Reconceptualizing Organizational Learning: A Multidimensional Interpretation." The International Journal of Educational Management 15(5): 212-219.

Lave, J. and E. Wenger (1991). Situated Learning: Legitimate Peripheral Participation. Cambridge, Cambridge University Press.

Lave, J. and E. Wenger (2000). Legitimate Peripheral Participation in Communities of Practice. Strategic Learning in a Knowledge Economy: Individual, Collective and Organizational Learning Process. M. Crotty and S. B. Israelit. Melbourne, Butterworth Heinemann: 167-182.

Limerick, D., B. Cunnington, et al. (1998). Managing the New Organisation: Collaboration and Sustainability in the Post-Corporate World. Warriewood, New South Wales, Business and Professional Publishing.

Lincoln, Y. S. and E. Guba, G. (2000). Paradignmatic Controversies, Contradictions, and Emerging Confluences. Handbook of Qualitative Research. N. K. Denzin and Y. S. Lincoln. London, Sage Publications: 163 - 188.

Loermans, J. (2002). "Synergizing the Learning Organization and Knowledge Management." Journal of Knowledge Management 6(3): 285-294.

Luhman, J. T. (2005). "Narrative Processes in Organizational Discourse." E:CO 7(3-4): 15-22.

Lyotard, J.-F. (2004). The Postmodern Condition. The Postmodernism Reader. M. Drolet. London, Routledge: 122-146.

Lytras, M., A. Pouloudi, et al. (2002). "Knowledge Management Convergence - Expanding Learning Frontiers." Journal of Knowledge Management 6(1): 40-51.

MacDonald, C., M. Gabriel, et al. (2000). "Factors Influencing Adult Learning in Technology Based Firms." Journal of Management Development 19(3): 220-240.

Maddox, H. (1993). Theory of Knowledge and Its Dissemination. Castlemaine [Vic.], Freshet Press.

Malhotra, Y. (2002). Why Knowledge Management Systems Fail - Enablers and Constraints of Knowledge Management in Human Enterprises. Handbook on Knowledge Management 1: Knowledge Matters. C. Holsapple. Heidelberg, Springer-Verlag: 577-599.

Marquardt, M. J. (1999). Action Learning in Action: Transforming Problems and People for World-Class Organizational Learning. Palo Alto, Calif., Davies-Black Pub.

Marquardt, M. J. (2002). Building the Learning Organization: Mastering the 5 Elements for Corporate Learning. Palo Alto, CA, Davies-Black Pub.

Marshall, N. and B. Simpson (2005). Socially Constructing Emotion and Learning in Organisations: A Pragmatist Perspective. The Passion for Learning and Knowing, Trento, Italy, University of Trento.

Marsick, V. J. and K. E. Watkins (1999). Facilitating Learning Organizations: Making Learning Count. Aldershot, Hampshire, England; Brookfield, Vt., USA, Gower.

Martensson, M. (2000). "A Critical Review of Knowledge Management as a Management Tool." Journal of Knowledge Management 4(3): 204-216.

Matthews, J. (2005). Capturing Passion and Knowledge for Innovation. The passion for learning and knowing: Proceedings of the 6th international conference on organizational learning and knowledge, Trento, Italy, University of Trento.

Maturana, H. R. and F. J. Varela (1992). The Tree of Knowledge: The Biological Roots of Human Understanding. Boston, Shambhala.

McAdam, R. and S. McCreedy (1999). "A Critical Review of Knowledge Management Models." The Learning Organisation 6(13): 91-101.

McElroy, M. W. (2000). "Integrating Complexity Theory, Knowledge Management and Organizational Learning." Journal of Knowledge Management 4(3): 195-203.

McElroy, M. W. (2003). Ashen and Relationships. ActKM, Email communication.

Mezirow, J. (1990). Fostering Critical Reflection in Adulthood: A Guide to Transformative and Emancipatory Learning. San Francisco, Jossey-Bass Publishers.

Mezirow, J. (2000). Learning as Transformation: Critical Perspectives on a Theory in Progress. San Francisco, Jossey-Bass.

Miller, L., R. McDaniel, et al. (2001). "Practice Jazz: Understanding Variation in Family Practices Using Complexity Science." The Journal of Family Practice 50(10): 872-878.

Mirvis, P. H. (1996). "Historical Foundations of Organization Learning." Journal of Organizational Change Management 7(5): 13-31.

Moffett, S., R. McAdam, et al. (2003). "An Empirical Analysis of Knowledge Management Applications." Journal of Knowledge Management 7(3): 6-26.

Moran, D. (2000). Introduction to Phenomenology. London, Routledge.

Morel, B. and R. Ramanujam (1999). "Through the Looking Glass of Complexity: The Dynamics of Organizations as Adaptive and Evolving Systems." Organization Science **10**(3): 278-293.

Morrison, K. (2002). School Leadership and Complexity Theory. New York, Routledge/Falmer.

Muscatello, J. (2003). "The Potential Use of Knowledge Management for Training: A Review and Directions for Future Research." Business Process Management Journal **9**(3): 382-395.

Nahapiet, j. and S. Ghoshal (1998). "Social Capital, Intellectual Capital, and the Organizational Advantage." Academy of Management Review **23**(2): 242-267.

Nicolini, D. and M. Meznar (1995). "The Social Construction of Organizational Learning: Conceptual and Practical Issues in the Field." Human Relations **48**(7): 727-746.

Nonaka, I. (1988). "Toward Middle-up-Down Management: Accelerating Information Creation." Sloan Management Review **29**(3): 9-30.

Nonaka, I. (1991). "The Knowledge-Creating Company." Harvard Business Review **69**(6): 96-105.

Nonaka, I. (1994). "A Dynamic Theory of Organizational Knowledge Creation." Organization Science **5**(1): 14-39.

Nonaka, I. and H. Takeuchi (1995). The Knowledge-Creating Company: How Japanese Companies Create the Dynamics of Innovation. New York, Oxford University Press.

Nyhan, B., P. Cressey, et al. (2004). "European Perspectives on the Learning Organisation." Journal of European Industrial Training **28**(1): 67-92.

O'Donnell, D. (1999). "Habermas, Critical Theory and Selves-Directed Learning." Journal of European Industrial Training **23**(4/5): 251-161.

Orr, J. (1990). Talking About Machines: An Ethnography of a Modern Job, Cornell University. **PhD:** 247 pages.

Oval, R. (2003). Changing Pedagogy: Contemporary Vocational Learning. Sydney, University of Technology, Sydney: 25.

Pears, D. (1971). What Is Knowledge? London, Harper & Row.

Phelps, R. (2004). <u>The Potential of Reflection in Studying Complexity 'in Action'</u>. Complexity Science and Educational Research Conference, Chaffey's Locks, Canada.

Polanyi, M. (1967). <u>The Tacit Dimension</u>. London, Routledge.

Polanyi, M., Ed. (1969). <u>Knowing and Being</u>. London, University of Chicago Press.

Ponelis, S. and F. A. Fairer-Wessels (1998). "Knowledge Management: A Literature Overview." <u>South African Journal of Library & Information Science</u> **66**(1): 1-9.

Prusak, L. (2001). "Where Did Knowledge Management Come From?" <u>IBM Systems Journal</u> **40**(4): 1002-1008.

Ragin, C. C. (1992). "Casing" and the Process of Social Inquiry. <u>What Is a Case? Exploring the Foundations of Social Inquiry</u>. R. L. Ruggles and H. S. Becker. Melbourne, Cambridge University Press.

Reger, J. (2004). "The Organizational "Emotion Work" through Consciousness-Raising: An Analysis of a Feminist Organization." <u>Qualitative Sociology</u> **27**(2): 205-222.

Revans, R. W. (1978). <u>The A.B.C. Of Action Learning: A Review of 25 Years of Experience</u>. Altrincham, Greater Manchester, R.W. Revans.

Rhodes, M. L. and G. MacKechnie (2003). "Understanding Public Service Systems: Is There a Role for Complex Adaptive Systems Theory?" <u>Emergence</u> **5**(4): 57-85.

Robertson, M. and G. O'Malley Hammersley (2000). "Knowledge Management Practices within a Knowledge-Intensive Firm: The Significance of the People Management Dimension." <u>Journal of European Industrial Training</u> **24**(2/3/4): 241-153.

Rossett, A. and E. Mohr (2004). "Performance Support Tools: Where Learning, Work and Results Converge." <u>TD</u>(February): 35-39.

Roth, J. (2003). "Enabling Knowledge Creation: Learning from an R&D Organization." <u>Journal of Knowledge Management</u> **7**(1): 32 - 48.

Rugg, G. and M. Petre (2004). <u>The Unwritten Rules of PhD Research</u>. Berkshire, Open University Press.

Sanchez, R. and A. Heene (2000). A Competence Perspective on Strategic Learning and Knowledge Management. Strategic Learning in a Knowledge Economy: Individual, Collective, and Organizational Learning Process. R. Cross and S. Israelit. Melbourne, Butterworth Heinemann.

Scarbrough, H. (2003). "Knowledge Management, HRM and the Innovation Process." International journal of manpower 24(5): 501-516.

Scarbrough, H., M. Bresnen, et al. (2004). "The Processes of Project-Based Learning: An Exploratory Study." Management Learning 35(4): 491-506.

Scarbrough, H., J. Swan, et al. (1999). Knowledge Management - a Literature Review. London, Institute of Personnel and Development.

Schein, E. (1999). "Empowerment, Coercive Persuasion and Organizational Learning: Do They Connect?" The Learning Organisation 6(4): 163-172.

Schostak, J. F. (2002). Understanding, Designing and Conducting Qualitative Research in Education. Buckingham, Open University Press.

Schwandt, T. A. (2003). Three Epistemological Stances for Qualitative Inquiry - Interpretivism, Hermeneutics and Social Constructionism. The Landscape of Qualitative Research - Theories and Issues. N. K. Denzin and Y. S. Lincoln. London, Sage: 292-331.

Scott, P. (2005). "Knowledge Workers: Social, Task and Semantic Network Analysis." Corporate communications: An international journal 10(3): 257-277.

Senge, P. (1992). The Fifth Discipline - the Art and Practice of the Learning Organisation. Sydney, Random House.

Senge, P. (1999). The Dance of Change - the Challenges of Sustaining Momentum in Learning Organizations. London, Nicholas Brealey.

Senge, P. M. (1995). The Fifth Discipline Fieldbook: Strategies and Tools for Building a Learning Organization. London, Nicholas Brealey.

Shelton, C. and J. Darling (2003). "From Theory to Practice: Using New Science Concepts to Create Learning Organizations." The Learning Organization 10(6): 353-360.

Sherlock, J. and M. Nathan (2004). "Producing Actionable Knowledge: Applying Mezirow's Theory to the Managerial Learning Context." Best Papers Proceedings - Academy of Management: E1-E6.

Silverman, D. (2000). Doing Qualitative Research: A Practical Handbook. Thousand Oaks, Calif.; London, Sage.

Simon, H. (1962). The Architecture of Complexity. American Philosophical Society.

Sims, H. P. and D. A. Gioia (1986). The Thinking Organization. San Francisco, Calif., Jossey-Bass.

Slater, S. and J. Narver (1995). "Market Orientation and the Learning Organization." Journal of Marketing 59(3): 63-75.

Snowden, D. (2006). "The Gurteen Knowledge Website." Retrieved 15 March, 2006, from http://www.gurteen.com/gurteen/gurteen.nsf/id/X00070912/.

Snowden, D. J. (2000). "Knowledge Elicitation: Indirect Knowledge Discovery." Knowledge Management 3(9): 1-6.

Snowden, D. J. (2002). "Complex Acts of Knowing: Paradox and Descriptive Self-Awareness." Journal of Knowledge Management 6(2): 100-111.

Snowden, D. J. (2003a). Ashen and Relationships. ActKM, Email communication.

Snowden, D. J. (2003b). Leadership in a Complex-Complicated World. Centrelink and Family and Community Services, Canberra.

Snyder, W., E. Wenger, et al. (2004). "Communities of Practice in Government: Leveraging Knowledge for Performance." The Public Manager 32(4): 17-21.

Sorohan, E. (1993). "We Do: Therefore, We Learn." Training and Development 4(10): 47-55.

Spencer, B. (2001). Changing Questions of Workplace Learning Researchers. Sociocultural Perspectives on Learning through Work. T. Fenwick. San Francisco, Jossey-Bass: 31 - 40.

Spencer, B. (2002). "Research and the Pedagogics of Work and Learning." Journal of Workplace Learning **14**(7): 298-305.

Spender, J.-C. (1996). "Organizational Knowledge, Learning and Memory: Three Concepts in Search of a Theory." Journal of Organizational Change Management **9**(1): 63-78.

Spender, J.-C. (2003). "Exploring Uncertainty and Emotion in the Knowledge-Based Theory of the Firm." Information Technology and People **16**(3): 266-288.

Spender, J.-C. (2006a). "Getting Value from Knowledge Management." The TQM Magazine **18**(3): 238-254.

Spender, J.-C. (2006b). "Method, Philosophy and Empirics in KM and IC." Journal of Intellectual Capital **7**(1): 12-28.

Srivasta, S. (1983). The Executive Mind. San Francisco, Jossey-Bass.

Stacey, R. D. (2001). Complex Responsive Processes in Organizations: Learning and Knowledge Creation. London, Routledge.

Stacey, R. D. (2003a). "Learning as an Activity of Interdependent People." The Learning Organization **10**(6): 325-331.

Stacey, R. D. (2003b). Strategic Management and Organisational Dynamics: The Challenge of Complexity. Harlow, Prentice Hall.

Stewart, T. and S. Kirsch (1991). "Fortune." Fortune **123**(11): 44 - 55.

Steyn, G. (2003). "Creating Knowledge through Management Education: A Case Study of Human Resource Management." Education **123**(3): 514.

Storey, J. and E. Barnett (2000). "Knowledge Management Initiatives: Learning from Failure." Journal of Knowledge Management **4**(2): 145-156.

Strauss, A. and J. Corbin (1998a). Grounded Theory Methodology - an Overview. Strategies of Qualitative Inquiry. N. K. Denzin and Y. S. Lincoln. Thousand Oaks, Calif., Sage Publications: 158-185.

Strauss, A. and J. M. Corbin (1998b). Basics of Qualitative Research - Techniques and Procedures for Developing Grounded Theory. London, Sage.

Strauss, A. L. and J. M. Corbin (1990). Basics of Qualitative Research: Grounded Theory Procedures and Techniques. Newbury Park, Calif., Sage Publications.

Sturman, A. (1999). Case Study Methods. Issues in Educational Research. J. Keeves and G. Lakomski. New York, Pergamon: 103 - 111.

Sun, P. and J. Scott (2003). "Exploring the Divide - Organizational Learning and Learning Organization." The Learning Organisation 10(4): 202-215.

Swan, J. and H. Scarbrough (2001). "Knowledge Management: Concepts and Controversies." Journal of Management Studies 38(7): 913-921.

Taft, R. (1999). Ethnographic Research Methods. Issues in Educational Research. J. Keeves and G. Lakomski. New York, Pergamon: 113-120.

Thompson Klein, J. (2004). "Interdisciplinarity and Complexity: An Evolving Relationship." E:CO 6(1-2): 2-10.

Tsoukas, H. and E. Vladimirou (2001). "What Is Organisational Knowledge?" Journal of Management Studies 38(7): 973-993.

van Eijnatten, F. M. (2004). "Chaordic Systems Thinking: Some Suggestions for a Complexity Framework to Inform a Learning Organization." The Learning Organisation 11(6): 430-449.

van Eijnatten, F. M. and G. D. Putnik (2004). "Chaos, Complexity, Learning and the Learning Organization: Toward a Chaordic Enterprise." The Learning Organisation 11(6): 418-429.

Vaughan, D. (1992). Theory Elaboration: The Heuristics of Case Elaboration. What Is a Case? Exploring the Foundations of Social Inquiry. C. C. Ragin and H. S. Becker. Cambridge, Cambridge University Press: 173-202.

Vera, D. and M. Crossan (2003). Organizational Learning and Knowledge Management: Toward an Integrative Framework. The Blackwell Handbook of Organizational Learning and Knowledge Management. M. Easterby-Smith and M. Lyles. Carlton, Victoria, Blackwell: 122-142.

Visser, M. (2005). The Social Construction of Organizational Learning and Knowledge: An Interactional Perspective. The passion for learning and knowing: Proceedings of the 6th international conference on organizational learning and knowledge, Trento, Italy, University of Trento.

Von Krogh, G. N., Ikujiro Aben, Manfred (2001). "Making the Most of Your Company's Knowledge: A Strategic Framework." Long Range Planning **34**(4): 421.

Vygotsky, L. (1962). Thought and Language. Cambridge, Massachusetts, The M.I.T Press.

Waldrop, M. M. (1994). Complexity: The Emerging Science at the Edge of Order and Chaos. London, Penguin.

Walsh, J. and G. Ungson (1991). "Organizational Memory." Academy of Management Review **16**(1): 57-91.

Wang, C. L. and P. K. Ahmed (2003). "Organisational Learning: A Critical Review." The Learning Organisation **10**(1): 8-17.

Weick, K. E. (1995). Sensemaking in Organizations. Thousand Oaks, Sage Publications.

Weick, K. E. (2001). Making Sense of the Organization. Malden, MA, Blackwell Publishers.

Weick, K. E. and K. H. Roberts (1993). "Collective Mind in Organizations: Heedful Interrelating on Flight Decks." Administrative Science Quarterly **38**: 357-381.

Weick, K.E. and f. Westley (1996). Organizationa Learning: Affirming an Oxymoron. Handbook of Organization Studies. S.R. Clegg, C. Hardy and W.R. Nord (eds). London, Sage: 440-458.

Wenger, E. (2004). "Knowledge Management as a Doughnut: Shaping Your Knowledge Strategy through Communities of Practice." Ivey Business Journal(January/February): 1-8.

Wenger, E., R. A. McDermott, et al. (2002). Cultivating Communities of Practice: A Guide to Managing Knowledge. Boston, Mass., Harvard Business School Press.

Wheatley, M. J. (1999). Leadership and the New Science: Discovering Order in a Chaotic World. San Francisco, Berrett-Koehler Publishers.

Wiig, K. M. (1997). "Knowledge Management: An Introduction and Perspective." The Journal of Knowledge Management **1**(1): 6-14.

Winch, A. and H. Ingram (2002). "Re-Defining the Focus of Workplace Learning." International journal of contemporary hospitality management 14(7): 361-367.

Yeo, R. (2002). "Learning within Organisations: Linking the Theoretical and Empirical Perspectives." Journal of Workplace learning 14(3): 109-122.

Zuboff, S. (1991). "Informate the Enterprise." National Forum 71(3): 3-8.

PhD Research Project

Learning and Knowing in Organisations

Participants' information

This research aims to understand how workplace learning experiences support knowledge creation, development, sharing and institutionalisation. It aims to explore the experiences of organisational members in their learning and sharing of knowledge in order to develop theory and about learning and knowledge management in organisations.

Your role as a participant

Narrative workshop
As a narrative workshop volunteer you will be involved in a two-hour session with up to seven other organisational members. The researcher will facilitate the session and participants will be asked to share their experiences about knowledge in the organisation. The researcher will begin from a question like, 'What experiences have you had in the organisation that have led to the creation of new knowledge, or its development, sharing or institutionalisation?'. For example, questions like, 'Can you think of a time when you came up with a really good idea that had the capacity to make a difference to your work, your colleagues, your clients or your organization over time?', 'Can you describe a time when you learnt something new from a really odd source?', 'Tell us about a time when something that you thought of led to an organisational change', will be used to prompt narratives. The questions may vary, but will always relate to learning, knowledge and organisation.

The researcher or other narrative workshop participants might ask you questions about the experience you relate and you might ask questions of others, or share other experiences that relate to those you hear about. The atmosphere will be one of sharing, rather than critique.

The researcher will audio tape the workshop. These tapes will be confidential and kept secure at the University of Canberra. Once the tapes have been transcribed they will include no identifying features and you will receive your group's 'metanarrative' (combined narrative) summary. From this you will have the chance to provide feedback about the accuracy of the way your words are represented.

Theme finding workshops
One group of eight volunteers from the twenty-four or so narrative workshop participants will take part in two, three hour workshops. This is a substantial investment

of time for volunteers, but will be rewarded by a greater understanding of the relationship between learning and knowledge in their organisation, as well as an introduction to a novel group technique for problem solving and planning.

Participants in these workshops will work as a group to develop a list of emerging themes and categories from the narratives. These are highly participative sessions that draw on participants' own experience and understanding. Again, these sessions will be audio taped.

At the end of the first workshop, participants will have developed a list of themes that emerge from the narratives and have clustered associated concepts around those themes.

At the end of the second workshop, participants will have developed a map of the interrelationship between emergent themes – a learning and knowledge framework.

SUMMARY OF PARTICIPANT INVOLVEMENT IN RESEARCH

Phase 1 Group story telling workshop September 2004

Three groups of eight individuals share stories relating to experience of learning and knowing in organisation.
Researcher audio tapes interaction for further analysis and summary. Researcher selectively transcribes stories for analysis and from these develops short stories for group use.
Researcher may contact participant for clarification or further information.

Phase 2 Group sense-making and category development October/November 2004

One group of eight volunteers uses story summaries to make sense of experience elicited through story telling. Researcher facilitates discussion to draw out main themes in group and develop categories
Researcher audio-tapes interaction for further analysis and summary. Researcher selectively transcribes group discussion for analysis

Phase 3 Group connection-making April - June 2005

Group uses story summaries and emergent categories to investigate relationships.
Researcher adds group developed theoretical memos to those already accumulated

Participant feedback

You will be given a depersonalized transcribed summary of your narrative workshop's metanarrative and will be asked to let the researcher know if itaccurately reflects your experience. When the research is complete, you will be invited to hear about the findings of the study and the theoretical model that was developed from yours and others experiences.

Safeguards
This research has been approved by your organisation and by the University of Canberra committee for Ethics in Human Research.

When your narrative is transcribed, any identifiers are removed. This means that there will be no way of identifying you from your narrative or your interactions. The only person who will access the original audio tape is the researcher.

All the identifying records that relate to this study are kept in secure structures at the University of Canberra.

The transcribed (sterile) narratives and interactions will be available to you, the researcher, her supervisor and those involved in the theme-finding workshops.

Your participation in this research is entirely voluntary and you are free to leave the research at any stage, without reason or penalty. You are free to choose not to be involved in any process. Your choice about involvement in this research will have no impact on your work life.

Consent
If you are interested in taking part in either one stage (narrative workshop) or three stages (narrative and theme finding workshops) please complete and sign the Informed Consent Form which is attached.

When you sign the consent form you are not committing to the research. It is not a binding document. You are free to withdraw from the research at any stage.

Further information
Please contact me if you have any questions about the research or the involvement of participants.

Monica Kennedy
PhD Candidate
Division of Communication and Education
University of Canberra ACT 2601
Phone: 02 62012495
Fax: 02 6201
Email: monica.kennedy@canberra.edu.au

You may also contact my supervisor for further information.

Supervisor:
Dr Trish Milne
Associate Professor
School of Information Management and Tourism
Division of Communication and Education
University of Canberra ACT 2601
Phone: 02 62012053
Fax: 02 26012649
Email: trish.milne@canberra.edu.au

PhD Research Project

LEARNING AND KNOWLEDGE IN ORGANISATIONS

INFORMED CONSENT FORM

I, _____ , declare that I:
    (Participant's name)

Willingly volunteered to participate in this study
Am aware of the purpose of the study
Am aware of my role as a participant in the study
Understand that I may withdraw from the research at any time and for any reason
Am aware that in group sessions my identity will be known to other participants
Am aware that my narrative will be transcribed and that upon transcription my input
will be anonymous
Understand that the research report will not identify me
Agree that information collected from me may be used in the research and published

Signed: _____ Date: _____

Contact telephone number: _____

Email address: _____

I agree to participate in the narrative workshop
I agree to participate in the theme finding workshops
I wish to receive an electronic version of the final report at the email address provided
above

COMMITTEE FOR ETHICS IN HUMAN RESEARCH

Document for people who are participants in a research project

CONTACTS FOR INFORMATION ON THE PROJECT AND
INDEPENDENT COMPLAINTS PROCEDURE

The following study has been reviewed and approved by the Committee for Ethics in Human Research:

Project title: Learning and Knowledge in Organisations
Project number: 04/39 Principal researcher: Monica Kennedy

As a participant or potential participant in research, you will have received written information about the research project. If you have questions or problems which are not answered in the information you have been given, you should consult the researcher or (if the researcher is a student) the research supervisor. For this project, the appropriate person is

Research supervisor:
Dr Trish Milne
Associate Professor
School of Information Management and Tourism
Division of Communication and Education
University of Canberra ACT 2601
Phone: 02 62012053
Fax: 02 26012649
Email: trish.milne@canberra.edu.au

2.   If you wish to discuss with an independent person a complaint relating to
   •   conduct of the project, or
   •   your rights as a participant, or
University policy on research involving human participants,
you should contact the Secretary of the University Research Committee

---

Providing research participants with this information is a requirement of the National Health and Medical Research Council *National Statement on Ethical Conduct in Research Involving Humans*, which applies to all research with human participants conducted in Australia. Further information on University of Canberra research policy is available in *University of Canberra Guidelines for Responsible Practice in Research and Dealing with Problems of Research Misconduct* and the Committee for Ethics in Human Research *Human Ethics Manual*. These documents are available from the Research Office at the above address or on the University's web site at http://www.canberra.edu.au/secretariat/respprac.html (Research Guidelines) http://www.canberra.edu.au/secretariat/ethics/human_ethics/manual.html (Human Ethics Manual)

(02) 6201 2466, University of Canberra, ACT 2601.

Pattern of categorisation of the research data – All Nodes listing

(1) /Aggregate
(1 1) /Aggregate/Self-organisation
(1 1 1) /Aggregate/Self-organisation/Support
(1 1 1 1) /Aggregate/Self-organisation/Support/honesty
(1 1 1 2) /Aggregate/Self-organisation/Support/care factor
(1 1 1 2 1) /Aggregate/Self-organisation/Support/care factor/confidence
(1 1 1 2 2) /Aggregate/Self-organisation/Support/care factor/commitment
(1 1 1 2 3) /Aggregate/Self-organisation/Support/care factor/trust
(1 1 1 21) /Aggregate/Self-organisation/Support/sharing
(1 1 1 24) /Aggregate/Self-organisation/Support/support
(1 1 2) /Aggregate/Self-organisation/Stretch
(1 1 2 2) /Aggregate/Self-organisation/Stretch/challenge
(1 1 2 17) /Aggregate/Self-organisation/Stretch/motivation
(1 1 3) /Aggregate/Self-organisation/Protect
(1 1 3 18) /Aggregate/Self-organisation/Protect/ownership
(1 1 3 20) /Aggregate/Self-organisation/Protect/secrecy
(1 9) /Aggregate/dynamic of group
(1 9 12) /Aggregate/dynamic of group/interdependency
(1 10) /Aggregate/Improving fitness
(1 10 3) /Aggregate/Improving fitness/change
(1 10 3 3) /Aggregate/Improving fitness/change/energy required
(1 10 6) /Aggregate/Improving fitness/effectiveness
(1 10 6 1) /Aggregate/Improving fitness/effectiveness/finding solutions
(1 10 6 2) /Aggregate/Improving fitness/effectiveness/usefulness
(1 10 6 3) /Aggregate/Improving fitness/effectiveness/meeting the need
(1 10 6 4) /Aggregate/Improving fitness/effectiveness/cutting it
(1 10 11) /Aggregate/Improving fitness/source of innovation
(1 10 11 10) /Aggregate/Improving fitness/source of innovation/shifts the outcome
(1 10 11 12) /Aggregate/Improving fitness/source of innovation/work around
(2) /Tagging
(2 3) /Tagging/concern for the organisation
(2 3 25) /Tagging/concern for the organisation/valuing people
(2 3 26) /Tagging/concern for the organisation/valuing the work
(2 22) /Tagging/sphere of inclusion
(2 22 14) /Tagging/sphere of inclusion/knowledge seeking
(2 22 14 2) /Tagging/sphere of inclusion/knowledge seeking/brain space
(2 22 14 13) /Tagging/sphere of inclusion/knowledge seeking/knowing why
(2 22 14 15) /Tagging/sphere of inclusion/knowledge seeking/what we do with information

(2 22 14 15 1) /Tagging/sphere of inclusion/knowledge seeking/what we do with information/chinese whispers

(2 22 14 15 2) /Tagging/sphere of inclusion/knowledge seeking/what we do with information/learning stragegy

(2 22 16) /Tagging/sphere of inclusion/localisation

(2 22 16 10) /Tagging/sphere of inclusion/localisation/identity

(3) /Nonlinearity

(3 3) /Nonlinearity/perfect world

(3 3 2) /Nonlinearity/perfect world/consistency

(3 3 2 1) /Nonlinearity/perfect world/consistency/accountability

(3 3 2 3) /Nonlinearity/perfect world/consistency/control

(3 3 2 4) /Nonlinearity/perfect world/consistency/direction

(3 3 2 5) /Nonlinearity/perfect world/consistency/training

(3 3 2 6) /Nonlinearity/perfect world/consistency/expert

(3 3 2 7) /Nonlinearity/perfect world/consistency/in the book

(3 10) /Nonlinearity/real world

(3 10 1) /Nonlinearity/real world/flexibility

(3 10 2) /Nonlinearity/real world/crisis

(3 10 2 1) /Nonlinearity/real world/crisis/baptism by fire

(3 10 5) /Nonlinearity/real world/discretion

(3 10 8) /Nonlinearity/real world/individuality of customer

(4) /Flows

(4 9) /Flows/disconnection

(4 9 1) /Flows/disconnection/frustration

(4 9 8) /Flows/disconnection/recognition

(4 9 10) /Flows/disconnection/glory seeking

(4 9 11) /Flows/disconnection/inequity

(4 9 12) /Flows/disconnection/risk

(4 9 12 1) /Flows/disconnection/risk/danger

(4 9 12 2) /Flows/disconnection/risk/fear

(4 9 12 3) /Flows/disconnection/risk/hiding

(4 9 12 4) /Flows/disconnection/risk/survival

(4 9 12 12) /Flows/disconnection/risk/risk taking

(4 9 15) /Flows/disconnection/leadership

(4 9 19) /Flows/disconnection/rhetoric

(4 10) /Flows/power

(4 10 1) /Flows/power/politics

(4 10 3) /Flows/power/ivory tower

(4 10 8) /Flows/power/permission

(4 10 8 1) /Flows/power/permission/encouraged to explore

(4 10 8 2) /Flows/power/permission/blame

(4 10 8 3) /Flows/power/permission/blockers

(4 10 8 6) /Flows/power/permission/leadership

(4 10 8 9) /Flows/power/permission/permission to make mistakes

(4 10 8 11) /Flows/power/permission/ramifications

(4 14) /Flows/structure

(4 14 1) /Flows/structure/compartmentalise

(4 14 2) /Flows/structure/isolation
(4 14 3) /Flows/structure/direction
(4 14 4) /Flows/structure/job design
(4 14 5) /Flows/structure/narrow focus
(4 14 9) /Flows/structure/measurement
(4 14 9 1) /Flows/structure/measurement/measurement
(4 14 12) /Flows/structure/relationship
(4 14 13) /Flows/structure/resources
(4 14 13 1) /Flows/structure/resources/cost of learning
(4 14 13 2) /Flows/structure/resources/time
(4 14 13 3) /Flows/structure/resources/tools
(5) /Diversity
(5 1) /Diversity/naivety
(5 3) /Diversity/narrow focus
(5 4) /Diversity/skills
(5 5) /Diversity/survival
(5 9) /Diversity/role perspective
(5 9 1) /Diversity/role perspective/skills
(5 9 2) /Diversity/role perspective/specialisation
(5 9 23) /Diversity/role perspective/sphere of responsibility
(5 9 23 5) /Diversity/role perspective/sphere of responsibility/customer focus
(6) /Internal models
(6 1) /Internal models/a new way of thinking
(6 2) /Internal models/letting go
(6 3) /Internal models/capturing the learning
(6 4) /Internal models/developing people
(6 5) /Internal models/real learning needs
(6 6) /Internal models/different way of doing it
(6 7) /Internal models/learning from mistakes
(6 9) /Internal models/reconceptualising
(6 11) /Internal models/the normal confines
(6 11 1) /Internal models/the normal confines/make it work
(6 11 4) /Internal models/the normal confines/no room for anything else
(6 11 6) /Internal models/the normal confines/reinventing
(6 11 8) /Internal models/the normal confines/role modelling
(6 11 10) /Internal models/the normal confines/set in their processes~
(6 11 14) /Internal models/the normal confines/what you can't do
(6 12) /Internal models/the right thing
(6 12 1) /Internal models/the right thing/good faith
(6 13) /Internal models/what i know
(6 13 1) /Internal models/what i know/'I didn't become it, I came that way
(6 13 3) /Internal models/what i know/life experience
(6 15) /Internal models/memory of the organisation
(7) /Building blocks
(7 1) /Building blocks/real learning needs
(7 7) /Building blocks/repetition

Related research

Author (date)	Focus of research	Relationship to this study	Dissimilarity to this research	Relevant findings
Farrell (2000)	Integration of organisational change, market orientation, management behaviour and learning orientation in learning organisation investigation	Cross-disciplinary investigation into the impact of formal organisation on learning orientation. Investigates the practices and behaviours that facilitate learning.	Quantifies learning orientation through survey instrument. Targets managers and relates survey findings to business performance.	Learning orientation has a strong significantly positive effect on business performance
Griego, Geroy and Wright (2000)	Predictors of learning organisations	Investigates perceptions of organisational members in relation to training and education and information flow in the organisation.	Quantitative approach using Learning Organization Practices Profile. Investigates 5 dimensions of organisation through survey instrument, other issues may not emerge. Seeks to describe predictors of learning organisation. Focus on training and development as opposed to learning.	An environment of knowledge sharing and learning systems is an indication of learning organisation.
MacDonald, Gabriel and Cousins (2000)	Factors influencing adult learning in technology firms	Investigates the relationship between learning and the learning environment. Describes features of effective learning approaches and the role of constructivism.	Positivist approach seeking to confirm hypothesis related to conditions for learning. Traditional approaches to workplace training tested in specific program. Seeks to test rather than understand.	Applying principles of adult learning to a training program can increase program effectiveness.

Author (date)	Focus of research	Relationship to this study	Dissimilarity to this research	Relevant findings
Robertson and O'Malley-Hammersley (2000)	Role of HRD in facilitating knowledge management	Knowledge creation unsupported by systematic training. Learning recognised as central to knowledge management. Qualitative approach seeks to understand relationship between knowledge creation and learning strategy. Situates knowledge and learning within organisational context.	Interviews focus on specific research question which examines specific people management practice. Focus on organisational environment and on individual knowledge creation.	Knowledge creation facilitated and sustained through people management practices
Storey and Barnett (2000)	Analysis of failed knowledge management initiatives	Uses case study to analyse the social influences on knowledge management. Considers knowledge management within a complex socio-technical organisational context. Highlights relationship between knowledge creation, sharing and organisational change.	Follows the implementation of an IT-based knowledge management programme. Critically analyses implementation in order to explain failure. Draws recommendations from analysis of case rather than articulated experience of organisational members.	Learning organisation concept may be inspired by wider developmental values that IT led intervention.
Hensen and Haas 2002	A productivity perspective on knowledge sharing	Investigates knowledge sharing strategies in organisations and perceived quality.	Tests hypotheses relating to time and quality of different sources of knowledge in a particular project. Considers knowledge as existing outside of its context and apart from its creators. Analyses knowledge outcomes in terms of costs.	Personal expert knowledge leads to quality, documented knowledge leads to efficiency.

Author (date)	Focus of research	Relationship to this study	Dissimilarity to this research	Relevant findings
Winch and Ingram (2002)	Meaning making and learner centred workplace learning approaches	Investigates the process of learning undertaken by an individual in the context within which they work. Develops a model of individual and organisational learning that incorporates 'complex responsive processes'. Focuses on meaning making, both personal and collective. Recognises the limitations of training and the limitations of personal constructs that resist change. Attempts to reconcile individual and organisational learning.	Focus on the individual.	Process rather than content of learning key concern. Treat the organisation through the metaphor of a living system Emergence gives rise to a whole new way of approaching learning
ANTA(2003)	Training packages and the future	Explores limitations of current workplace learning strategy in Australia in relation to changing organisational contexts. Investigates changing nature of work, pedagogy and organisation	Reviews literature and practice in workplace learning in order to develop recommendations for future approaches to learning in organisations	Highlights need for new understandings of knowledge and learning for practice in changing organisational contexts

Author (date)	Focus of research	Relationship to this study	Dissimilarity to this research	Relevant findings
Harkema (2003)	Application of Complex Adaptive Systems theory to learning through simulation model	Investigates how people learn with a focus on complexity theory, looks at nonlinearity, dynamic behaviour, emergence and self-organisation. The implications of these phenomena for learning are explored. Provides an example of a learning study that explores the relationship between learning and theory derived from the new sciences. Situates learning within knowledge context. Focuses on individual and collective learning.	Manipulates knowledge types to facilitate emergence of characteristics in computer simulation, detached from context. Does not seek to explore relationship between individual learning experience and organisational knowledge. Exploration reductionist. Seeks to explain rather than understand.	Individual learning emergent, arising through the following factors: Who an agent met How often an agent met a certain other agent Which characteristics the agents respectively had The characteristics of the agents
Moffett, McAdam and Parkinson (2003)	The relationship between the cultural and technological aspects of knowledge management	Highlights relationship between knowledge management and the organisational context. Used exploratory approach through ethnographic and social constructionist studies.	Focuses exclusively on technical and cultural implications for success of knowledge management implementation. Does not consider learning experience in exploration.	Culturally led knowledge management programs are more likely to be successful

352

Author (date)	Focus of research	Relationship to this study	Dissimilarity to this research	Relevant findings
Muscatello (2003)	Use of knowledge management for training	Recognises relationship between strategies developed in knowledge management and opportunity for learning	Focuses on information technology (expert systems) as facilitating learning through its ability to 'employ expertise at all levels and increase expert development efforts'. Recognises learning as linear and direct transfer 'A knowledge system could support a learning organisation by reducing the amount of time required to transfer knowledge from a master to an apprentice' (2003, 38). Provides worked example but no empirical study.	Knowledge management systems may reduce the amount of structure required in an organisation
Roth (2003)	Increasing knowledge creation and sharing across project boundaries	Explores knowledge creation and sharing behaviours. Discusses role of groups and diversity in knowledge creation and tacit knowledge. Researches knowledge within a rich context	Tests a knowledge management approach through action research. Focuses on systems and steps in knowledge management	Encourage groups in the organisation to meet in constellations and create common knowledge. Take different forms and levels of knowledge into consideration as well as the relational and contextual factors of knowledge.
Rhodes and MacKechnie (2003)	Using complexity theory to better understand public service systems	Highlights the interactions among participants in contributing to outcomes of the system. Applies metaphors derived from complex adaptive systems. Seeks to integrate disparate strands of theory into a coherent model	Explicitly sets out to use overlay complexity theory in a specific case. Uses mixed methods for data collection – interview, documents and quantitative analysis of decision making practices. Focuses on the process of policy development rather than learning or knowledge sharing in organisations	Finds that complex adaptive systems theory is an appropriate lens for analysing organisational processes and integrating theoretical strands

Author (date)	Focus of research	Relationship to this study	Dissimilarity to this research	Relevant findings
Scarbrough (2003)	Knowledge management, human resource management and innovation	Considers knowledge management as a human and social function through 'collectivizing' knowledge and learning. Discusses the development of knowledge through the application of knowledge. Calls for a social view of knowledge generation	Focuses on a failed knowledge management implementation programme. Aims to explain failure rather than explore organisational members' experiences of success in learning and knowledge sharing.	Recognise networks of social relationships as a critical resource for the combination and exchange of knowledge required to promote new knowledge
Backstrom (2004)	Collective learning	Investigates learning using complexity theory focussing on competence development in a collective system	Interaction pattern is the unit of analysis for the study which uses secondary analysis of data derived from one-on-one conversations focused on intensity of work, competence, and leadership	Develops a model of collective learning on two dimensions, grasping and interacting.
Beesley (2004)	Relationships among knowledge creation, diffusion, and utilization	Focus on the emergent patterns that emerge in knowledge activities at individual, group, and organisational levels.	Interest too in inter-organisational levels of learning. Focus on the factors which influence the degree to which knowledge designed for organisational application is utilised.	Finds knowledge-creating processes are context-specific. The knowledge 'assets' of the organisation are in the pattern of relationships amongst its members.
Evans and Kersh (2004)	Tacit knowledge and competence	Seeks to understand adult learning within the context of work and organisation. Focus on understanding learners' experience of learning.	Focus on organisation as restrictive or expansive. Focus on performance independent of cognition. Focus on individual learners and individual knowledge.	Tacit skill development is nonlinear Occupational and learning biographies can be used to understand tacit skill recognition

Author (date)	Focus of research	Relationship to this study	Dissimilarity to this research	Relevant findings
Hill (2004)	Fugitive and codified knowledge in emergent citizen's groups	Case study of construction of group knowledge through engagement in activity. Highlights tension between emergent and codified knowledge and collective action. Highlights interdependency.	Focus on environmental conflict. Uses historical-organisational/observational case study to highlight issues of power and control in learning and community development.	Tension develops between the knowledge that emerges through collective engagement in environmental conflict and the attempts at control supported by canonical knowledge.
Phelps (2004)	Use of reflection in studying complexity in action	Posits an alignment of complexity theories with reflective practice and develops case analysis using metaphors provided by complexity	Focus on journal keeping and reflection.	Journal keeping can help learners to 'deal with a complex, ill-structured world' (citing Jonassen et al. 1997)
Scarbrough, Bresnen et al. (2004)	Tensions between learning at project level and the stocks and flows of organisational knowledge	Qualitative study which investigates learning experiences and transfer to organisational knowledge in case study	Focus on project group as unit of analysis. Assumes 'acquisition' perspective on knowledge, focus on learning-by-absorption and learning-by-reflection.	Differing types of learning occur at different stages of the project. There are inherent tensions in the processes which embed learning in organisational knowledge
Scott (2005)	Development of collective identity of knowledge workers	Study interest in interaction of organisational members and their informal and formal organisation through communication	Focus on communication rather than learning or knowledge development. Targets 'knowledge workers' exclusively. Uses network analysis on long interview data.	Knowledge workers connect beyond focal workgroup.

Journal excerpts

15 April 2004

I've reached a place in my research where I think I'm almost comfortable that the questions I'm asking and my rudimentary ideas about how to ask them will work. What a process this is ! I'm astounded by the amount I've learnt over the past 8 months. Pretty much reading over the period and trying to make sense of the interactions between all the themes I come across.

Is it just me, or does everyone experience the feeling that every single idea they come across relates to the research topic? Just yesterday, I picked up a "mind over matter" sort of a health book that discussed the relationship between the new sciences and holistic health, had a conversation with a friend about the effects of Newton's theory on culture, and while having a glass of wine with Jane about her research on the effectiveness of scaffolding in early childhood settings, had an insight into the way that adults scaffold each others' learning (I've been thinking about using Vygotsky in the lit review and now I know I must).

It's funny to think that only 4 months ago I presented to the research colloquium on what I though my research question was (I'd had another epiphany that week and thought I knew everything once again!). The question was quite close to my current one, but I stated it not as a problematic (which all my understanding now shows is an appropriate approach), but as an hypothesis. I was sure I needed to be able to state my research questions in a sentence that began "My thesis is that…" and all the research was about was proving the point. I now have a much fuller understanding of the ways interesting things might be investigated. The fact that I am now able to see the relationship between the focus of my research and the epistemological and methodological approach has been (again) like an epiphany! I struggled with the intertwining concepts, particularly where I had a focus in complexity theories, thought I'd like to use approaches being used in KM, but couldn't substantiate the techniques methodologically without preparing a PhD on the use of the strategies as methodologically sound techniques. Margaret's help in finding a sympathetic approach to the theory was fantastic.

17 April 2004

Thinking today about personal and shared mental models. While all I'm reading and thinking about is making mental models explicit so they can be challenged and adjusted to meet the environment, why is it that the new ideas I'm reading about and looking to research sit so comfortably with me? What is it about my own mental models that makes the logic of the new sciences, the idea of collective construction of meaning, the understanding of knowledge as contextual and alive, and my preference for interpretative approaches to research feel so right? Isn't it because of my mental models? Isn't it because of the experiences of my past that have cemented my preference for all things "thick", "deep" and paradoxical? Couldn't it be that my mental models are assisting me to pursue a specific type of exploration that is actually limiting my ability to learn. Couldn't it be that by researching in this area that I'm looking to cement the neural net that has led me to this type of research in the first place?

24 April 2004

It keeps playing on my mind that my focus on keeping my methodology in line with principles of complexity might limit the outcomes this study can deliver. I want to follow complexity to find out what emerges from the complex interaction of diverse agents, and yet I also want to be able to focus just on the key are of learning that I'm interested in. It's really risky to begin on a research program with the hope that what will emerge through an indirect question and boundaries to discussion relates to the research area that I'm defining. How frightening to think that I might spend 3 years of my life studying and researching in an area that, because I have selected one theoretical approach over another, results in no definite results! It could easily happen here. I have to accept that in using this theory I might find nothing at all!

As I'm writing this I'm thinking that my thinking is exactly the sort of thinking that limits individual (and organisational) learning. I'm going about this thing in a really different way in the hope that I can make sense enough of the changing world to add some new concept, some new understanding to this field of study, and yet in order to do so I have to be scared, I have to justify myself as being rigorous, and in the end I may have to deal with failure and all it brings. Life doesn't set us up for this. Life sets us up to take "considered" and "managed" risks and to avoid failure at all costs. But if I'm committed to working with complexity then it means going out on a limb, chancing looking stupid and wasting time and resources on the slight chance that something may emerge that will lead to generative change.

19 February 2005

I'm playing with the data today, using the codes we worked up. It's interesting how the codes have me looking at the data differently and finding lots of text to code under the categories. I keep thinking as I'm coding of what the group talked about as they talked about the code, and it makes the code much richer for me. I have been working on the last about 1/3 of group 1 narrative today. It's hard to keep focused on learning and knowing because the stories illustrate the integral nature of those constructs within the broader themes of organisation, relationships, leadership, personal ambition, emotion (and on and on until the whole world is described as the context!). This has been troubling me today (well, not troubling, but causing me reflection). How do I focus in on these when the whole context of life impacts on the learning and knowing that happens in that organisation for those individuals and groups? In this part of the text I've found "survival" (which was a group identified code) has been important. I wonder if I would have recognised it as an important theme without the perspective and discussion of the group. I know I never would have thought about it in the way it is used had I been asked to theories on this six months ago. It's worrying that people are using "survival" as a reason not to innovate! The difficulty with having permission to take a risk and the frustration with putting new ideas in practice are indicated as reason why. Something to think about...

23 February 2005

I'm starting to get worried about the broad ranging topics that are being discussed and I'm coding. The thing is, they all link to knowledge and learning – it's not like I can just say, no that doesn't relate to the research topic because it seems everything does – everything from fear to structure to disconnection to real world to leadership and everywhere else. I hope that I'll find a way to recognise this complexity and the interaction of all these dimensions somehow. I'm having trouble coding the concept that continually emerges – the need to know how to deal with entirely individual problems encountered and a related concept that is to do with the way people perceive their place and role in the organisation and its outcomes … can't quite grasp what's going on here yet.

Sample Narrative

2.4

Yeah, well I used to be in [another part of the organisation] and we looked at the ways we could help people [detail deleted] the problem was very complicated, but the bottom line was, we thought, well why don't we... and we had [clients] complaining, significant numbers of [clients] complaining about the amount of paperwork we were sending them for reviews ... so we thought we could look at a number of ways

(RESEARCHER)

When you say "we"... I'm sorry to interrupt...

2.4

Oh, me and my team... we did it as a meeting, you know we set up, we said well, OK what are some of the things that we can do, lets set up some hair-brained ideas, we brain-stormed together, the... you know, this is what we thought we might do, did a little bit of project scoping, well did a lot of project scoping and then off we went with a few ideas. And one of them was, [detail of strategy deleted]. And we'd worked it out that we could do it, but it became very costly. And we talked to Nationals about it and the pros and cons and all that sort of stuff and said, "Yeah, well, we still think it's worthwhile but there needs to be a much greater effort that what we can afford to put in, and expertise from IT people. Another way was [details of strategy deleted] and so we got the same outcome out of that and it was a lot cheaper, but we were still interested in this [first option]. We even went to a point where we went and spoke to an expert [in another government department about the way that they deal with similar situations] and we went over and had a chat with him, them we went down to Melbourne and spoke to a company [detail deleted] and we went and talked with them. We spoke with them at the conceptual level about would this work? Would you be prepared to be involved in it? We talked around [other issues] and then, Nationals – "No, there's not enough money, we couldn't possibly pursue this any further". And then, off the boiler it goes and we go and do other things and 12 months later [another part of the organisation] started up and we're now [doing just what we proposed]. But that came under someone else's bailiwick. So what you can see is, somebody saw what we were up to and thought, "Well, gee, that's a great idea. I can work that where I am, but we don't need to involve [4's previous team] in this". [Detail deleted]. Well, then about a week later I was in Nationals at a [deleted] workshop. And all the coordinators are sitting there, and there's this guy from Nationals talking about this project that he's running in Albury. And I'm just sitting there having a chuckle to myself because he's not working with us, he just thought he'd better consult with us after the event. And he said "This is the flagship, [my area] is a flagship", and I said, "well, if you don't mind me saying so it's a bit of a leaky old rowing boat because you've gone about it the wrong way, and these are the reasons. To this day, I don't know whether if what I had to say had any impact, but it should have. It should have.

2.6

Well, you probably won't know until you come across him and he's going to give you a job. That's when you'll find out.

2.4

Either way, I think that's buggered, so, you know, you look at that, and you say to yourself, "well there was a lot of information that wasn't transferred to the right people, and I wonder how much of it was glory seeking and how much of it was real genuine concern for the organisation

2.6

Well, there was probably someone sitting in a team in National and they said, "Get a project going" and that person's gone, "Oh, OK, well what will I do?", and they've gone off and they've looked up to see what they could pick up and they've come across what you were doing and they wouldn't even have thought, they've just gone, "Oh I know, I'll pick up that thing that [4] did" and they've just looked for something they can touch up, because that's what they do, they just redo everybody's old projects. And I know through people who've worked there. That's what they do. It's not all of what they do, but it's a lot of what happens, especially if a team hasn't got a lot of work on at the time.

INTRODUCTORY STATISTICAL MECHANICS

PHYSICS SERIES

Consulting Editor   **Paul Davies**
                         University of Adelaide